To: SHAD
From: DADDY

Wm L Banks
1 JOHN 3:22

HAPPY B-DAY!!!

2015

LOVE YOU
SWEETHEART!!
Always!!!

WORDS FROM THE WORD

A Study of Some Commonly Used
Figures of Speech Found in the Scriptures

William L. Banks, D. Min.

ISBN 0-7414-5145-X

Published by:

PUBLISHING.COM

1094 New DeHaven Street, Suite 100
West Conshohocken, PA 19428-2713
Info@buybooksontheweb.com
www.buybooksontheweb.com
Toll-free (877) BUY BOOK
Local Phone (610) 941-9999
Fax (610) 941-9959

Printed in the United States of America

Published February 2009

Table of Contents

Foreword

Abbreviations

Bibliography

Foreword

If you enjoy "word pictures" you will be pleased with this book. It is simply marvelous to read the many figures of speech the Bible contains—they number in the hundreds! God's heavenly word is down to earth, verbally inspired as the Lord communicates His will through the use of metaphors, symbols, idioms, proverbial sayings, phrases, and colloquial expressions. No device so common to all languages should be overlooked or thought insignificant.

Although our daily conversations are colored with words and phrases found in the Bible, apparently many people do not realize that commonly used figures of speech are derived from the Scriptures or that the Bible has greatly influenced our language. One of the purposes of this work is to reveal to the reader by way of Bible exposition, the heart of God who so wonderfully makes known His will in His Word, through Jesus Christ, the Word made Flesh.

In addition, some experiences and customs of Black American Christians and their churches—insights probably unknown to the majority of White Americans—are revealed. Ignorance remains a factor in poor race relations in our country. Our prayer is that as we grow in Christ we come to appreciate His working in such varied ways among those who love Him, and that we come to love each other more. May even the humorous thoughts and cartoons add to our understanding of the Book of Books, and draw us closer to its Author.

Thanks to editorial cartoonists Tony Auth of The Philadelphia Inquirer and Tom Stiglich of The Leader Newspaper, for the use of their cartoons. Thanks also to Joyce Rigdon of the Alliance of Confessing Evangelicals (*Eternity Magazine*), Philadelphia, Pa; to Mr. Tom Rice of The Evening Bulletin of Philadelphia (Aunt Het cartoons); and to the *Leadership Journal* cartoon used by permission.

I am grateful also to the Palmer Theological Seminary Library; the Montgomery Library of the Westminster Theological Seminary; and the Krauth Memorial Library of the

Lutheran Theological Seminary. Many hours of research were spent in these institutes, and their librarians were more than helpful to me.

I thank the Lord for Thelma my wife of 54 years, for her love, patience, and encouragement, for throughout the years we have been co-laborers in the vineyard of our Savior.

Abbreviations

ABMJ	American Board of Mission to the Jews
AHD	American Heritage Dictionary of the English Language.
ATR	A.T. Robertson, *Word Pictures in the NT*
BAGD	Bauer, W., W. F. Arndt, F. W. Gingrich, and F. W. Danker, *Greek-English Lexicon of the New Testament and Other Early Christian Literature.* 2d ed. Chicago, 1979
BDB	Brown, F., S. R. Driver, and C. A. Briggs, *A Hebrew and English Lexicon of the Old Testament.* Oxford, 1907
BSac	*Bibliotheca sacra*
CBQ	*Catholic Biblical Quarterly*
CEV	Contemporary English Version
DBI	*Dictionary of Biblical Imagery*
ExpGT	*Expositor's Greek Testament*
ExpTim	*Expository Times*
EvQ	*Evangelical Quarterly*
HTR	*Harvard Theological Review*
ICC	International Critical Commentary: *Critical and Exegetical Commentary;* Edinburgh: T& T Clark
ISBE	*International Standard Bible Encyclopedia,* ed. James Orr. 4 vols. Peabody, Mass.: Hendrickson, 1994
JBP	JB Phillips NT in Modern English
JFB	Jamieson, Fausset and Brown
JQR	*Jewish Quarterly Review*
JSOT	*Journal for the Study of the Old Testament*
JBL	*Journal of Biblical Literature*
JTS	*Journal of Theological Studies*
K&D	Keil, C. F., and F. Delitzsch, *Biblical Commentary on the OT.* Reprint, 10 vols. Peabody, Mass.: Hendrickson, 1996
KJV	King James Version
LB	Living Bible
Moffatt	A New Translation, James Moffatt
Montg	NT in Modern English, Helen B. Montgomery
MCED	Mounce's Complete Expository Dictionary of OT and NT Words

Nelson	*Nelson Study Bible-NKJV*
Neot	*Neotestamentica*
NASB	New American Standard Bible
NBC	New Bible Commentary
NEB	New English Bible
NICOT	New International Commentary on the OT
NIV	New International Version
NIB	*New Interpreter's Bible*
NKJV	New King James Version
NLT	New Living Translation
NRSV	New Revised Standard Version
NT	New Testament
OT	Old Testament
OED	Oxford English Dictionary
Parallel	KJV Parallel Bible Commentary
Pilgrim	New Pilgrim Bible, KJV
RH	Random House Dictionary
RSV	Revised Standard Version
Sco	Scofield Study Bible III (NKJV)
Thayer	J. H. Thayer, *Greek-English Lexicon of the NT*
TDNT	*Theological Dictionary of the NT.* Edited by G. Kittel and G. Friedrich, Translated by G. W. Bromiley. 10 vols. Grand Rapids: Eerdmans, 1964-1976
TWOT	*Theological Wordbook of the Old Testament.* Edited by R. L. Harris, G. L. Archer Jr., and Bruce K. Waltke, 2 vols. Chicago: Moody Press, 1980
TEV	Today's English Version (Good News Bible)
VT	*Vetus Testamentum*
WTJ	*Westminster Theological Journal*
WBC	Word Biblical Commentary
WBD	World Book Dictionary, 2 vols.
Weymouth	New Testament in Modern Speech, R. F. Weymouth
Wycliffe	*Wycliffe Bible Commentary*

Bibliography

Adam, Ben. *The Origin of Heathendom.* Minneapolis: Bethany Fellowship, 1964.

Aesop. *The Fables of Aesop.* N. Y.: Books, n. d.

Alexander, Joseph. A. *The Prophecies of Isaiah.* Grand Rapids: Zondervan, 1974.

Allis, O. T. "The Parable of the Leaven." *EvQ* 19 (1947): 254-273.

Anderson, Sir Robert. "Sin and Judgment to Come." *The Fundamentals.* Grand Rapids: Baker, 2003.

Ayer, Wm. W. "The Pulpit Prophet." *BSac.* 124 (1967): 291-302.

Baptist Standard Hymnal. Nashville: Sunday School Publishing Board, NBC, U.S.A., Inc., 1924.

Barnes, Albert. Barne's Notes, Electronic Database. 1997, 2003 by Biblesoft, Inc.

Barnhouse, Donald Grey. *The Invisible War.* Grand Rapids: Zondervan, 1965.

_____. *Revelation.* Grand Rapids: Zondervan, 1971.

_____. *Illustrating the Gospel of John.* Grand Rapids: Revell, 1998.

_____. *Romans.* 4 vols. Grand Rapids: Eerdmans, 1999 reprint.

Barr, James. "The Literal, the Allegorical, and Modern Biblical Scholarship." JSOT 44 (1959): 3-17.

Bennett, Thomas J. "Matthew 7:6—a New Interpretation." *WTJ* 49 (1987), 371-86.

Berkhof, Louis. *Systematic Theology.* Grand Rapids: Eerdmans, 1986 reprint.

Boice, James M. *Romans.* Vol 2. Grand Rapids: Baker, 2001.

_____. *Acts.* Grand Rapids: Baker, 2002.

Bradford, Charles E. "The Word Whose Time Has Come." *The African American Pulpit* 9, (2006): 44-46.

Brewer's Dictionary of Phrase and Fable. Revised by Adrian Room. N.Y.: HarperCollins, 1995.

Brown, F., S. R. Driver, C. A. Briggs. *A Hebrew and English Lexicon of the Old Testament.* Oxford University, 1952. BDB

Brownlee, Wm. H. "The Placarded Revelation of Habakkuk." *JBL* 82 (1963): 319-25.

Bruce, F. F. *The Gospel of John & the Epistles of John.* Grand Rapids: Eerdmans, 1994, 1997.

Brueggemann, Walter. "Of the Same Flesh and Bone (Gn 2,23a)." *CBQ* 32 (1970): 532-42.

_____. *Genesis.* Atlanta: John Knox, 1982.

Brunk, M. J. "The Seven Churches of Revelation Two and Three." *BSac* 126 (1969): 244-46.

Bullinger, E. W. *Figures of Speech Used in the Bible: Explained and Illustrated.* Grand Rapids: Baker, 2005.

Burton, Ernest De Witt. *Syntax of the Moods and Tenses in NT Greek.* Chicago: University of Chicago, 1893.

Byatt, Anthony. *New Testament Metaphors.* Edinburgh: Pentland, 1995.

Caird, G. B. *Language and Imagery of the Bible.* Grand Rapids: Eerdmans, 1980.

Calvin, John. *Sermons from Job.* Grand Rapids: Eerdmans, 1952.

_____. *Commentaries.* Grand Rapids: Baker, 1996.

Carr, Arthur. *The Expositor* (Eighth Series, 6, 1913): 511-17.

Chafer, Lewis Sperry. *Systematic Theology.* 8 vols. Dallas: Dallas Seminary, 1964.

Chenu, Bruno. *The Trouble I've Seen.* Valley Forge: Judson, 2003.

Cheyne, T. K. *Hosea.* Cambridge: University, 1887.

Chilvers, Gordon. "A Delicate Distinction." *Evangelical Christian.* (June 1961).

Clarke, Adam: Commentary. Electronic Database by Biblesoft, Inc. 1996, 2003.

Contemporary English Version. *The Holy Bible.* N.Y.: American Bible Society, 1995. CEV

Dana, H. E. and J. R. Mantey. *A Manual Grammar of the Greek NT.* NY: Macmillan, 1955.

Davies, W. J. and G. S. S Ellison. "Was His Father Lying Dead at Home?" *ExpTim* 62 (1950/51): 92.

Davis, Barry C. "Ecclesiastes 12:1-8: Death, an Impetus for Life." *BSac* 148 (1991): 298-318.

Ebony Magazine, 47 (Jan 1961). "What Happened to Hell?"

Ehrenstein, H. "Your Questions Answered." *Eternity* (Oct 1966), 39.

Eidevall, Goran. *Grapes in the Desert; Metaphors; Models, and Themes in Hosea 4-14.* Stockholm: Almquist and Wiksell International, 1996.

Evans, J. Ellwood. "The Song of Habakkuk." *BSac* 113 (1956): 57-65.

Family Word Finder. Pleasantville, N. Y.: Reader's Digest Association, 1975.

Faur, Jose. "Biblical Idea of Idolatry." *JQR* 69 (1978/79): 1-15.

Faussett's Bible Dictionary. Electronic Database Biblesoft 2003, 1998.

Feinberg, Charles L. *Habakkuk, Zephaniah, Haggai and Malachi.* NY: ABMJ, 1951.

_____. *Hosea: God's Love for Israel.* N.Y.: ABMJ, n.d.

_____. "The Scapegoat of Leviticus Sixteen." *BSac* 115 (1958): 320-333.

_____. *God Remembers: A Study of the Book of Zechariah.* NY: ABMJ, 1965 second printing.

_____. *The Prophecy of Ezekiel.* Chicago: Moody, 1969.

Fowler, H. W. *A Dictionary of Modern English Usage.* Oxford: Oxford University, 1983 reprint.

Freeman, James M. *The New Manners & Customs of the Bible.* ed. H. J. Chadwick. Gainesville, Fla.: Bridge-Logos, 2004.

Fremont, Carson. "The Meaning of Commitment." *The Message,* (Spring 1989), 11-12, 18.

Fulghum, W. B. *A Dictionary of Biblical Allusions in English Literature.* NY: Holt, Rinehart & Winston, 1965.

Fundamentals, The. Eds. RA Torrey, AC Dixon, et al. Two Volume Set (4-vols). Grand Rapids: Baker: 2003 reprint.

Gaebelein, Arno C. *The Revelation.* NY: Our Hope, 1915.

_____. *The Prophet Ezekiel.* NY: Our Hope, 1918.

_____. *Moses - His First and Second Coming.* NY: Our Hope, 1940.

_____. *The Fundamentals.* "Fulfilled Prophecy a Potent Argument for the Bible." Grand Rapids; Baker (2003 reprint), 2:112-143.

Gill, John. *Exposition of the Bible.* Online CD-Rom.

Girdlestone, Robert B. *Synonyms of the OT.* Grand Rapids: Eerdmans, 1953.

Glasson, T. F. "Chiamus in St. Matthew 7:6." *ExpTim* 68 (1957).

Grudem, Wayne. *I Peter.* ed. Leon Morris. Tyndale NT Commentaries. Grand Rapids: Eerdmans, 1989 reprint.

Ham, Ken; Carl Wieland, Don Batten. *One Blood; the Biblical Answer to Racism.* Green Forest, Arizona: Master, 2005.

Harrison, Everett F. "The Importance of the Septuagint for Biblical Studies, Part II." *BSac* 113, (1956): 37-45.

Harrison, R. K. *Jeremiah and Lamentations.* Downers Grove, Ill.: InterVarsity, 1973.

Hendrickson, Robert. *The Facts on File Encyclopedia of Word and Phrase Origins.* NY: Checkmark, 2004, 3rd edition.

Hendry, George S. "Judge Not: A Critical Test of Faith." *ThTo* 40, (1983): 113-129.

Henry, Matthew. *Commentary on the Whole Bible.* Hendrickson, New Modern Edition, Electronic Database 1991, Inc.

Hiebert, D. Edmond. "Selected Studies from Jude." *BSac* 142 (1985): 355-65.

Hodges, Zane C. "Problem Passages in the Gospel of John." *BSac* 135, (1928):139-52.

_____. "Problem Passages in the Gospel of John." *BSac* 137, (1980): 41-50.

Holt, John Marshall. "So He May Run Who Reads It." *JBL* 83 (1964), 298-302.

Hoste, Wm. & Rodgers, Wm. *Bible Problems and Answers.* Scotland: John Ritchie, 1986.

Howard, H. G. "Was His Father Lying Dead at Home?" *ExpTim* 61, (1949/50): 350-1.

Hughes, Philip Edgcumbe. "Bible Book of the Month," Galatians. *Christianity Today.* (18 Jan 60), 18 [318].

Ironside, Harry A. *Lectures on the Book of Revelation.* NY: Loizeaux, 1958.

Jackson, Basil. "Maturity in the Pastor and Parishioner." *BSac* 132 (1975): 99-113.

Jamieson, Fausset, and Brown Commentary. Electronic Database, 2003 by Biblesoft, Inc.

Jeffrey, David L. edit. *A Dictionary of Biblical Tradition in English Literature*. Grand Rapids: Eerdmans, 1992.

Johns, Claude H. W. "Babylonian Law; the Code of Hammurabi." Encyclopedia Britannica, 1910-1911, eleventh edition. Internet.

Johnson, J. Weldon & Johnson, J. Rosamond. *The Books of American Negro Spirituals*. NY: Viking, 1969.

Johnson, S. Lewis. "The Gospel that Paul Preached." *BSac* 128, (1971): 327-340.

Joyce, P. M. "Individual Responsibility in Ezekiel 18?" StudBib (1978). JSOTSup11. 185-196.

Juan, Stephen. *The Odd Body*. Kansas City, Mo: Andrews McMeel, 2004.

Kaiser, Walter C. Jr., P. H. Davids, F. F. Bruce, Manfred T. Brauch, *Hard Sayings of the Bible*. Downers Grove, Ill.: InterVarsity, 1996.

Keach, Benjamin. *Preaching from the Types and Metaphors of the Bible*. Grand Rapids: Kregel, 1972.

Kennedy, James M. "Peasants in Revolt: Political Allegory in Genesis 2—3." *JSOT* 47 (1990): 3-14.

Kidner, Derek. *Genesis – An Introduction and Commentary*. Downers Grove, Ill.: InterVarsity, 1973 reprint.

Kirkpatrick, A. F. *The Book of Psalms*. Cambridge: University, 1903.

Kitchens, Ted G. "Perimeters of Corrective Church Discipline." *BSac* 148 (1991): 201-213.

Kuyper, J. "The Meaning of Isaiah XL. 6." *VT* 13 (1963): 489-92.

Larkin, Clarence. *The Book of Revelation*. Philadelphia: Larkin, 1919.

Lategan, B. C. "The Truth that sets man free (John 8:31-36)." *Neot* 2 (1968), 70-80.

Lenski, R. C. H. *Interpretation of the New Testament*. Twelve vols: Minneapolis: Augsburg, 1961.

Leupold, H. C. *Exposition of the Psalms*. Grand Rapids: Baker, 1972.

_____. *Exposition of Genesis*. Grand Rapids: Baker, 1974.

Levy, David M. *Revelation: Hearing the Last Word*. Bellmawr, NJ: Friends of Israel Gospel Ministry, 1999.

Lindars, Barnabas. "Ezekiel 18 and Individual Responsibility." *VT* 15 (1965): 452-467.

Lindsay, Thomas M. *The Gospel according to St. Luke, Chapters I-XII.* Edinburgh: T&T Clark, 1887.

Loewen, J. W. *Sundown Towns.* NY: Simon & Schuster, 2005.

Loewenstamm, Samuel E. "The Making and Destruction of the Golden Calf." *Biblica* (48) 1967, 431-490.

Lovell, John Jr. *Black Song: the Forge and the Flame.* NY: Macmillan, 1972.

Lowery, David K. "The Head Coverings and the Lord's Supper in 1 Corinthians 11:2-34." *BSac* 143 (1986), 158.

Luck, G. Coleman. *Daniel.* Chicago: Moody, 1958.

_____. "The First Glimpse of the First King of Israel." *BSac* 123, (1966): 60-66.

MacBeath, A. *The Book of Job – a Study Manual.* Grand Rapids: Baker, 1966.

MacDonald, Wm. ed. Art Farstad. *Believer's Bible Commentary.* Nashville: T. Nelson, 1995.

Machen, Gresham. *NT Greek for Beginners.* NY: Macmillan, 1961.

Man, Ronald E. "The Value of Chiasm for NT Interpretation." *BSac* 141 (1984) 146-54.

Manson, T. W. *The Sayings of Jesus.* London: SCM, 1949.

Mason, Clarence E. Jr. *Prophetic Problems with Alternate Solutions.* Chicago: Moody, 1973.

McCane, B. R. "Let the Dead Bury Their Own Dead." *HTR* 83 (1990): 31-43.

McClain, Alva J. "The Greatness of the Kingdom-Part II." *BSac* 112 (1955): 107-124.

Merrill, Eugene."Paul's Use of 'About 450 years' in Acts 13:20." *BSac* 138, (1981): 246-54.

Meyer, F. B. *The Way into the Holiest.* Fort Washington: Christian Literature Crusade, 1961.

_____. *Joseph: Beloved—Hated—Exalted.* London: Morgan & Scott, 1910.

Mikliszanski, J.K. "The Law of Retaliation and the Pentateuch." *JBL* 66 (1947): 295-303.

Moffatt, J. *A New Translation Bible.* NY: Harper, 1950.

Montgomery, Helen B. *The New Testament in Modern English.* Philadelphia: Judson, 1949.

Morris, H. "Seven Reasons for Opposing Evolution." *BSac* 122 (1965): 254-69.

_____. *The Revelation Record.* Wheaton: Tyndale, 1988.

_____. *Defender's Study Bible.* Grand Rapids: World, 1995.

Morris, Leon. *The Epistles of Paul to the Thessalonians.* Grand Rapids: Eerdmans, 1957.

_____. *The Gospel according to John.* Grand Rapids: Eerdmans, 1971.

Mounce, Wm. D. MCED: Grand Rapids: Zondervan, 2006.

Myers, Edw. P. *Biblical Interpretation: Principles and Practices.* Grand Rapids: Baker, 1986.

Nee, Watchman. *Song of Songs.* Fort Washington: Christian Literature Crusade, 1974.

Nelson Study Bible, NKJV. Nashville: T. Nelson, 1997.

New American Standard Bible, Carol Stream, IL: Creation House, 1971. NASB

New English Bible: New Testament. Cambridge: Oxford University, 1961. NEB

New International Version of the Holy Bible. Colorado Springs, International Bible Society, 1984. NIV

New Pilgrim Bible KJV. NY: Oxford University, 2003.

Newell, Wm. R. *The Book of the Revelation.* Chicago: Moody, 1935.

Parsons, G. W. "Guidelines for Understanding and Proclaiming the Book of Proverbs." *BSac* 150 (1993): 151-70.

Perry, Alfred M. "Pearls Before Swine." *ExpTim* (46) (1934/1935): 381-2.

Peters, George W. "Perspectives on the Church's Mission." *BSac* 136 (1979): 3-15.

Philips, J. B. The New Testament in Modern English. NY: Macmillan, 1958. JBP

Pink, Arthur W. *An Exposition of Hebrews.* Grand Rapids: Baker, 1967.

Practico, Gary D. & Miles V. Van Pelt, *Basics of Biblical Hebrew Grammar.* Grand Rapids: Zondervan, 2001.

Quine, Jay A. "Court Involvement in Church Discipline." *BSac* 149 (1992): 60-73.

Rice, John R. *The King of the Jews: A Commentary on the Gospel according to Matthew.* Murfreesboro, Tenn: Sword of the Lord, 1975.

Robertson, A. T. *Robertson's Word Pictures in the New Testament. Electronic Database. Biblesoft,* 1997, 2003.

Robertson, E. "The Apple of the Eye in the Masoretic Text." *JTS* 38 (1937): 56-59.

Robertson, F. W. *The Biblical Illustrator.* Ages Software & Biblesoft, 2002, 2003.

Robertson, Palmer. "Habakkuk." NICOT. Grand Rapids: Eerdmans, 1990.

Revised Standard Version of the Bible. NY: T. Nelson, 1952. RSV

Ross, Allen. *Creation and Blessing.* Grand Rapids: Baker, 1988.

Rushdoony, "Judging: Part I: Hypocritical Judgment." *Chalcedon Report* #245 (Dec 1985), n. p.

Sale-Harrison, L. *The Wonders of the Great Unveiling.* NY: Loizeaux Bros., n.d.

Saphir, Adolph. *The Epistle to the Hebrews: an Exposition.* NY: Loizeaux Bros., Bible Truth Depot, n.d.

Scofield Study Bible NKJV. NY: Oxford University, 2002

Scott, Otto. "Fashion." *Chalcedon Report* (Dec 1993), 3-4.

Seiss, J. A. *The Apocalypse: Lectures on the Book of Revelation.* Grand Rapids: Zondervan, n.d.

Selwyn, Edward G. *The First Epistle of St. Peter.* London: Macmillan, 1958.

Shedd, Wm. G. T. *Commentary on Romans.* Grand Rapids: Baker, 1980.

Simcox,, Thomas C. "The Yom Kippur Scapegoat." *Friends of Israel* (Sep/Oct 2006): 32.

Snaith, Norman H. "The Exegesis of Isaiah 40.6." *ExpTim* 52 (1941), 394-6.

Spurgeon, C. H. *The Treasury of David, 3 vols.* McLean, Va: MacDonald, n.d.

Stevens, W. C. *Revelation, the Crown-Jewel of Biblical Prophecy.* Harrisburg, Pa: Christian Alliance, 1928.

Stevenson, Burton. *Home Book of Proverbs, Maxims, and Familiar Phrases.* NY: Macmillan, 1948.

Tasker, R. V. G. *The Gospel according to St. Matthew.* Grand Rapids: Eerdmans, 1983.

Tatford, Frederick A. *The Climax of the Ages: Studies in the Prophecy of Daniel.* London: Oliphants, 1964.

Tenney, Merrill C. *Interpreting Revelation.* Grand Rapids: Eerdmans, 1957.

_____. "Eschatology and the Pulpit." *BSac* 116, (1959): 30-42.

_____. "The OT and the Fourth Gospel." *BSac* 120 (1963): 300-308.

_____. "The Imagery of John." *BSac* 121 (1964): 13-21.

_____. "The Meaning of Signs: Part II." *BSac* 132 (1975): 145-160.

Thayer, Joseph Henry. *Greek-English Lexicon of the New Testament.* Grand Rapids: Zondervan, 1965.

Thiessen, Henry Clarence. *Lectures in Systematic Theology.* Grand Rapids: Eerdmans, 1986 reprint.

Thomas, Robert L. "The Glorified Christ." *BSac* 122 (1965): 241-7.

Thomas, W. H. Griffith. "The Plan of the Fourth Gospel, Part II." *BSac* 125, (1968): 313-23.

Today's English Version (Good News for Modern Man). NY: The American Bible Society, 1966. TEV

Traver, J. H. "The Biology of Salvation." *BSac* 120 (1963): 251-258.

Trench, Richard C. *Parables of Our Lord.* London: Macmillan, 1877.

_____. *Synonyms of the New Testament.* Grand Rapids: Eerdmans, 1985.

Unger, Merrill F. "Some Observations, Scientific Biblical Criticism and Exegesis." *BSac* 121 (1964): 58-65.

Varner, Wm. *Jacob's Dozen.* Bellmawr, NJ: Friends of Israel, 1987.

Waltke, Bruce K. "1 Corinthians 11:2-16: An Interpretation." *BSac* 135 (1978): 46-57.

Walvoord, John. "The Judgment of the Church in Heaven." *BSac* 123 (1966): 99-103.

_____. "The Kingdom of Heaven." *BSac* 124 (1967): 195-205.

_____. "The Doctrine of Grace in the Interpretation of Prophecy." *BSac* 140 (1983): 99-107.

Weymouth, R. F. *The New Testament in Modern Speech.* Fort Worth, Tex: Kenneth Copeland, 1996.

White, Wilbert Webster. *Studies in OT Characters.* NY: Young Men's Christian Association, 1909.

Williams, David J. *Paul's Metaphors: Their Context and Character.* Peabody, Mass.: Hendrickson, 1999.

Wilson, Kenneth T. "Should Women Wear Head Coverings?" *BSac* 148 (1991): 442-62.

Word Biblical Commentary: WBC. Dallas (Waco), Texas: Word.

World Book Dictionary, 2 vols. Eds. Clarence L. Barnhart and Robert K. Barnhart. Chicago: World Book, 1983.

Wyrtzen, David B. "The Theological Center of the Book of Hosea." *BSac* 141 (1984): 315-325.

Young, Edward J. *The Book of Isaiah.* 3 vols. Grand Rapids: Eerdmans, 1999.

Young, Robert. *Analytical Concordance to the Bible.* McLean, Va: MacDonald Publishing Co., n.d.

<u>William L. Banks</u>

Northeast High School – 1945
U.S. Army, honorably discharged – 1949
University of Pennsylvania – B. A. – 1953
Lincoln Seminary – B. D. – 1957
Eastern Baptist Theological Seminary – M. Th. – 1959
Carver Bible College – D. D. – 1973
Eastern Baptist Theological Seminary – D. Min. -- 1982

Adam's Ale and Adam's Apple

Adam's ale is a humorous, facetious and colloquial expression for water, the only drink of our first parents, Adam and Eve. It contained no alcohol, for it is believed there was no fermentation in the Garden of Eden. When visiting other cities, I often remark to my audiences, "Adam's ale here tastes better than Schuylkill Punch" (the Schuylkill River runs through Philadelphia).

Adam's apple: Take literally the Garden of Eden, with many fruit trees there. God's test of obedience: *Of every tree of the garden you may freely eat; but of the tree of the knowledge of good and evil you shall not eat, for in the day that you eat of it you shall surely die* (Gen 2.16-17). The Bible does not describe the fruit Adam and Eve ate. No mention is made of an apple. We are simply told that Eve "took of its fruit and ate. She also gave to her husband with her, and he ate" (Gen 3.6). Tradition and superstition, **not** the Bible, claim that a piece of the apple stuck in Adam's throat and formed the lump or projection (the thyroid cartilage of the larynx) we call "Adam's apple", seen at the front of the neck. It is normally more prominent in men than in women (Brewer's, 9).

Thought: "The sin in the Garden of Eden was not about the apple on the tree, it was about the pair on the ground." Thomas Hood:
When Eve upon the first of Men,
The apple press'd with specious cant,
Oh! What a thousand pities then,
That Adam was not adamant.

All Flesh Is Grass
Isa 40:6: *All flesh is grass* (1 Pet 1:24-25)

Grass grows rapidly after the winter and spring rains in Palestine; when the summer heat and the blistering desert wind strike, it withers just as quickly. Observation of the ephemeral nature of grass leads to comparing man's life as a here-today-and gone-tomorrow existence. [1] Life is like grass that is cut down, withering as the green herb, flourishing as a flower of the field, only to have its fading glorious beauty perish beneath the sun's burning heat (Pss 37:2, 103:15; Isa 28.1, 4, 37:27, 51:12; Jas 1:10-11). The phrase *all flesh* is found 43 times; it first occurs in Gen 6:12 describing the earth as corrupted; it closes with 1 Pet 1:24 describing *all flesh* as grass. In its widest sense *all flesh* includes the entire animal world, though primarily descriptive of humanity, and of human flesh.[2]

> The universal rule of decay and death is prominent in NT theology. The creature has been made 'subject to futility,' and is under the 'bondage of decay,' groaning and travailing in pain together (Rom 8.20-22). The earth and its atmospheric heavens are 'waxing old like a garment,' and shall be 'folded up,' and 'perish' (Heb 1.11-12). [3]

Flowers are appropriate figures of humanity's condition; their life cycle is relatively short, their perishability is readily observable. Human flesh is weak, frail, mortal; man's stay is precarious, short-lived, transitory, fleeting, insignificant, and impermanent. Spurgeon puts it: "Here is the history of the grass—sown, grown, blown, mown, gone; and the history of man is not much more." [4] One aspect of a *metaphor* is to show the connection expressed or understood between two things, both mentioned and taken literally, in this case *flesh* and *grass*. In Isa 40:6, note that "*All flesh* **is** *grass.*" *Is* distinctly affirms that one thing is another thing; all the figure lies in the verb "is". Thus the figure of speech has as "its one true and proper signification: that of *representation*."

In 1 Pet 1:24, note "*All flesh is* **as** *grass.*" This is called *simile*, the figure gently states that one thing is **like** or **resembles** another, whereas "*metaphor* carries the figure *across* at once . . . boldly and warmly declaring that one thing **is** the other." [5] Another way of looking at man's flower emphasizes his glory—his splendor, fame, strength, honor, art, education, learning, virtue, achievements, power, inventions, wealth, etc. As the flower of the field is dried up by the scorching rays of the sun and blown away by the wind, so quickly disappears all in which the ungodly take pride.[6]

Summary: The main thought is the terrific contrast between the ephemeral nature of human flesh and the permanence of God's Word! Feeble man's transitory beauty fades into oblivion, while God's Word basks in its eternal beauty. Man's flesh is weak;

2

God's Word is powerful. Man is unreliable; God's Word is steadfast and sure. Earthly beauty is short; God's Word is everlasting.[7]

Thought: A lady and her new maid were dusting some pictures on the wall of a bedroom. The maid asked if a certain photo was one that her employer had taken many years before. The lady acknowledged that it was. "My," the maid blurted out, "ain't time a wrecker!"

For years Cyclone Mitchell, former coal miner, amazed audiences with his feats of strength. He pulled heavily loaded wagons with his teeth; took cat naps on a bed of nails; allowed an automobile to roll over boards on his powerful chest; and with a heavy mallet his aids smash stones on his chest. He gave up barnstorming and became a part-time policeman. One day he suffered a heart attack and on the way to the hospital, he gasped in disbelief to a friend: "All this strength, and I'm powerless. There's nothing I can do." He was DOA.

[1] Yamauchi, *TWOT* 1:315.
[2] Alexander, 2:97; Lenski, *Peter,* 74; Grudem, 92; Baumgartel, *TDNT* 7:106. The flesh is part for the whole person; this is called *synecdoche,* Bullinger 642; Michaels, (WBC 49) 78.
[3] H. Morris, *(BSac* 122): 259.
[4] Oswalt, *TDNT* 1:135; Jacob, *TDNT,* 9:623; E. J. Young, 3:33. Keach, 133; Byatt, 7-9; Spurgeon, *Treasury,* (Psa 90:6) 2:62. *DBI,* 349: Grass: "symbol of human transience, mutability and mortality."
[5] Bullinger, 735-6.
[6] Calvin: Isaiah describes frail human life so as to "reduce to nothing all the excellence which men think that they possess." Not only is the outward man described, but mental gifts such as "prudence, courage, acuteness, judgment, skill in the transactions of business, etc . . . all men, with all their glory are nothing else than grass." Young, 3:33-4: "Isaiah is speaking, however, not merely of the frailty of human existence. His thought penetrates as well to the inner life of man. The mind, with all its qualities and attributes, as well as the spiritual life, is included in the prophet's thought."
[7] Kuyper, *VT* (13) 492; Snaith, *ExpTim* (52) 395; Bigg, *Peter & Jude,* ICC 124.

Amen Corner

The word *amen* occurs some 78 times. The NT Greek word *amen* is a transliteration of the Hebrew verb (*aman*) meaning to be firm, to confirm or to support. Used as an adverb, it asserts or confirms a matter. When repeated (verily, verily; truly, truly; surely, surely; or certainly, certainly), it has the "force of a superlative, *most assuredly*." Exclaimed at the end of a prayer or hymn, amen means, "So be it," or "so let it be!" *Amen Corner* is not found in the Bible, but refers to a place near the pulpit of some Protestant churches, occupied by a group of fervent worshipers or ardent believers of the congregation, who support and assist the preacher by their responsive "amen." Their vocal response may be occasional and irregular; it depends on some point emphasized in the prayer or in the sermon. Figuratively, *amen corner* is "any rallying place" (Hendrickson, 22).

Thought: An interesting use of the word *amen* is often heard in Afro-American church circles. When the person introducing the preacher at a revival or banquet is long-winded, someone (or more) may be heard to shout, "Amen!" The tone of voice, the inflection given this two-syllable word is such that it means, "Sit down, you've said enough. Let us hear the preacher!" Amen!

Apple of Your Eye: Psa 17:8 - *Keep me as the apple of Your eye.*

We know that God sees, and since we see with our eyes we say God has eyes. This language of accommodation (*anthropo-morphism:* man form) with which we describe ourselves is also applied to the LORD. Literally, the text reads, keep me as the *pupil, daughter of Your eye.* The word *pupil* means *little man (ishon).* This Hebrew usage or idiom (*Hebraism*) expresses a filial (son or daughter; *ishon bath*) relation; it implies affectionate, tender care. Even as the eye is "the tenderest part of the body" to us, so are God's people to Him.[1]

Prov 7:2 – *Keep my commands and live, and my law as the apple of your eye.* Hold God's Word in esteem just as we highly treasure our eyes. Jehovah keeps, guards and cares for us is with utmost diligence.

4

Lam 2:18: *Give thyself no rest; let not the apple of thine eye cease* (KJV). *Give yourself no relief; give your eyes no rest* (NKJV). Having failed to obey the LORD, Jerusalem now experiences abject sorrow, and is exhorted to continue wailing, day and night. Jehovah commands "Give your eyes no respite; let your crying be perpetual." The Hebrew reads, "Do not let the pupil of your eye cease" from crying. The pupil [rendered *apple*] is a surrogate or substitute for the whole eye, describing the functions of this extremely sensitive organ.[2]

Zech 2:8: *For he who touches you touches the apple of His eye.* This verse has two references: 2:8 (English) and 2:12 (Hebrew). In the Hebrew text chapter one has 17 verses; and chapter two starts with what is v18. See the importance of the intimate covenant relationship between Jehovah and the Jewish people. Whoever seeks to strike out the eyes of Israel will not only fail, but will have their own eyes plucked out! Imagine the enemies of Israel "pulling out their eyes by their own fingers!" Anti-Semitism is suicidal! And so the LORD encourages, "Have no fear of the unbelievers! When they afflict you, they afflict Me." Calvin believed that Jehovah's love towards the faithful is so tender that when *they* are hurt *He* burns with such displeasure as though one attempted to pierce His eyes. As we protect our eyes, so our Lord tenderly, affectionately protects us.[3] The Hebrew word used (only) here, and translated *apple*, determined to be of uncertain derivation by some scholars, is said by others to be derived from a root meaning gate or door. [4] This would suggest that *apple of the eye,* or eyelid or pupil is the orifice of the eye, "literally, the gate through which the light enters the eye, so the *pupil.*" [5]

Deut 32:10 – *He kept him as the apple of His eye.* When you look into a person's eye you see a miniature picture (*ishon: little man*), a reflection of yourself. [6] Look into God's eyes and see Israel. This text is "the primary passage for this bold figure, which is the utterance of loving entreaty." [7] Jehovah's miraculous deliverance of Israel from Egypt illustrates this truth. No nation succeeded in permanently hindering the Jews from passing through to the Promised Land. God provided victory in battle, food, water, and the pillar of cloud by day that became by night a pillar of fire. He guarded Israel "from harm as carefully as one guards his sensitive eyeball." [8]

Our eyes are a complex and delicate part of the body, protected in a number of ways. They are seated within strong frontal bony orbits or sockets; our eyebrows are like hedges, helping to break off light rays and help keep perspiration out of our eyes. Incidentally, eyebrows are not to be shaved off and painted on again! The eyelids are like curtains; they may be drawn very rapidly and are closed in sleep. Eyelashes are like fences or barriers against dust or perspiration. Note how quickly the hand goes up to protect the eyes.

I remember one day I tripped while running and fell into an iron fence. This resulted in having three stitches in my left eyelid; the scar remains. In recent years I have had laser repair of my right retina, and there are still small tears in the left eye retina; and I wear bifocals. If you suffer from cataracts or from glaucoma you know how valuable the gift of eyesight is. Because Christ is our Lord, we are more precious to God than our eyes are to us. The phrase, *apple of His eye*, is an English idiom that declares we too are precious to Him. [9]

Thought: *I love Thy Church, O God! Her walls before Thee stand, Dear as the apple of Thine eye, And graven on Thy hand.* (T. Dwight).

[1] Briggs & Briggs, *Psalms,* ICC 1:130.
[2] Harrison, R. K., 220.
[3] Scheper, cf. Jeffrey, 52.
[4] *TWOT* 1:89; E. Robertson, *JTS* (38): 56.
[5] Feinberg, *God Remembers* 49.
[6] Christensen, (WBC 6B) 797.
[7] K&D cited in Psa 17:8; describes Deut 32:10.
[8] E. Robertson, ibid. Calvin: Great precautions are taken against the injury of "the most tender part of the body."
[9] Schultz, *TWOT* 2:663; Fulghum, 17.

Appointed for Men to Die Once

Heb 9:27: *And as it is appointed for men to die once, but after this the judgment, so Christ was offered once to bear the sins of many.*

I have heard Heb 9:27 used often at funeral services to assure us that physical death is inevitable. It is true that, "Man who is born of woman is of few days and full of trouble" (Job 14:1). Our days are determined, months counted, time appointed, and our steps numbered. However, it is inaccurate to describe the dying here as **physical** death.

The reference is to **spiritual** death; in this way we maintain the analogy *appointed once to die* and *offered once to die*. God appointed humanity to die once in Adam; this was a spiritual death. We entered the world with a sin nature, "dead in trespasses and sins" (Eph 2:1, 5). Physical death, which comes as a result of spiritual death, has not been the lot of every human being. There are believers who *will not die* physically (1 Cor 15:51).

The verb translated *appointed* means to lay away, reserve, to lay up so that it can be counted on, to come upon someone as destiny; figuratively, it means "there is awaiting man." *Appointed* expresses the certainty of man's future established by the will of God; it is already fixed, cannot be changed or broken, for man is subjected to the divine ordination. [1] The pronouncement of judgment for this death has no intervening time link; there is an inevitable and immediate connection between sin that leads to death, and death that leads to judgment. [2] It is an open and shut case: Death, Judgment! Jehovah warned Adam that "in the day that you eat of it [the tree of the knowledge of good and evil], you shall surely die." This "penal appointment" for disobedience brought instant fractured fellowship, broken communion with God. Adam and Eve died spiritually that very moment; however, they did not drop dead physically. Centuries later, at the age of 930, Adam died physically, fulfilling Gen 3:19.

Consider the difficulties encountered when we define death in this passage solely as physical death: **(1) some human beings have died twice physically**. Though once restored to human life, eventually they died again. "For those there was one cradle, two coffins; one birth, two burials." [3] **(2) some human beings did not see physical death**: Enoch, Gen 5:24, Heb 11:5. Elijah, 2 Kgs 2:11. We reject R. Bultmann's interpretation of Heb 7:3, 16-17 that includes Melchizedek.[4] **(3) Some Christians shall never see physical death**: 1 Thess 4:17: "then we who are alive remaining" at the Second Coming of Christ. I Cor 15:51-52: "We shall not all sleep, but we shall all be changed." **(4) Unbelievers will experience what the Bible calls a "Second Death,"** Rev 20:14; without faith in the shed blood of Jesus Christ, the unregenerate will die a "second death," eternal separation from God. These variables move some scholars to talk of "exceptions," or "acts of Divine Sovereignty." [5]

> The cup was not His physical death on the cross, but the second death that was His due as the One who was made sin for us (2 Cor 5:21), who was made a curse for us (Gal 3:13). This meant nothing less than the second death (Rom 6:23). [6]

This "Second Death" refers to the "Lake of Fire". It is not second in relation to the physical death of the wicked. We do not compare physical death with eternal death. What occurred in the lives of Adam and Eve in the Garden of Eden was the "First Death." Failure to accept Jesus Christ leads to the Second Death.

2 Cor 5:14b – *that if One died for all, then all died*—helps us in our interpretation of Heb 9:27. First, the word rendered *all* means universal; all humanity died. Second, the verb translated *died* is a tense (*aorist*) that signifies **finality.** Rom 6:3-6 emphasizes a positional truth; because Christians are in Christ, when He died, we died; when He was baptized, we were baptized; when He was buried, we were buried; and when He rose, we too rose. We categorize these truths as **Positional** because they point out that God the Father sees us through the eyes of Jesus Christ. It is His desire that Positional truths affect our **Condition**, so that we become more like our position, more like that which the Lord has declared us to be already.

Considering the old self-life dead is not the issue in Heb 9:27, nor is it the point stressed in 2 Cor 5:14. The death all humans died is the sentence declaring us spiritually dead in sins and trespasses, the result of being in Adam. If Jesus Christ had not died for us, we would remain in this terrible condition forever and face the Second Death. Since Christ was separated from God the Father for all of us, then all of us were separated from God. Do not bring in the matter of physical death at this point. Death of the physical body is the result of spiritual death or separation from God. Do not confuse spiritual death with physical death. Maintain the order that Jesus Christ became sin and died (separated from God the Father); His atoning death dealt with total-depraved, dead human beings. Spiritual death, not physical death is stressed in Heb 9:27. Corporeal death may or may not be our lot. Christians face only the judgment for rewards for the deeds done in these bodies (2 Cor 5:10). This is not the judgment that condemns!

[1] Buchsel, *TDNT* 3:655.

[2] Saphir 2:603.

[3] F. B. Meyer, *The Way* 125. Christ alone has been resurrected, but there were many restorations: Son of the Zarapheth widow (1 Kgs 17:22); son of the Shunammite (2 Kgs 4:35); dead man touched Elisha's bones (2 Kgs 13:21); Jairus' daughter (Matt 9:25); son of the widow of Nain (Luke 7:15); Lazarus of Bethany (John 11:44); Dorcas (Acts 9:40); Eutychus (Acts 20:10). As for the saints restored after Christ resurrected (Matt 27:52) see my *Three Days and Three Nights*, 21. I believe Moses and Elijah will be the two witnesses (Rev 11:3). Moses appears along with Elijah; both are slain and restored to life (11:11). Christ alone has a glorified body; we cannot say that Moses received a resurrected body when Christ rose. A glorified body cannot be slain. Moses and Elijah represent the Law and the Prophets of Israel; as the two witnesses they stress the role of Israel in the Second Coming of Christ. Enoch has no relationship with Israel in this matter.

[4] Bultmann, *TDNT* 3:14n61.

[5] Pink, *Hebrews* 525.

[6] Barnhouse, *Romans,* God's Glory: 4:36.

As a Man Thinks in His Heart, So Is He - Prov 23:6-8

I.   Evil Eye: In certain contexts an evil eye refers to enchantment. Bewitchment, casting spells, the 'double-whammy', or some mysterious mischievous power is not the issue here; [1] rather an evil eye is the product of envy and selfishness. [2] One who has an evil eye is a miser; he is stingy; [3] he squeezes a penny so tight that he gives Abraham Lincoln a headache. The Hebrew word for evil here is variously rendered: calamity, distress, adversity, grief, affliction, misery, sorrow, trouble, sore, noisome, hurt, heavy, vex, wretchedness, harm, ill, mischief, wicked, naughty (good for nothing), and bad; it signifies "*breaking up* or *ruin* . . . and binds together in one the wicked deed and its consequences." His conduct is injurious "both to himself and to every one around him." [4] In the NT an evil eye may be diseased, blind, disordered, in poor condition (Matt 6:23; Luke 11:34), or bad in an ethical sense, as it is considered in Matt 20:15 (KJV): "Or is your eye evil because I am good?" [5]

II. Warning: Watch the company you keep. Sometimes the table is a trap, and the purpose of the invitation is to gain goodwill and later use the one considered a debtor. Doing "mental arithmetic with each bite," [6] the host calculates the cost of entertaining his guest. Do not be the guest of such a person, for while his words of invitation may be warm and friendly, his motives are impure. Though he invites you to help your self, and says, "Have some more," he counts every spoonful you take. He secretly hopes you will choke on the first bite, but dismisses the thought inasmuch as there is no one there to administer the Heimlich maneuver. His mask of hospitality is one of hypocrisy; his invitation is one of insincerity. What he says with his mouth is not what he thinks in his heart. Therefore do not desire his delicacies, his dainties, for he is duplicitous. [7] "In any case the paragraph is a maxim of social intercourse, a caution against indiscriminant dining out." [8]

When you realize how phony his welcoming words are, you will wish you had not eaten a crumb. Or that you could throw up what you did eat (return the food to him?). Eating food with an avaricious person is like "a hair in the throat," a phrase suggesting a vomiting reaction. [9] Not only *his* words, but the thought of *your* expressions of thanksgiving for the hospitality and meal you have just eaten may make you ill.

III. The Eyes of the Heart: We are on the outside what we are in our heart. Oftentimes our cover is blown, and we reveal what we really think; thoughts are put into action. The Hebrew word translated 'think' means to calculate, reckon, divide, decide, or estimate. This host estimates what it costs him to feed you, and his heart says, "Please don't eat too much." The part played by the human eye is significant, for "The eye is used to express knowledge, character, attitude inclination, opinion, passion and response. The eye is a good barometer of the inner thoughts of a man. . . .The eyes are a mirror of man's inner being. The eyes reflect generosity, stinginess, design, arrogance, humility, mockery, pity and avarice." [10] Figuratively, the eye is the heart or mind, the organ of spiritual reception . . . an index of the mind and disposition of man. [11]

Summary

Often I hear the words, "As a man thinks in his heart, so is he," used with total disregard to the context! The danger is: If a man thinks good thoughts, is he therefore a good man? We may suggest all men at some point in life have some good thoughts—but who judges them good? God does not, for without faith in Him it is impossible to please Him; in His sight the unbeliever has no pure thoughts. [12] When citing Prov 23:7, be sure to remember its context. It describes a hypocrite with an evil eye who regardless of what he says is still what he thinks in his heart. This does not mean that if he thinks good or pure thoughts, that he is good or pure. Only Christians are capable of thinking thoughts that are pleasing to the Lord (Phil 4:8).

Thought

Family Circus

"... But remember, Billy — what you think ..
you ARE!"

[1] M. Henry: Not an eye of evil enchantment as used in superstition.
[2] Van Leeuwen, *NIB* 5:206: "Bad of eye" is an idiom for selfishness.
[3] Prov 28:22: "A man with an evil eye (a stingy man) hastens after riches, and does not consider that poverty will come upon him."
[4] Girdlestone, 80.
[5] Weymouth, NIV: Are you envious (Thayer) because I am generous? RSV: Do you begrudge my generosity? Moffatt: Have you a grudge because I am generous? Montgomery: Or is your eye evil because I am generous? JBP, CEV: Must you be jealous

11

because I am generous? NEB: Why be jealous because I am kind? NASB: Or is your eye envious [evil] because I am generous [good]? BAGD: an evil eye is one that looks with envy or jealousy upon other people.

[6] Hawkins, *Parallel* 1240.

[7] K&D: his calculating, grudging look poisons your every bite.

[8] Toy, ICC *Proverbs* 430.

[9] Murphy, (WBC 22) 175; Gill; Van Leeuwen, ibid. Bulllinger 424: not taken literally, but is hyperbole or exaggeration, expressing "the suffering of regrets at having received benefits from such a host."

[10] Carl Schultz, *TDNT* 2:662-3.

[11] Luering, *ISBE* 2:1069.

[12] Christ describes what is in the heart of man: Mark 7:21-23, 10:18; Matt 19:17; Luke 18:19.

Ashes to Ashes, Dust to Dust: Gen 3:19: *In the sweat of your face you shall eat bread till you return to the ground, for out of it you were taken; for dust you are, and to dust you shall return* (cf. Gen 2:7).

"Earth to earth, ashes to ashes, and dust to dust" is a phrase we often hear at funeral services held in the church, but more often at the funeral parlor or at the grave site. It is part of what is called the *committal,* which is then followed by the interment or cremation. [1] Jehovah had warned Adam not to eat of the tree of the knowledge of good and evil, "for in the day that you eat of it you shall surely die" (Gen 2:16-17). Communion with God was broken, and the germ of death entered Adam's body the moment he disobeyed. Eventually at the age of 939, physical death returned his body to the earth to be dissolved into primitive dust. *Ashes* and *dust* describe poetically the mortal remains of a dead body after decay or cremation. The words are joined by common usage of the conjunction *and* for emphasis.[2] Jehovah formed man's body out of the elements of the earth, the same materials He created and used to form plants and animal bodies.

> The fact that man comes from the dust of the earth is a
> reminder of the sovereignty of God in his creative acts,
> and of the insignificance of man apart from the
> intervening 'breath of life' of his goodness. Man as a

fashioned artwork owes praise and obedience to the Potter who fashioned him of clay. Dust-man became living-man by God's grace; therein lies his humility and his dignity. (R.B. Allen, *TWOT 2:*687) [3]

Gen 18:27: *Then Abraham answered and said, "Indeed now, I who am but dust and ashes have taken it upon myself to speak to the LORD."* (Cf. Job 10:9, 30:19, 34:15). By calling himself a man created out of the dust and ashes of the ground, Abraham humbly contrasted himself with his Creator. Imagine a vile, unworthy, mortal, frail, feeble abject piece of clay interceding with a Holy God for whatever number of righteous folks may live in the city of Sodom. Abraham speaks with 'strong words of self-abasement,' [4] reminding us that although we have access to God the Father through Jesus Christ, our approach always must be with reverence.

Job 42:6: *Therefore I abhor myself, and repent in dust and ashes.* He repents of the disrespectful speeches he made in his anger, and humbles himself. [5] Job admits his worthlessness, lamenting that God has reduced "his native earth before he has lived out his life." His penitence expresses the truth and sincerity of repentance. Job's physical condition is described as half-dead, looking like a corpse, and covered with dust and ashes. The philosophy appears to be to let our external appearance correspond to our internal feelings; "outward expressions of godly sorrow well become penitents" (M. Henry).

Eccl 3:20: *All go to one place: all are from the dust, and all return to dust.* Bringing back man's mind to his origin, this reflection upon from whence we came, and where our bodies are going—*from* dust *to* dust—is calculated to humble us. Dust is figurative of self-abasement, humiliation; ashes point to insignificance. [6] Since the Fall, both man and beast are on their journey from dust to dust. Annihilation is not taught; humans do not cease to exist upon dying. Although from the writer's point of view [under the sun], *there is no work or device or knowledge or wisdom in the grave* (9:10), there is no biblical basis for assuming that death ends it all. How disconcerting it must be for the proud to be told their commonality with beasts is demonstrated by the corruption of their bodies in death. H. Morris (*Defender's* Gen 3:19) speaks of the "universal tendency for systems to decay and become disordered . . . for the living to die." This is called the law of increasing *entropy* ("in-turning"). It is a fundamental principle of nature that runs smack dab over the concept of evolution.

Psa 103:14: *For He knows our frame; He remembers that we are dust.* (Cf. 104:29). "Ashes" is a word often used in the Bible to denote insignificance, evanescence, or worthlessness; and dust symbolizes man's frailty and mortality. [7] We need to remember our infirmity. Failure to glorify God's majesty leads to our own self-exaltation. Failure to see the sinfulness of sin leads to self-righteousness. Failure to think high thoughts of the God of the Bible leads to thinking highly of our selves. Failure to remember how helpless we are against Satan, evildoers, disease, natural catastrophes, and our own natures—easily leads to self-confidence and pride. And pride leads to a downfall.

> Our heavenly Father never overlooks us, and never fails to give us strength equal to our day, because He always takes our frailty into account when He is apportioning to us our lot. Blessed is His holy name for this gentleness towards His frail creatures. (Spurgeon, *Treasury* [Psa 103:14] 2:281)

> Many pastors have had the mournful opportunity to stand at an open grave, and commit the ashes of someone dear to others standing there. I always shudder when I listen to the burial ceremony which says, "Earth to earth, ashes to ashes, dust to dust," as if that were all. It isn't. We are not looking to the sod, but to the stars. Our hope does not lie in the grave, but in the Lord. The effect of this doctrine on personal hope is tremendous. 'If we believe that Jesus died and rose again, even so them also which sleep in Jesus will God bring with Him.' The preaching of this hope is to stimulate, to comfort, and to strengthen those who need it. (Tenney, *BSac* [116] 40-41)

Thought: "Ashes to ashes and dust to dust, If God won't have him the Devil must" (Brewer's, 59).

[1] Man's "under the sun" point of view denotes total finality, a "when you're dead, you're done!" Like animals, we "all go to one place: all are from the dust, and all return to dust" (Eccl 3:20). *Above* the sun is God's Word reassuring us that absent from the body is to be present with the Lord (2 Cor 5:8). Burning the bodies of the dead was an ancient custom, but not the customary or ordinary method used by the Hebrews to dispose of the deceased; cf. Eager, *ISBE* 2:744.

[2] Bullinger, 442.

[3] The joke is told that a proud scientist said to God, "We no longer need you now that we can clone humans, and create people!" God said, "Fine, can you create a man the same way I made Adam?" This would be difficult thought the scientist, but he agreed to try. He stooped to get some soil, but the Lord stopped him and said, "Not so fast. You must create your own dirt, too."

[4] Zimmerli, *TDNT* 5:659n25; Jeffrey, 217-8; Fulghum: Hence the phrase expresses humility, worthlessness, and repentance, 61-2.

[5] Fichtner, *TDNT* 5:395; Clines, (WBC 17) 248.

[6] Ashes are mentioned first, and dust is but refined ashes. Metaphorically, both signify contempt, misery, frailty, vileness, great calamity, sadness and mourning that follow (Keach, 128).

[7] Eager, *ISBE* 1:269; Edwards, *ISBE* 2:883. See 2 Sam 13:19; Job 2:8; Isa 58:5, 61:3; Jer 6:26; Lam 3:16; Ezek 27:30, 28:18; Jonah 3:6 and Matt 11:21.

At Ease in Zion: Amos 6:1: *Woe to you who are at ease in Zion.*

In Philadelphia, PA, the name *Zion* is a popular one in Black churches. [1] This is true in most of our large urban centers. Zion refers to Jerusalem the capital of Judah, the southern kingdom. Samaria was the capital of Israel, the northern kingdom. Both nations are warned, for both are guilty of having sinned against Jehovah, after having enjoyed for nearly a generation both economic prosperity and the security of a strong military (Nelson, 1483). They believed they were God's chosen, and that Jehovah would never allow the calamity that Amos preached to fall upon them. Israel is especially condemned for its idolatry and spiritual insensitivity.

However, Zion (Judah) is named first, perhaps suggesting "a ring of decadence to it beyond" what the reference to Mount

Samaria connotes. [2] The first woe (Amos 5:18) is announced against those who desire the Day of the LORD (*Yom Yahweh*), unaware that it will be a day of judgment. The second woe begins with chapter six. *Woe* is an interjection or exclamation used to express sorrow, dismay, grief, trouble, distress or warning, it is onomatopoeic—a word formed by imitating the sound associated with the thing designated. *Hoy* usually expresses dissatisfaction and pain, "Ah, Alas, or Ha." [3]

To be *at ease* is to lean confidently, rest securely without pain or anxiety, to be quiet, comfortable, all with a collateral idea of recklessness, carelessness, arrogance and wantonness. Amos aims directly at the *notable persons*—nobles, leaders, officials, ruling classes, the chief men, the influential, those responsible for administering justice and helping the poor. Their philosophy appears to be, "get rich in bad times;" their self-indulgence and disregard for others is rebuked (Calvin).

Amos describes their evil behavior, their complacent, decadent luxury-loving lifestyle. [4] (1) They show no concern for the threatened judgments, or for their own soul salvation (Clarke); by putting off the day of doom, they hasten its arrival. (2) They lie on beds "inlaid with ivory" and stretch out on couches. (3) They eat lambs from the flock and calves from the midst of the stall (carefully selected for their special fatness or daintiness); and choose calves reared artificially in a stall in order to be easily fattened.

(4) They sing idly to the sound of stringed instruments they invented; "who sing [twitter] idly, used sarcastically of the music rendered at feasts." Amos indicates "contempt for the perhaps really not unmusical songs with which feasts were enlivened." [5] (5) They drink wine abundantly from bowls—not ordinary drinking vessels, but large size, "another token of self-indulgence." [6] (6) They anoint themselves with the best ointments, expensive perfumes and colognes. (7) They show no concern for the affliction of Joseph. (8) They recline at banquets. H. Morris (*Defender's*: Amos 6:1) sees in this state of things in Zion a "frighteningly obvious" parallel to Western Christianity today.

Thought

[1] The 2007-08 Verizon Yellow Book Philadelphia directory reveals: Zion AME; **African Methodist Episcopal Zion** (Alleyne, St James, Varick, Wesley); **Baptists** (Celestial Zion, Love Zion, Mt Zion [Germantown, Holmesburg, West Phila], New Mt Zion, Second Mt Zion, Zion, Zion Hill, Zion Hill Memorial, Zion Tabernacle). Mt Zion Fire Baptized Holiness; Mt Zion United Methodist; Zion Assemblies of God Church; Endtime Zion Church of Jesus Christ; Mount Zion Apostolic Church of Christ; Zion Tabernacle Church of Jesus Christ, Inc.; **Pentecostal** (Mt Zion, Mt Zion Church of Christ, Mt Zion Holy Church, Mt Zion Holy Tabernacle, Mt Zion Mission of Deliverance; New Mt Zion Church of God in Christ, Zion Hill COGIC; Trumpet of Zion Tabernacle, Mt Zion Pentecostal Faith; Zion Pent[a]costal Church of God House of New Direction; Zion Temple, Inc.); Mt Zion Lutheran African.

[2] Stuart, (WBC 31) 358; Fink, *Parallel* 1709: "The people of Zion mistook God's favor for favoritism."

[3] Another word, *oy*, is more distinctly, *woe,* an impassioned expression of grief and despair (Isa 6:5).

[4] Fulghum, 20; Barnes: a luxury and ease that make the soul sensual, dull, stupid and callous (hard-hearted).

[5] Harper, *Amos & Hosea,* ICC 147.

[6] Bowl, basin (vessel for *throwing or tossing a liquid*); the verb means "to toss, throw, scatter in abundance;" the noun refers to drinking-bowls (Amos 6:6); Van Groningen, *TWOT* 1:254.

Babbler: Acts 17:18: *"What does this babbler want to say?"*

The noun **babble** (a word that is imitative of babies' chatter) is variously defined: blather, gabble or gab; blabber or blab, drivel, twaddle; jabber, prattle, chatter, chitchat, murmur, clamor, hubbub, din; incoherent, irrational, inarticulate or foolish talk; "running off at the mouth;" it is rapid, foolish, excited and incomprehensible talk; it is a meaningless confusion of words or sounds.[1] We find the word **Babbling(s)** three times in the Scriptures. It occurs first in "one of the sharpest attacks on drunkenness in the Bible" (Nelson, 1066), and with razor sharp satire and vivid imagery. Prov 23:29 asks, "Who hath babbling?" (KJV) "Who grumbles?" (Moffatt); "Who has complaints?" (NKJV, NIV, NASB). The Hebrew word signifies meditation and speech; here it is sorrowful thought and complaint (K&D).

In the other two passages, the Apostle Paul warns Timothy to avoid "profane and vain babblings" (1 Tim 6:20; 2 Tim 2: 16). Here the word translated *babbling* is literally, "empty sound" *(kenophōnia),* "empty chatter" (NASB), "profane jargon" (Moffatt), "frivolous talk" (Weymouth), "godless chatter" (NIV). Thayer calls such talk "uttering emptiness, empty discussion, or discussion of vain and useless matters." Shun what is falsely called science, for its path "leads away from faith, and turns to error rather than to knowledge." Thus Paul exhorts his spiritual son to avoid the moral and religious consequences of such babblings.[2]

The word **Babbler** occurs twice in the Bible. **(1)** Eccl 10:11 (KJV): Surely the serpent will bite without enchantment (NKJV: when it is not charmed); and the slanderer (NKJV: babbler) is no better (NKJV: different). NIV: "If a snake bites before it is charmed, there is no profit for the charmer" (cf. NASB). Moffatt: "the charmer's skill is useless." Note the various renderings: *babbler, slanderer,* and *charmer.* The idea is that a man (master) of tongue, one with an enchanting tongue, thus a charmer, wastes his skill if the serpent bites before it is charmed. An unused skill is a waste (Nelson, 1093).

(2) This brings us to the word **Babbler** in Acts 17:18, *spermológos,* literally, seed-collector. The paraphrasers and translators have much to say here. In mocking Paul some of the philosophers in Athens called the apostle an "ignorant showoff" (TEV); a "jester, a silly or paltry trifler" (Calvin). He's "a dreamer" (LB), an "intellectual beach-comber" (Rieu). "Whatever does the fellow mean with his scraps of learning?" (Moffatt) What is "this babbler with his scrap-picked learning trying to say?" (Amplified); this "picker-up-of-scraps" (Rotherham). He is an "idle babbler" (one who makes his living by picking up scraps: NASB; BAGD). "What can this charlatan be trying to say" (NEB). "What would this seed-picker say" (Lenski). Goodspeed calls him a "ragpicker" (incorrect, says Lenski). "What has this beggarly babbler to say?" (Weymouth). He is "a babbler with second-hand ideas." [3] Because birds flitter about, picking up seeds, "following the plough or haunting the corn markets," what is said about birds is applied to men.[4] "What is this cock sparrow trying to say" (JBP). He is a "gutter sparrow, a small bird that snatches up scraps of food" (Nelson, 1852).

It is suggested we have here a bit of Athenian slang applied to a man picking up fragmentary ideas here and there and passing them on without digesting or thinking through what he teaches. He has no real knowledge of their meaning; consequently, what he says amounts to nothing! He is a dilettante, a dabbler, and trifler. Here is another reminder that the world despises Christians. To the materialist, the secularist, the worldly philosopher, the doctrines of the Bible are nonsense. And so, to the list of names Paul's enemies called him—persecutor of the church, trouble-maker, jail-bird, one who sought to turn the world upside down, insincere, not to be trusted, a fool, mad (beside himself)—add, *babbler*!

[1] Family Word Finder, 74; Association with *Babel* (Gen 11:9) may have affected the definitions, but no direct connection can be traced. AHD modern definition of *babble*: "A tape recording of several dozen voices talking at the same time, used as an antibugging device to make private or secret conversations inaudible to eavesdropper."
[2] Bietenhard, *TDNT* 5:283; Foerster *TDNT* 7:190.
[3] Bertram, *TDNT* 4:845n110.
[4] Byatt, 51.

Blind Leading the Blind: Matt 15:14: *And if the blind leads the blind, both will fall into a ditch* (Luke 6:39).

Both the scribes and Pharisees criticized the Lord for allowing His disciples to eat bread without first washing their hands, a failure they considered as transgressing "the tradition of the elders." Christ condemned their disobedience of God's commandments, as well as their loyalty to tradition. Later, the disciples asked the Lord whether He knew that the Pharisees were offended (*scandalized*: displeased, made indignant) by His scathing denouncement. Christ responded by exhorting the disciples not to be troubled with the Pharisees' feelings. Whatever God the Father has not planted will be uprooted. By stumbling on a plain road, it is obvious that they are willfully blind (Calvin). Do not worry about their rage. The tense of Christ's command suggests, "Let them go! Give them up! Have nothing to do with them! Have no kind of religious connection with them. Let them alone to do their worst." Their case is hopeless; reform is impossible; their road leads to ruin and cannot be avoided. [1]

What follows is a general proverb, "a way side saying, a saw or adage," one that shows the absurdity of the spiritual condition of the Pharisees and their followers. [2] *"Blind leaders of the blind"* is a saying that describes the ignorance of both leaders (literally, escorts or guides) and followers. They are blind in that they equate the will of God with their own traditions and customs; they are blind to the truth of the words of the Lord Jesus. Their arrogance, pride and self-righteousness have closed their eyes to spiritual truths.

Nonetheless they assert their ability as teachers of the truth; they believe that people who do not know the Law and tradition as *they* know them are the ones who are really blind. They think they are "leaders of the blind" when in truth they are "blind leaders." [3] In essence, blindness means unbelief. [4] We cannot give to others what we do not have; we cannot teach what we do not know. The attempt to do so inevitably leads to falling into a ditch or more accurately, into an "open cistern in the field." [5] Disobedience to God's word causes stumbling (1 Pet 2:8). They fall into the cistern of ignorance, error, immorality, distress, despair, temporal ruin and destruction, eternal damnation, and the lake of fire (Gill). "Man is by nature (from birth) blind to the light of revelation." [6]

20

Nor is this blindness a mere misfortune or only the natural blindness of men that is due to their inherited sinful state. Theirs is that self-willed and obdurate blindness which consists in a fixed and final opposition to the light. They deliberately chose the darkness, rather than the light (John 3.19) and proudly called that blindness sight (John 10.40-41), desiring to be designated as *the Seeing Ones.* (Lenski, *Matthew* 591)

"The falling of both together will aggravate the fall of both; for they that have thus mutually increased each other's sin, will mutually exasperate each other's ruin." [7] The picture of lostness here is a vivid expression of the devastating consequences of false teaching. One might say that these religious leaders are guilty of putting obstacles in the way of a blind man or leading him astray whether deliberately, or ignorantly (Lev 19:14; Deut 27:18).

God often suffers one man to lead many to ruin. A rich and profligate man, an infidel, a man of learning, a politician, or a teacher, is allowed to sweep multitudes to ruin. This is not unjust, for those who are led are not compelled to follow such people. They are free in choosing such leaders, and they are answerable for being led to ruin (Barnes).

Thought: Arabian Proverb: He who knows not and knows not that he knows not, he is a fool; shun him. He who knows not and knows that he knows not, he is simple; teach him. He who knows and knows not that he knows he is asleep; wake him. He who knows and knows that he knows he is wise; follow him.

---

[1] Clarke; ATR; AB Bruce, *ExpGT* 1:214.
[2] Bullinger, 755.
[3] Schrage, *TDNT* 8:293; Rom 2:19, Matt 23:16, 24.
[4] Stahlin, *TDNT* 7:351.
[5] Kent, *Wycliffe* 956.
[6] Schrage, *TDNT* 8:290.
[7] M. Henry; cf. Isa 9:16.

Bone of My Bones: Gen 2.23: *And Adam said; "This is now bone of my bones and flesh of my flesh; she shall be called Woman, because she was taken out of Man."*

Bones last longer than any other part of a dead body; and the skeleton is like the framework of a building, supporting the entire edifice. [1] Because the word rendered *bone* means substance, self, power or might, there is a figurative meaning of close relationship; *bone* signifies more than sharing the same bodily heritage. [2] In this first statement of personal intimacy, the Hebraic idiom *bone* is equated with the totality of one's being, or what one writer calls an equal and complementary relationship shared by the two sexes. [3]

> The word **Ish**, being first used by man of himself in contradistinction to a second being of his own kind and springing from him, must represent some personal feeling of a kind [hitherto strange to Adam]. Instead of being isolated and without a fellow, having God far above him, and the beast of the earth below him, Adam found that he had a companion of a nature congenial to his own, 'a help,' as Scripture says, 'meet for him;' there was an *I* and a *Thou*, a personal relationship between two *selves* or *existences*, an **Ish** and an **Ishah**, the one springing from the other, and reflecting the other's nature—the same, yet distinct. (Girdlestone, 48-9)

Bone and flesh is a Hebrew phrase meaning "having the same nature, and the nearest relation"; since they have the same source the figurative expression indicates "family kinship . . . formed from the same parents, or from the same family." [4] *Bone of my bones* is the Hebrew "genitive superlative" seen in such phrases as 'servants of servants,' 'holy of holies,' 'King of kings,' and 'Song of songs'. [5] Adam's first words are, "This is now," literally, "This time." Behind those words is the idea, "Now at last, at length, finally . . . in contrast with the whole animal creation Adam had just named" (Nelson, 9). In the Hebrew the word *this* is repeated three times: "**This** now at length *is* bone from my bones and flesh from my flesh for **this** [one] shall be called *ishah* for from *ish* was taken out **this** one." Such animated language indicates the anticipation with which Adam looked forward to this event. He immediately recognized "the most complete physical congruity

22

[agreement, harmony] of this new person with himself." [6] Adam knew something was lacking in his life; it is as if he said, "This living creature which at the present time passes before me, is the companion which I need, for it is bone of my bones, and flesh of my flesh." [7] In short, he expresses joyous astonishment at the suitable helpmate God has provided. Eve was a mirror of Adam, a perfect match, yet different, and he expresses his joy by the words, "She is bone of my bones and flesh of my flesh." [8]

Thought: If man is the head, she is the crown, a crown to her husband, the crown of the visible creation. The man was dust refined, but the woman was dust double-refined, one remove further from the earth . . . That the woman was made of a rib out of the side of Adam; not made out of his head to rule over him, nor out of his feet to be trampled upon by him, but out of his side to be equal with him, under his arm to be protected, and near his heart to be beloved (M. Henry).

[1] Jacob, *TDNT* 9:623-4.
[2] Oswalt, *TWOT* 1:136. Brueggemann, *CBQ,* (vol 32) 533: It is with "an assertion that is not concerned simply with physical relationship but includes also psychological dimensions of interaction."
[3] Jeffrey, 97-100, cites Waukkonen; Psa 35.10; cf. Waltke, *BSac* (135) 47. So far as their humanity is concerned Adam and Eve are equal; yet they are set apart from the animals. Because Adam was created first, and had the privilege of naming the woman, "she is expected to be subordinate to him," Wenham, (WBC 1) 69. Gen 3:16; 1 Cor 11:3, 8-9; 1 Tim 2:11-13.
[4] Leuring, *ISBE* 1:495. Schrader, *Parallel* 19; Gen 29.14: And Laban said to him (Jacob), "Surely you are my bone and my flesh." Judg 9.2: Abimelech, son of Gideon, said: "Remember that I am your own flesh and bone." 2 Sam 5.1: Then all the tribes of Israel spoke, saying, "Indeed we are your bone and your flesh." 2 Sam 19.12-13: You are my brethren, you are my bone and my flesh . . . And say to Amasa, "Are you not my bone and my flesh?"
[5] Fulghum, 33; cf. Pratico and Van Pelt, 110.
[6] Leupold, *Genesis* 1:136. *DBI* 113: "conveys Adam's sense of the fact that, unlike the animals he has named, this new individual is profoundly and essentially him."
[7] Calvin (editor); K&D.

Bullinger 689: "Though the bone and flesh of Adam were changed and made into Eve, yet the name of the original source, 'bone,' etc., is retained."

Brand Plucked out of the Fire

Amos 4:11: *And you were like a firebrand plucked from the burning.* Zech 3:2: *Is this not a brand plucked from the fire?* Jude 23: *But others save with fear, pulling them out of the fire.*

Perhaps originally the Hebrew word rendered *brand* or *firebrand,* referred to a bent stick used to stir fire. The Old English word translated *brand* means 'torch' and is related to the word *burn.* [1] The word brand has a "double signification of an object on fire and of objects used to feed a fire." [2] See then the firebrand plucked from the burning as a stick with one end already on fire, a proverbial phrase vividly describing God's deliverance of Israel in what we call "the nick of time." **Amos** reminds Israel that throughout its history Jehovah chastened them with famine, drought, crop failure, plague, etc. However, "As God overthrew Sodom and Gomorrah, and you were like a firebrand plucked from the burning; yet you have not returned to Me."

Even as God pulled Lot's family out of Sodom's terrible destruction (Gen 19), so He often rescued Israel at the last moment! The destruction of Sodom and Gomorrah is mentioned more than twenty times.[3] Hear the broken heart of God repeat this solemn refrain, "Yet you have not returned to Me!" (Amos 4:6, 8, 9-11). No matter what the disaster, whether earthquakes or fire, the people remained unmoved. Such was their "stubborn infidelity," even after the Lord in mercy delivered the nation by snatching it out of the fire, as "a log pulled away from the conflagration!" [4] The sin of ingratitude soon leads to spiritual amnesia.

Zechariah's emphasis is upon the retrieval of Israel for God's future purpose, for He has further plans for that nation. Scholars who dismiss Israel from God's Plan for the Ages are in error. The Church has not taken Israel's place. In this vision Joshua, the priest, represents Israel. Satan, a great observer and student of history, is acutely aware of Israel's backsliding and wickedness, and vehemently opposes Joshua. For a number of reasons Satan hates Israel (Rom 3:2; 9:4-5). Obviously, he despises the concept of grace, and considers the nation unfit to carry out any priestly function. Jehovah announces that by His sovereign grace, Israel was delivered from the *fire* of captivity in Babylon. Satan's hatred cannot prevent the LORD from snatching, plucking, and pulling Israel out of her trouble. And though Israel faces still further *fire,* rest assured God's plans shall be fulfilled. Jehovah maintains the integrity of His choice, a choice not based upon Israel's goodness or upon Joshua's sinlessness. He brought Israel out of exile (captivity) in Babylon, to demonstrate His purpose. And He will continue to pluck brands from the fire!

Jude's comment on *pulling them out of the fire* also echoes the proverbial phrase used by Amos, and finds its source more probably in Zechariah.[5] The verb translated *pulling out (harpazo)* means "to take something forcefully (rapaciously, quickly, or firmly); it is to 'snatch' out of the fire with the thought of speed." [6] The fire here is seen as "a common image for the judicial wrath of God," depicting what "is mostly the irresistible power of destruction." [7]

Because of the words in Jude 7, "suffering the vengeance of eternal fire," Lang believes the *fire* is that of judgment, hell-fire. [8] Some scholars believe reference is to those already in the fire. MacDonald says they are on the verge of the precipice, ready to fall over into the flames of apostasy. Bauckham states that while the fire is that of final judgment in hell, Jude does not teach that the people are already in the fire, but that they are on the edge of it; they can be snatched back before they fall into it. [9]

Jude does not explain how they are to be snatched out, except to say there is to be a continuous effort (present imperative, to save; present participle, snatching). Lenski likens the deliverance to snatching some one out of a burning house. Litfin writes about confronting cults and whether the use of "deprogramming" is justified by the words *save with fear, pulling them out of the fire.* It is God's desire that all of us grow in Christ. For some there will be the need to deal with patience and tender, loving care. On the other hand, drastic action is needed for those at the very brink of hell, those who are "on the verge of slipping off into apostasy," who have "all but embraced the heresy of the false teachers." [10]

---

[1] Hendrickson, 101.

[2] *ISBE* 1:514.

[3] Sodom and Gomorrah: Gen 13:10, 18:20, 19:24, 28; Deut 29:23, 32:32; Isa 1:9, 13:19; Jer 23:14, 49:18, 50:40; Lam 4:6; Amos

4:11; Zeph 2:9; Matt 10:15, 11:23-24; Mark 6:11; Luke 10:12, 17:29; Rom 9:29; 2 Pet 2:6, and Jude 7.

[4] Stuart (WBC 31) 339. Calvin: The people were indeed worthy of complete destruction; but it was God's will that some remnant should continue, lest anyone should think that He had forgotten His covenant. He had to contend with the wickedness and hypocrisy of the people *while* showing that His covenant was not entirely void. Cf. Walker, *ISBE* 2:1112; Fisher, *TWOT* 2:594.

[5] Bauckham, (WBC 50) 115.

[6] Foerster, *TDNT* 1:472.

[7] Lang, *TDNT* 6:935.

[8] *Ibid*, 6:946.

[9] Bauckham, ibid: "They are sinners who are in imminent danger of judgment at the *parousia* [Second Coming]. They are evidently church members who under the influence of the false teachers are indulging in sinful behavior, but will repent when their error is pointed out to them."

[10] Litfin, *BSac* (135): 239-40. OED 2:488: cf. "A person delivered from imminent danger."

Cast in His Teeth: Matt 27:44: *The thieves also, which were crucified with him, cast the same in his teeth* (KJV).

Note that the crowd—the populace, chief priests, scribes, Sadducees, and Pharisees—spat their venom at the Lord Jesus, but we do not read of any "reflections on the thieves that were crucified with Him." [1] The Greek word translated *thieves* is properly rendered **"robbers."** A thief is one who is sneaky, takes property by stealth; the robber is in-your-face, and may resort to violence. Compared with Christ, it was as if the robbers were saints, and we hear of no cry of revenge directed at them. Consider the variety of translations and paraphrases of the words, *cast the same in His teeth*: "Reviled" (NKJV; RSV; BAGD); "hurled abuse" (JBP); "taunted" (NEB); [2] "were casting the same insult at Him" (NASB); [3] "denounced" (Moffatt); "heaped insults" (NIV; Weymouth); "said cruel things" (CEV); "kept reviling" (Montgomery); "reproached" (Expositor's); [4] "chided" (Hagner, WBC); and "upbraided" (Barnes).[5] "Even those who were crucified with Him reviled Him" (Mark 15:32b).

Does it appear odd that the two robbers would join in with these mockers? Could it be that they probably felt a momentary superiority by maligning Him (ATR). Imagine being in their situation and joining in with the religious leaders cursing the claims of the Lord to be the Messiah, the King of Israel, and the Son of God. When Christ did not answer, one of the criminals began blaspheming Him, saying, "Are You not the Christ (Messiah)? Save Yourself and us!" The original Greek word (*oneidizo*) means to reproach, upbraid, revile; and is used both of deserved and unjust reproach; it is to heap insults upon. [6] *To cast in someone's teeth* means to throw reproof at someone; [7] understand then that "the passion of Jesus includes being despised even by those who were crucified with Him." [8]

[1] M. Henry also speaks of the crowd's "insatiable revenge" that was not satisfied with the death of Christ.
[2] Hindson, *Parallel* 1959: "repeated similar taunts."
[3] NASB: Luke 23:39: "And one of the criminals who were hanged there was hurling abuse at Him."
[4] ATR: "began to reproach"; cf. Hagner, (WBC 33B) 840.
[5] Barnes calls *cast the same in His teeth* "a most unhappy translation." Gill states the robbers *twitted* Him. *Twit* means to taunt, ridicule, or tease, especially for embarrassing mistakes or faults (AHD); jeer at, reproach, blame (WBD).
[6] Schneider, *TDNT* 5:239: *to cast [the same] in his teeth:* to scold, bring reproaches against someone, lay something to a person's charge, and raise a complaint against something. "The objects of *oneidizo* [reproach] are God, Israel, the righteous, or men of the nearest and closest circle of life."
[7] Brewer's, 189: refers to knocking someone's teeth out by stones.
[8] Schneider, *TDNT* 5:240.

Cast Your Bread upon the Waters: Eccl 11:1: *Cast your bread upon the waters, for you will find it after many days;*

There is "no certain explanation of this proverb"; its interpretation is obscure, "the exact meaning of this expression or where it originated is unknown." [1] The **first** interpretation we may eliminate signifies *bread* is the seed of human life, and so borders on the licentious. [2] A **second** interpretation is called the *Agricultural*: Sow seed on muddy ground, or fertile soil flooded by the early rains; the seeds will take root, grow, and produce a rich harvest. [3] If bread means seed or corn then that seed cast on flooded land will take root. Once the waters recede, there will be a profitable harvest for the one who sows. [4]

A **third** interpretation is one we would call *Uncertainty*. Because bread cast on water dissolves, such casting is a metaphor representing doing something that makes no sense. However, because we are ignorant of what the future holds and totally unaware of its possibilities, when one casts bread upon the waters, it may "nevertheless paradoxically lead to an unexpected successful result." [5]

A **fourth** interpretation is called the *Commercial Trade*. It alludes to merchants who commit their goods (grain, etc.) by sea. The longer the voyage and the more ships sent out, the greater the profit.[6] Moffat writes: Trust your goods far and wide at sea, till you get good returns after a while. Hawkins says: "Let your bread of charity go out upon the waters, as ships do in their travels, carrying precious cargo hither and yon." [7] Here the "idea is that in traveling by sea with commerce, take a commercial risk that has some possibility, but not certainty, of success . . . take a calculated risk, since there may be a good result from it." [8]

A **fifth** interpretation is labeled *Liberality*. It teaches: Venture forth wisely, doing good to others, with love and generosity, without expecting gain or advantage, and without assurance of reward. There is a certain amount of risk, but *nothing ventured, nothing gained.* [9] If you do not take a chance you may not learn that generosity is always repaid, nor may you expect to gain anything. [10] Given a spiritual twist, "The metaphor is that of spreading spiritual seed far and wide, trusting eventually to find its fruit in redeemed lives." [11] This traditional interpretation is correct. [12] As Christians we diversify our investments in the lives of others, through prayer, support of missions, works of charity, and help in times of disaster. Let our love for Christ overflow so that our love for other Christians overflows to love those who do not know the Lord in the pardoning of their sins.

Thought

Persian saying: Cast
thy bread upon the water,
God will know of it if the
fishes do not.

[1] Laurin, *Wycliffe* 592; Brewer, 189; Freeman, 338-39.

[2] Barton, *Ecclesiastes,* ICC 181, "this interpretation is undoubtedly wrong."

[3] Barnes; Clarke; MacDonald, 911.

[4] Bullinger, 564. Barton, ibid, rejects this interpretation, claiming that "Bread never means seed."

[5] Murphy, (WBC 23A) 106-7, continues: Misfortune one knows not of may be lurking ahead. The uncertainties (which may just possibly go in one's favor) are such that one cannot rely on careful moves. Precautions will bring no security . . . one cannot rely even on uncertainty itself.

[6] Gill; M. Henry; MacDonald, ibid.

[7] Hawkins, *Parallel* 1278.

[8] Murphy, ibid. Barton, ibid: rejects this fourth interpretation because "bread does not mean merchandise."

[9] Nelson, 1094; WBD, RH: "Bread"; Fulghum, 41; Jeffrey, 105, calls this "The injunction to disinterested benevolence."

[10] Brewer's, 189; Freeman, 338-9.

[11] H. Morris, *Defender's* 709.

[12] Barton, ibid. Murphy, ibid disagrees: "the action of letting bread go upon the water does not of itself suggest almsgiving."

Casting Pearls before Swine: Matt 7:6 – *Do not give what is holy to the dogs; nor cast your pearls before swine, lest they trample them under their feet, and turn and tear you in pieces.*

Here we have four parallel lines in a sentence:

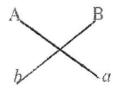

A   Do not give what is holy to the dogs,
B   nor cast your pearls before swine
b   *lest they trample them under their feet,*
a   *and turn and tear you in pieces.*

A and B are parallel; a and b are parallel. Connect A with a, and B with b to form an X. This is called *Introversion,* literally "a turning or bending inward." When subjects are introverted the correspondence is called *Chiasmus* (Latin) or *Chiasmos* (Greek) because of its likeness to the Greek letter *Chi* (X). [1] We then read: (1) Do not give what is holy to the dogs [lest] *they turn and tear you in pieces* (2) Do not cast your pearls before swine [lest] *they trample them under their feet.* [2] In other words, the dogs turn and tear you to pieces, but do not trod upon the pearls. Undiscerning pigs may at first think the pearls are acorns or pellets of food. Rushing out to gobble them up they trample the pearls under their feet in the mud, but do not turn and tear you to pieces. "Pearls are things of value to many people, but pigs will despise them because they cannot eat them." [3]

Second, consider the words *dogs* and *hogs.* Wycliffe said, "Men should not give holy things to hounds." [4] In Matt 15:26 (Mark 7:27) the Lord uses the term *little dogs* (*kunarion*), the diminutive of *kuōn*; this is a house dog or lap-dog "in contrast to a dog of the street or farm, but also used with no diminutive force at all, little dog," or just dog. These unclean animals, for the most part having no owners, were street scavengers living on offal: dead bodies, garbage, etc. They were not hugged and pampered household pets, well-fed, bathed, taken to the veterinarians and given shots. Jews were not allowed to throw to the dogs flesh offered in sacrifice to God. The Jews were not allowed to keep hogs, or eat their flesh (Lev 11:7).

"You dirty dog!" and "You greedy pig!" are expressions I often heard as a boy. It is true that Gentiles were considered "dogs," and in addition, men who were sodomites were called "dogs" (Deut 23:18). It is held then that both terms, dogs and hogs, are used as metaphors, figures of speech, to describe all classes of human beings whether Jews or Gentiles. [5] On the other hand, there are those who consider such language derogatory, insulting and unworthy of coming from the lips of Christ or any Christian.

Opinions vary, e.g.: Make the application to all people, not just the heathen or Gentiles.[6] Dogs and swine are not unbelievers, so that it seems best not to limit this verse unnecessarily but to regard it as applicable to both Jews and Gentiles—to all who are receptive; [7] Christ did not classify men as dogs and swine, but borrowed these terms from the lips of hypocrites who judged others as such animals, and thus the Lord indirectly condemned the use of such terms. [8]

Others comment: In Matthew 7:6, both terms refer to individuals who hear the message of truth and deliberately reject it.[9] They are described as violent, furious persecutors, and impudent blasphemers. Their behavior is impure; after having heard the gospel preached, "They return to their vicious, filthy nature", [10] like dogs returning to their vomit (Prov 26:11), or the washed sow returning to wallow in the mud (2 Pet 2:22). They are more than mere unbelievers, or those ignorant of the Gospel. These dogs and swine are neck-hardened (Prov 29:1) scorners who despise and ridicule the Word of God. Paul warned the saints at Philippi to beware of *dogs*, "Jewish or Judaising opponents" and "false teachers . . . who perverted the gospel and substituted something else for the blood of Christ." [11]

Calvin calls them "incurable opponents of the Word of God." Taken out of context, and approached from a secular point of view, Matt 7:6 is interpreted exhorting us to be cautious in dealing with people (uncultured Philistines) who are incapable of properly evaluating that which is valuable (pearls: *margarites*), the precious finer things of life. [12] In antiquity, pearls were valued precious stones, used for necklaces and other ornaments. We see how "the word came to be a figure of speech for something of supreme worth." [13]

One author suggests that the proper place to insert Matt 7:6 is in Matt 6:1-8, prohibiting ostentation (showing off) (1) in the giving of alms, (2) in prayer, and (3) in fasting. "It is in this context [the author believes it is apparently the original one] that Matt 7:6 becomes a further warning against those who would practice parading their religion (or their religious practices).

Keeping the expressions 'dogs' and 'hogs' in this context further amplifies the lack of appreciation some people have for the significance and value of holy things—almsgiving, prayer, and fasting. Ostentation not only displeases the Lord, but also excites the contempt and derision of men." [14] Here is the major thrust of this text. As in the secular world it is important to distinguish those capable of holding in high esteem intellectual or artistic matters, it is much more important to be able to discern those capable of treasuring spiritual values.

> It is counterproductive to try to teach the treasures of biblical truth to those who reject and ridicule the Scriptures. Their hearts must first be prepared by the Holy Spirit, supplemented by a gracious presentation of Christian evidence . . . Our zeal against sin must be guided by discretion, for as it is often said, 'Want of common sense does great harm to religion.' (H. Morris, *Defender's* 1015) . . . The meaning must be that holy words, things, and truths have to be treated with reverence and are not to be permitted to become the butt of jests and ridicule of wicked people. (M. Henry) [15]

Matthew 7:6 warns against offering or giving a valuable thing to a person who is incapable of appreciating it; (1) the gift will be unappreciated (2) and may be dangerous to the donor. [17] The "general sense is clear: objects of value, special privileges, participant in sacred things should not be offered to those who are incapable of appreciating them." [17] Holy Spirit perception or insight is necessary because we do not want to overlook witnessing to others who may not fit certain schemes of social values. We want nothing to do with a "holier than thou" (Isa 65:5) attitude that assumes "outcasts of society" are *dogs and hogs.*

1. Bullinger (356-62, 374-79) is helpful in our study of this "stylistic literary figure." Cf. Byatt 40. Man, *BSac* (141) 146; Barnes.
2. TEV gives us the X already formed: Do not give what is holy to dogs—they will only turn and attack you; do not throw your pearls in front of pigs—they will only trample them underfoot.
3. Kaiser, *Hard Sayings* 370 (Matt 7:6): Annoyed that they cannot eat them, they trample them under foot.

4. Hendrickson, 136; Chilvers, 9.

5. Michel, *TDNT* 3:1102

6. Glasson, *ExpTim* (68), 302.

7. Hagner, (WBC 33A), 172.

8. Bennett, *WTJ,* 385.

9. Hindson, *Parallel* 1884.

10. Lenski, *Matthew* 291.

11. Phil 3:2; Michel, *TDNT* 3:1103; Roustio, *Parallel* 2444.

12. Brewer's, 189; Freeman, 418.

13. Hauck, *TDNT* 4:472-73.

14. Perry, *ExpTim* (46) 381-2

15. Tasker 80; BAGD, 461

16. Caird, 163.

17. Kaiser, ibid.

Changing Skin Color

Jer 13:23: *Can the Ethiopian change his skin or the leopard its spots? Then may you also do good who are accustomed to do evil.*

A rhetorical question is one asked only for effect, not for information; it is a question to which no answer is expected. "Instead of making a plain and direct statement . . . he puts what he was about to say or could otherwise have said, into the form of a question, without waiting for an answer." [1] This axiomatic (self-evident) proverb has been taken by some as an insult. However, it is not racially derogatory. The God of the Bible is no respecter of faces or races. Judging by the context, if I were a member of the nation of Israel in Jeremiah's day I would be angry! The prophet points out that wickedness has become so ingrained, so habitual, so second nature to the Jewish people that they can no more cease from their evil ways than an Ethiopian can wash out the blackness of his skin.

There is nothing racially disparaging here. *Ethiopia* means "burnt face [sunburned]," but there is no suggestion the Ethiopian is cursed with his blackness any more than the leopard is cursed with its spots, or the tiger and zebra with their stripes; or that the white man is blessed with his whiteness. [2] The permanence of evil in the children of Israel and their apparent inability to change their condition is the purpose of the comparison. "Judah preferred the filth of her harlotry to the purity offered by God." [3] Man has no ability to morally reform, for custom in sin is a very great hindrance to conversion from sin. [4] So firmly entrenched in their evil, so hardened in their wickedness, it is impossible for them to repent.[5] This verse is a proverbial expression for laboring in vain, attempting to do that which is not to be done. Their idolatry had become second nature; and inveterate habits of sin cannot be altered. No amount of washing or cleansing as a religious ceremony of purification, fulfilling moral obligations, ordinances, outward signs of fasting and repentance can change our hearts. Only God—not environment, not heredity—can change us. [6] Jehovah stands ever ready to forgive Israel. However, with the inability to change there comes judgment! Judah must be scattered (Jer 13:24).

Thought: When I was an occupation soldier in Germany after the Second World War, a little German boy ran up to me, grabbed my right hand, and rubbed the back of it. I imagine that he was quite surprised that nothing rubbed off! At this writing, I am 80 years old, and the color has not come off yet!

[1] Bullinger: 763, 943, and 956; cf. Hendrickson 433.
[2] Ham, *One Blood,* 57-88. 'Whiteness' study shows surprises (Philadelphia Inquirer, A3; 24 Sep 06); Hopfensperger, Minneapolis Star Tribune: Caucasian Americans don't take their race for granted, as supposed. "White people consider their race to be an important part of who they are, and most are aware that being white gives them advantages in America, according to an unusual survey by the University of Minnesota." Cf. *Critical Whiteness Studies,* Internet.
[3] F. G. Kroll, *Parallel* 1453.
[4] Brewer's 626: "leopards"; M. Henry.
[5] Craigie et al, (WBC 26) 193. Calvin: There is no hope of their repentance. So given up to their vices that they were no longer healable; so corrupt they could not repent, no longer had any discernment, and could not discriminate between good and evil. They harden themselves long beyond repentance; their wickedness had become inherent, firmly fixed in their hearts.
[6] H. Morris, *Defender's* 793; Wurthwein, *TDNT* 4:987: Jeremiah, for all the hopeful and winsome notes evoked by his profound love for the people, is well aware of the difficulty of conversion. And after the rich experiences of his life he no longer expects from men

a comprehensive renewing of the people. He expects this only from God, who will write His law on the people's hearts (31:33).

Charity Begins at Home: 1 Timothy 5:4, 8: *But if any widow has children or grandchildren, let them first learn to show piety at home and to repay their parents; for this is good and acceptable before God . . . But if anyone does not provide for his own, and especially for those of his household, he has denied the faith and is worse than an unbeliever (infidel: KJV).*

Charity begins at home is believed to be an ancient saying expressed by the Roman playwright and poet, Terence (185-159 BC), in one of his comic plays. [1] I believe this saying has 1 Tim 5:4, 8 as its biblical counterpart. [2] As a pastor I heard this expression used by church members who were not in favor of supporting *any* missions program. "Why spend money on those people in other countries when there is such a need here at home?" They were not all that supportive of "home missions" either. The word "charity" does not have the same meaning today it had in 1611 when the King James Bible used the Latin word *charitas* to translate the Greek *agape* for *love*. Do not read 1 Cor 13 using the word *charity;* instead use the word *love*. Today charity means something given to the poor, benevolence, and helping the needy.

Rules for receiving help from the early church were stringent; this was in order not to bankrupt the local assemblies. Recall they suffered persecution at the hands of those who rejected Jesus as the Messiah. If the widow had any descendants, children, nephews or grandchildren, [3] those family members were obligated to take care of her first, before coming to the church for help. Note the use of the word "piety," to act piously, respectfully, or reverently. Then consider the phrase "at home." Failure to take care of one's own family, those with whom one has natural physical ties, is a poor testimony to the Christian faith; indeed, such failure amounts to denying the faith. Children capable of helping their elderly parents but who fail to do so disobey the Fifth Commandment. How can we repay them for all of their care for us when we were children! "No acts of 'piety' toward God will make up for impiety towards parents" (ATR).

How do we connect 1 Tim 5:4, 8 with our obligation to evangelize, and to support Missions? There are those who see "charity begins at home" in Acts 1:8: "You shall be witnesses to

Me in Jerusalem, and in all Judea and Samaria, and to the end of the earth." Jerusalem is considered "at home." Historically, Acts 1:8 was fulfilled; and yet present-day Missionary activity still operates in the uttermost parts of the earth. Indeed, the command of Matt 28:19 to "Go therefore and make disciples of all the nations" is still in force. Does taking care of a parent at home preclude supporting missions in other countries? Is it scripturally correct to use the Timothy passage *against* Foreign Mission activity? My answer: No.

Thought
Charity begins at home and usually stays there (Stevenson, 322).

Aunt Het

Dennis the Menace

"IF WE GIVE HIM HIS MONEY NOW, WILL HE LET US GO HOME EARLY?"

I believe in supportin' missionaries to save the heathen, but it seems wrong to overlook our own and pick out the easy ones in Africa.

[1] Hendrickson 143; Thomas Browne (1605-1682) said: "Charity begins at home, is the voice of the world." Henry James (1843-1915) stated, "I think patriotism is like charity—it begins at home." J. McHenry Jones wrote (1896): "The charity of the most of us, I fear, too often begins and ends in the same place—at home." Jermain W. Loguen, born in slavery in Tennessee in 1813, said: "'Charity begins at home' is a truism as old as mankind. The charge of the apostle is founded on it." Cf. Encarta: "charity", and Africana Editors' Notes.
[2] Brewer's 205; OED 3:43: Used to express the prior claims of the ties of family, friendship, etc., to a man's consideration.

[3] Pilgrim, 1689; Bullinger, 859 (Nephew).

Clothed in His Right Mind: Mark 5:15: *Then they came to Jesus, and saw the one who had been demon-possessed and had the legion, sitting and clothed and in his right mind* (Luke 8:35).

In certain church circles it is common to hear someone pray, "I thank Thee Lord, for waking me up this morning, **clothed in my right mind**." The phrase has come to mean to be mentally alert, sane, well, or normal. I do not deny this expression makes good sense even when taken out of context. It reminds me of a slang expression, "He's not wrapped too tight," meaning he's *not* "clothed in his right mind." A proper reading of the demoniac's condition at Gadara will reveal that the words *clothed* and *in his right mind* do not run together. The commas in the KJV help here: "And they come to Jesus, and see him that was possessed with the devil [demon], and had the legion, sitting, and **clothed,** and in his right mind."

Incidentally, two demoniacs are mentioned in Matt 8:28 as being at Gergasa (Gadara). This is not a contradiction to Mark and Luke. It would be, however, if either Gospel said, "Only **one** demoniac" was there. There were two, but for God's purposes Christ's relationship with one is stressed. The demon possessed man is described as (1) living in the tombs, and not in a house (2) exceedingly fierce (3) preventing people from passing by that way (4) with superhuman strength breaking fetters and chains (5) untamable (6) screaming and crying out aloud (7) cutting himself with stones or upon the stones (8) restless, running here and there day and night (9) and note in **Luke 8:27**, that he *"wore no clothes."* This latter point is important for the correct exposition of the phrase, "clothed, (note KJV comma) and in his right mind."

Come as You Are

It is interesting that in a society as fashion-conscious as we are that we should hear the invitation from church leaders to "come as you are." Often I say under my breath, "Yeah, and leave as you came." Furthermore, in this age of increasing obesity, how we look, what shape we are in becomes more and more noticeable. Perhaps my comments are the products of yesteryear, a time when we wore our best to church—shoes (not sneakers) that were shined, and

37

neckties. And when we came home, we took off our "Sunday Best." [1]

Now if *Come as You Are* would be interpreted, *"Bring your sinful self to the Savior,"* I would have no problem accepting the slogan. It does not matter what we humans wear; all of our righteousnesses are like filthy rags in the sight of God (Isa 64:6). So if we consider *Coming as We Are* to mean for the sinner—undone, Hell-bound, lost, unregenerate, without Christ, "having no hope and without God (atheist) in the world"—to come, then O.K.

1 Samuel 16.7: *But the LORD said to Samuel, "Do not look at his appearance or at his physical stature, because I have refused him. For the LORD does not see as man sees; for man looks at the outward appearance, but the LORD looks at the heart."* This is the verse I hear most often used to support the invitation to "come as you are". Jehovah had sent Samuel to choose Saul's successor as the king of Israel. When Samuel saw Eliab, oldest son of Jesse the Bethlehemite, he said, "Surely the LORD's anointed is before Him!" It was at this point that Jehovah spoke the words of v7. God does not choose by sight of outward appearance, but looks on the heart, the inner person, mind and will. [2] The antithesis of *heart* is *outward appearance* or "eye." The idea seems to be that we can look in a man's eyes and see a "liveliness and sprightliness that appear in them," but God peers into man's heart and sees his thoughts and intents. We contend that whereas it is true the LORD looks at the heart, this does not mean He is not concerned with what we wear. [3] To establish the point that the God of the Bible has thoughts about what we wear, consider the following Scriptures:

Gen 3:21: *Also for Adam and his wife the LORD God made tunics of skin, and clothed them.* Recall that Adam and Eve had attempted to hide their nakedness with fig leaves (Gen 3:7). **Exod 39:1:** *Of the blue, purple, and scarlet thread they made garments of ministry.* In the Book of Exodus much is made of the priestly garments (robes, turbans, sashes, tunics, breastplate, ephod, etc.) for Aaron and his sons—with respect to color, material, style, workmanship, etc. **Deut 22.5:** *A woman shall not wear anything that pertains to a man, nor shall a man put on a woman's garment, for all who do so are an abomination to the LORD your God.* Any departure from custom with respect to dress, which has

38

as its aim the obliteration of the signs of difference and marks of distinction between the sexes, is an act of rebellion, an effort to escape from the God-ordained dress code. An attempt by women to defeminize or to masculinize their physical appearance is always a step downward. The unisex approach seeks to blur the distinction between men and women, and can lead only to moral deterioration. When God says something is an abomination to Him, it is unimaginable that His attitude is based purely upon social or cultural customs. I know that we are not Jews, and we are not under a law system. But do not claim the God of the Bible is not concerned about what we believers wear. [4]

1 Cor 11.5-7: *. . . head uncovered . . . not covered . . . covered . . . a man ought not to cover his head.* In this passage we learn that the woman ought to be under authority, and the head covering in Corinth was a sign of her submission to the authority of her husband (Gen 3:16; Eph 5.22-24). The saintly women at Corinth were told to wear a veil or covering for their head when attending public worship as a symbol of their subordination. Christian men, as representatives of Christ are told not to wear hats in the church. Different interpretations of this matter impress us still that God is interested in what we wear. When fashions and styles become attempts to declare independence from God's will then it is a matter of importance. Whatever interpretation we make of this passage we admit God regards our outward adornment. And such concern does not support the *Come as You Are* invitation to church.[5]

1 Tim 2.9: *In like manner also, that the women adorn themselves in modest apparel, with propriety and moderation, not with braided hair or gold or pearls or costly clothing, but, which is proper for women professing godliness, with good works.* **1 Pet 3:3:** *Do not let your adornment be merely outward—arranging the hair, wearing gold, or putting on fine apparel—rather let it be the hidden person of the heart, with the incorruptible beauty of a gentle and quiet spirit, which is very precious in the sight of God.* Both Paul and Peter condemn the dependence upon outward things and the focus of attention to fashion.[6] Ostentation and the desire to draw special attention to one's appearance is a hindrance to "good works." True beauty "ain't paint!" The source of true beauty is a gentle and quiet spirit.

To read these verses and still maintain a *Come as You Are* church dress-code is to be guilty of blatant disregard for the Word of God. Jehovah's caution to Samuel is not based upon culture, the society in which we live, the times, mores, or customs (nor costumes). There is a deeper principle involved; there is a biblical matter to be considered. Indeed, "Christian faith implies a different standard of dress and adornment from" that of the world.[7]

Thought: Mark Twain: Clothes make the man. Naked people have little or no influence on society. Henry Ward Beecher: Clothes and manners do not make the man; but, when he is made, they greatly improve his appearance.

THE BETTER HALF

"You'll be pleased to know last week's sermon against women's slacks scared the pants off my wife."

[1] Otto Scott: says "The term 'Sunday Best' is unknown to the present generation."
[2] 1 Kgs 8:39; Bowling, *TWOT* 1:466: "'Heart' became the richest biblical term for the totality of man's inner immaterial nature . . . the most frequently used term for man's immaterial personality functions . . . the most inclusive term for them since, in the Bible, virtually every immaterial function of man is attributed to the 'heart'."

[3] *DBI* 317: "The imagery of garments and clothing is of the major importance in the Bible. Its significance can be physical, economic, social, moral or spiritual . . . clothing can protect, conceal, display or represent a person's current state and can be symbolic of moral and spiritual qualities." Wenham, (WBC 1) 84: On a cultural level, "Clothing, besides its obvious protective function, is one of the most pervasive of human symbols through which a person's position and role in society is signaled."

[4] *DBI* 319: Jehovah makes it very clear that He disallows 'cross-dressing' [transvestism] between men and women.

[5] S. L. Johnson, *Wycliffe* 1247: the apostle gives three reasons (theological, biblical and physical) for his comments. More important than wearing proper physical clothing is obedience to the command to put off the old man and put on the new; and also wearing the whole armor of God (Eph 4:22-24; Col 3.9-10; Eph 6:11-17; 1 Thess 5:8).

[6] *DBI* ibid: "As an antidote to the feminine tendency toward extravagant clothing, two NT epistles warn against placing unwarranted value on external apparel and commend modesty in clothing."

[7] Paine, *Wycliffe* 1448.

Darkness That May Be Felt: Exod 10:21: *Then the LORD said to Moses, "Stretch out your hand toward heaven, that there may be darkness over the land of Egypt, darkness which may even be felt."*

I. Sun God

Each plague was a strike at an Egyptian god or goddess. In this ninth plague Jehovah's triumphant stroke is against the Egyptian god of the sun, Ra or Re.[1] This land of perpetual sunshine 365 days in the year was now suddenly eclipsed with the swiftness that brought life to an immediate halt. By shutting in the glories of the sun, Jehovah, the Creator of the sun, proved that the supreme deity of ancient Egypt was powerless. [2] The devotees of Ra suffered miserably: They went without food for three days, groping in darkness so thick with moisture that candles and torches could not be lit, so that they were unable to see each other. [3] In short, the God of the Bible caused Ra to disappear, unmasking his impotence. [4] In Psa 105.28 the plague of darkness is mentioned first. Several reasons are given for this. [5] For one thing, it is suggested that this plague especially convicted the Egyptians of the power of Jehovah, seeing what He had wrought against their sun-god. [6] It may have struck an unusual fear into their hearts, breaking their resistance to God's demand to release the Israelites; and fitly describing the entire period of the plagues. [7]

II. Symbolism of Man's Darkness

In this plague we see the essence of man's spiritual condition, for darkness symbolizes blindness, sorrow and sin; and men love darkness rather than light. This theme appears often and in many ways throughout the Scriptures. [8] The darkness of our hearts moves us to rebel against God's light, and we are plunged into greater darkness. This plague also points to the gathering of the dark clouds of judgment that will afflict the earth when the Lord Jesus, the Sun of Righteousness appears.[9] The ultimate condition of the unbeliever is given in 1 Sam 2:9: *But the wicked shall be silent in darkness.* Such a condition is changed only by faith in the Lord Jesus Christ, the Light of the World. A foreshadowing of such favor and blessing upon the people of faith is demonstrated; in that section of the land where the Jews lived, there was no darkness, only light (Exod 10:23b).

III. Supernatural

Was the cause behind this darkness natural or supernatural? Both points of view are held. I believe the correct answer favors the supernatural. It was not a solar eclipse. It was not a *simoom* (*simoon or samiel*), the name for the strong, hot, dry, suffocating wind laden with fine sand (dust) and coarse sand that blows across the Sahara and Arabian deserts during the spring and summer, generally for three days without interruption. Though this wind causes a yellow dimness, it does not bring a darkness that can be felt. [10] In addition to an emphasis on wind-driven sand, there is an explanation which includes thick aqueous vapors floating in the air and preventing the rays of the sun from penetrating. In light of the supernatural nature of all of the plagues against Egypt as recorded in Exod 7:14—12:30, "it is unquestionably a supernatural darkness." [11]

IV. Sensitivity

Should this verb translated *felt* be taken literally? Calvin "holds "that the darkness was so thick that it might be felt by hand." [12] Or should it be interpreted to mean "*a darkness so thick people will have to feel their way around,"* that is to say, the darkness will cause them to grope. Consider the use of this Hebrew verb *mashash*: [13] (1) Then Isaac said to Jacob, "Please come near, that I may *feel* you, my son, whether you are really my son Esau or not." So Jacob went near to Isaac his father, and he felt him. Isaac *felt* Jacob in order to identify him as Esau (Gen 27:21).

(2) And Laban **searched** all about the tent but did not find them . . . And he **searched** but did not find the household idols . . . "although you have **searched** all my things, what part of your household things have you found?" (Gen 31:34, 35, 37). Laban *felt* about among the goods packed up in Jacob's tents looking for his missing Teraphim idols.[14]

(3) Deut 28:29: And you shall **grope** at noonday, as a blind man **gropes** in darkness. This verse depicts the blind 'feeling around anxiously.' (4) Judg 16:26: Then Samson said to the lad who held him by the hand, "Let me *feel* the pillars which support the temple, so that I can lean on them." These verses support the suggestion of a palpable darkness; and we take literally the idea of a darkness that could be *felt* or *touched;* [15] this interpretation goes beyond saying that the darkness was so thick that the Egyptians had to grope or feel their way.

Thought: On July 13, 1977, a heat wave caused a blackout in New York City. In the twenty-five hours before power was finally restored, looting and vandalism inflicted $150 million in damages on the city. What a terrifying picture of the 'people walking in darkness' (Isa 9:2). Here was darkness the citizens of NYC felt.

---

[1] Two other names of sun gods of ancient Egypt are **Horus** and **Aton.** The name Ra helps to correctly spell Pha*ra*oh, a title that means not only the king but also the sun. He considered himself as the representative of the sun and thus deserving of divine honors.
[2] Gaebelein: *Moses,* 141; Freeman, 108.
[3] K&D disagree, stating we must not infer that the Egyptians were unable to kindle any lights even in their houses.
[4] Barnhouse: *Invisible War,* 210; MacDonald, 96.
[5] The order of the plagues in Psa 105 verses 29-36: turning their waters into blood [1st], invasion of frogs [2nd], swarms of flies [4th] and lice [3rd], hail and flaming fire [7th], locusts [8th] and finally, the destruction of the firstborn [10th].
[6] Kirkpatrick, 621; Nelson, 988

[7] Leupold, *Psalms* 740; Spurgeon, *Treasury* (Psa 105:28): 2:344.

[8] Ice, *BSac* (145): 297.

[9] Gaebelein, ibid; Rev 16:10: *Then the fifth angel poured out his bowl on the throne of the beast, and his kingdom became full of darkness.* Sale Harrison, 162: this plague is symbolic, while the ninth plague of Egypt was literal and typical. Nelson 2190 does not associate the pain with the darkness; stating it more likely refers to the scorching by the sun in earlier verses. Seiss 373: "And great are the miseries of that darkness; for it causes those who feel it to bite their tongues by reason of the distress which it adds to all the rest of their torments." Stevens, *Revelation* 265: "a darkness racking all with pain and aggravating their ulcers." Levy, *Revelation* 184: "The darkness will be so thick that it will cause intense psychological pain to people already in physical agony due to festering boils and burning flesh," causing them "to gnaw 'their tongues for pain'." Cf. Larkin, *Revelation,* 143.

[10] Gaebelein, ibid; Kyle, *ISBE* 4:2405; Spurgeon, ibid. 2:343: "It was no natural or common darkness to be accounted for by the blinding dust of the simoon, it was beyond all precedent and out of the range of ordinary events."

[11] Durham, (WBC 3) 141: This darkness is inexplicable, comparable to nothing the Egyptians or the Israelites ever before have known. Cf. Clarke: "an extraordinary thick mist supernaturally, i.e., miraculously, brought on"; H. Morris, *Revelation,* 306.

[12] Kyle, ibid: it is . . . a "darkness which may be felt."

[13] To feel, touch, grope; *TWOT* 1:535.

[14] The etymology (true sense, derivation) of the word Teraphim is dubious: "a kind of idol, an object of reverence, and means of divination." Young's Concordance: *nourishers:* "a kind of household gods, probably in the human form."

[15] Freeman, 109: in a cavern in Georgia, "the darkness was so absolute that it literally could be felt; it pressed against your eyes as you strained to see a minuscule of light somewhere."

David, a Man after God's Own Heart: 1 Sam 13:14: *The LORD has sought for Himself a man after His own heart.*

Imagine describing David—the adulterer, the murderer, the one so constantly engaged in warfare and bloodshed—as a man after God's own heart! A study of David's life causes misgivings with respect to describing him thus. We know of his affair with

Bathsheba and the resultant tragedies; we have record of his many wives and concubines (2 Sam 5:13). First Kings 2:9 also comes to mind: "Now therefore, do not hold him guiltless, for you are a wise man and know what you ought to do to him; but bring his gray hair down to the grave with blood." This is part of David's charge to Solomon given just before David dies. There are those who believe that David suggested Solomon "take care of Shimei" for maliciously cursing him (2 Sam 16:5-13); and in 1 Kgs 2:44-46, Solomon had Shimei slain.[1]

> Misunderstanding the phrase, where David is called 'a man after God's own heart' (as though it referred to David's *character*, instead of to David's *calling*, being *chosen* by God and not, as Saul was, by *man*), infidels have pointed to 1 Kings 2:9 to show David's faithless and blood thirsty character! But if, as in so many other cases, we repeat the negative from the preceding clause, there is no such difficulty: 'but his hoar head bring thou [*not*] down to the grave with blood.' True, Solomon did put Shimei to death, but this was for quite another reason, and as Solomon said, Shimei's blood was upon his own head (verse 37). Thus the passage is brought into agreement with David's oath to Shimei, which is repeated in immediate connection with this verse (1 Kgs 2 verse 8 from 2 Sam 19:23). (Bullinger, 93-4)

To be after the heart of God is to yearn to know His mind, to think His thoughts, to want to please Him; it is to desire to know His will and to do His will once known. Do not let David's faults blind you to the grace of God that worked in this man's life. First, note David's confidence that moved him to cry out (Psa 70:1, 5), to call on God when in trouble (Psa 27:1-3), but also to give God credit for every success (1 Sam 17:36-7). Second, see David's contrition (godly sorrow); he was humbled by guilt, repentant for his sins, and broken in spirit. It is difficult to convince some people they are wrong. They hardheadedly resist the convicting power of the Holy Spirit. They seek no forgiveness, experience no godly sorrow, and make no confession. After David committed adultery with Bathsheba, and caused the death of her husband Uriah, the LORD sent the prophet Nathan to announce, "You are the man!" Convicted by the Spirit, David confessed his sin (Psa 51:1-7, 10). Contrition led to cleansing.

Third **is the basic thrust:** Fleshly pride motivated the people to choose Saul, but David was Jehovah's choice to rule Israel. God picked the one man in all Israel who came closest to fulfilling what Israel needed. We see that there was a spiritual sensitivity that caused David to be mindful of his relationship to the LORD and made him desirous of executing Jehovah's will for the nation Israel; David wanted what God wanted; and the LORD used him as the king of Israel to achieve that purpose.

> When Samuel, speaking of David, said that he was a man after God's own heart, he did not mean that he was a man sinlessly perfect, but that he was a man who would go right where Saul had gone wrong; a man who would regard himself not as supreme in the state, but as God's vicegerent there, and in the government of the people would aim at fulfilling not his own will, but the will of God. (W. W. White, 99, cites Macgregor) [2]

[1] Read the charge concerning Joab the son of Zeruiah, 1 Kgs 2:5-6.
[2] Pilgrim, 614 (1 Chron 14:10). Cf. 1 Kgs 11:4; 14:8.

Dead Bury the Dead

Matt 8:22: *But Jesus said to him, "Follow Me, and let the dead bury their own dead."* Luke 9:60: *Jesus said to him, "Let the dead bury their own dead, but you go and preach the kingdom of God."*

A procedure called *Secondary Burial* involves re-interring the bones of the deceased. This burial ritual signifies Christ did not talk about the "spiritually" dead burying the physically dead, but that He expressed "a thought that was both ironic and eschatological," namely: let the "other dead [*bones*] in the family tomb rebury your father's bones." This final act of mourning took place about a year after the death of the father, and was carried out by the members of the immediate family. [1] Although it is said that this was a widespread custom among the Jews in first-century Palestine, nothing is said in the Bible about it; we reject it as an interpretation of our LORD's command.

One principle of hermeneutics (interpretation) to keep in mind: "An expression must be figurative when a literal meaning

46

would involve an impossibility." [2] Our Lord taught "Let the spiritually dead bury the physically dead;" "leave the spiritually dead to bury their naturally dead." [3] Some modern explanations of the text are softer than the blunt, "Let the dead bury the dead!" For example, "Don't worry about things over and done with; forget what happened in the past." [4] "Let bygones be bygones. Don't rake up old scores and dead grievances." [5] "Reject psychologizing explanations" offered to soften our Lord's remarks. [6] We were born dead spiritually—dead in trespasses and sins (Eph 2:1). "It is a fact that men who are bound to natural life can be called dead in spite of their natural vitality." [7] To die in such a condition is to face eternal separation from God. If the Lord Jesus tarries all of us will die physically. However harsh this sounds, it is truth, and it is reality.

Some scholars hold that this man's father probably was not even sick. [8] This seems unlikely, for the Lord would have dismissed the disciple immediately, rather than allow continued indecision. Another suggestion is that the disciple "has just received word about his father's death." [9] From the words, "Lord, let me first go and bury my father," it seems he had intentions of returning to Christ. However, it is also "tacitly assumed that the temporizer will not come back." [10] Answer Christ's call right now! Let it not be said: "My name is *Might Have Been*. I am also called *Too Late, No More* and *Farewell"* (D. Rosetti).

No longer able to earn a living, the aged father probably was frail and ailing. [11] It is understandable why the young man desired to go home and await his father's death. How long this would be he did not know, so that it is an indefinite postponement of his calling to be a disciple. [12] It is unlikely that the Lord would forbid the young man to go to his father's funeral if he were dead already, [13] indeed, "The phrase can hardly mean that his father is dead, for burial in the East follows immediately after death." [14]

Because this young man was a disciple, our Lord's words were sharp. Self-commitment to Christ is one that severs all other ties. [15] Domestic duty does not displace the disciple's devotion. It is as if the Lord said, "Your job, your duty is to follow Me. Doing what I bid you do is more important than attending your father's funeral." [16] His hesitation signifies a weak allegiance to his calling. [17] Indeed, the time is now, not later, to follow the Lord; procrastination is inexcusable. So those words are calculated to show the importance of being about that business which really counts in time and in eternity.

Proper burial for a loved one is "an outstanding work of love," [18] so that the Lord Jesus does not desire any one to disrespect or disregard his family. However, do not set aside the gospel ministry when there are unbelievers who can take care of dead bodies, for "While it is a good deed to bury the dead, it is a better one to preach Christ" (ATR). What a radical call to discipleship—one that "involves self denial, sacrifice, suffering, persecution and perhaps even death." [19] We are not to waste our lives on trivia. With clear priorities we are to put first things first. Let those who are not saved handle certain duties, while we do the work the Lord has called us to do. This requires full surrender to the Lord's calling.

> [The Lord] does not condemn burial . . . He intended only to show, that whatever withdraws us from the right course, or retards us in it, deserves no other name than *Death*. Those only live . . . who devote all their thoughts and every part of their life, to obedience to God; while those who do not rise above the world—who devote themselves to pleasing men, and forget God—are like *Dead* men, who are idly and uselessly employed in taking care of the dead. (Calvin)

[1] McCane, *HTR* (83): 36, 43.
[2] Myers, 92; Nolland, (WBC 35B) 543: "this understanding of Jesus' words is only absurd if taken literally."
[3] Pilgrim, 1442; MacDonald 1233.
[4] Hendrickson, 435.
[5] Brewer's 626.
[6] Nolland, ibid 542; Black, *ExpTim* (61) 219-20: 'Spirit dead' sounds somewhat harsh to us in our ignorance of the circumstances, "though it may have been the incentive that was ever needed."
[7] Bultmann, *TDNT* 2:863n267.
[8] Fremont, *Message* 12.
[9] Lenski, *Luke* 561.
[10] Schrenk, *TDNT* 5:982n235.
[11] JFB; Nelson 1589; H. Morris *Defender's* 1017; Hindson, *Parallel* 1906.

[12] Howard, *ExpTim* (61) 350; Davies and Ellison, *ExpTim* (62) 92.
[13] Rice, 134.
[14] Lindsay, (Luke 9:59) 148.
[15] Kittel, *TDNT* 1:213.
[16] Borland, *Parallel* 2036.
[17] Grundmann, *TDNT* 3:547.
[18] Hagner, WBC (33A), 218.
[19] Gutbrod, *TDNT* 4:1063.

Doubting Thomas: John 20:24-29

A *Doubting Thomas* is one who is slow to believe, sees the darker side of things, manages to think up all the problems that may arise, and experiences periods of despondency. Early readers of the Bible gave this name to any faithless doubter. [1] The dictionaries define the term *Doubting Thomas* as one who is habitually doubtful, undecided, skeptical, and refuses to believe without proof; and of course, they relate the term to the apostle Thomas and his reluctance to believe the disciples had seen the risen Savior. I believe that the epithet *Doubting Thomas* is unfair and gives an inaccurate picture of the character and personality of this fascinating apostle.

Thomas was no more a doubter than the other disciples. [2] Keep in mind that **all** of them heard the Lord's repeated predictions concerning His death and resurrection, yet none of them took the forecast to heart. According to various writers, Thomas (1) was "an honest skeptic," [3] willing, however, to be convinced by sound evidence. Two different negatives are used by Thomas, *ou* and *mn*, giving us literally, "Not [*ou*] not [*mn*] will I believe." The purpose of the double negative is to strengthen the assertion. [4] In spite of his asseveration the mind of Thomas was indeed changed. (2) Fitting in with his skepticism was his gloomy outlook, a man possessed of little natural buoyancy of spirit. [5] Others would call him a pessimist. Recall when the Lord planned to return to Judea, Thomas reminded Him that the Jews sought to stone Him there, then said to his fellow disciples, "Let us also go, that we may die with Him" (John 11:16).

(3) This shows courage and (4) a love and devotion to Christ (5) as for his dependence upon sight, the faith of all the disciples present was the outcome of sight, even that of John (20:8). [6] (6) Thomas' incredulity is attributed not to a distrust of his fellow

disciples, but to a belief that they "had been victims of some hallucination." [7] (7) Thomas was the type of person who preferred to suffer his grief in solitude. [8] His sensitivity was so shocked by his Master's death that he found it difficult to believe Christ had conquered the grave. His excessive concern with the print of the nails in Christ's hands and the wound in His side (John 20:25) indicates the deep impression made upon his heart. [9] (8) His pertinacity in refusing to accept the Apostles' testimony does not originate from a reluctance to believe so much as it does from his fear of making a mistake concerning such an important matter—an error akin to Nathanael asking, "Can anything good come out of Nazareth?" (John 1:46).

> I do not wonder that Thomas, with that honest, accurate mind of his, wishing that the news were true, yet dreading lest it should be false, and determined to guard against every possible illusion . . . dreaded the possibility of delusion, however credulous the others might be. (F. W. Robertson, *Biblical Illustrator NT*)

It is wrong to claim Thomas was an unbeliever in the sense of lacking any faith whatsoever, and to assert that Thomas "does not doubt, [but] he is openly unbelieving." [10] This is very harsh and unsupported by our understanding of the different levels of interpretation of the word *belief.* It may be used of unbelievers or non-Christians, folks on their way to Hell (Mark 16:16). The same verb (*pisteuo*) is used in Jas 2:19, "Even the demons **believe**—and tremble!" Christ called the disciples, a "faithless generation" (Mark 9:19), using *unbelieving* in a more general sense. [11]

Failure to trust or have confidence in one issue does not cause the believer to lose salvation, or become an unbeliever in any absolute sense. A believer is a believer: hear the cry of the distraught father, "Lord, I believe; help my unbelief!" (Mark 9:24). Do not make Thomas an unbeliever because of his doubts; do not make Simon Peter an unbeliever because of his denials. Do not make the disciples unbelievers because of their desertion. Remember: *Christians* must continue to hear the Gospel in our ongoing need to cleanse the heart-spots of unbelief. Some scholars are unusually harsh in their judgment of Thomas, assigning ill motives for his absence at the first meeting and for his refusal to believe the testimony of his fellow peers. One asserts Thomas was absent because of his obstinate refusal to believe. [12] However, we simply do not know why Thomas was not present when the Lord first showed Himself to the disciples, and we are not persuaded that his absence was intentional, or from sullen obstinacy.

> [Thomas' ground of the incredulity is unknown.] It is probable, however, that it was, in part, at least, the effect of deep grief, and of that despondency which fills the mind when a long-cherished hope is taken away. In such a case it requires proof of uncommon clearness and strength to overcome the despondency, and to convince us that we may obtain the object of our desires. Thomas has been much blamed by expositors, but he asked only for proof that would be satisfactory in his circumstances. The testimony of ten disciples should have been indeed sufficient, but an opportunity was thus given to the Savior to convince the last of them of the truth of his resurrection (Barnes).

When Thomas saw the resurrected Christ for himself he cried out, "My Lord and my God!" This expression of faith in acknowledging the deity of our Lord is one of the strongest in the New Testament, [13] and is called "the greatest and fullest [testimony] in all Christianity" of the profession of His deity. [14] The Lord accepted that faith as genuine. [15] We agree that Thomas should have been willing to believe what his fellow disciples kept on telling him. As Christ pointed out, "Blessed are those who have not seen and yet have believed." However, in summary, I do not believe the phrase *Doubting Thomas* justifiably applies to the apostle. It is an expression that accentuates the negative while hiding the wonderful positive qualities of his character, attitudes and speech.

[1] Hendrickson 220; Brewer's 1069.
[2] F. F. Bruce, 393: "Had he been with them on the evening of that first Easter Day, his doubts would have been removed at the same time as theirs. As it was, he had to wait a further week."
[3] H. Morris, *Defender's* 1172.
[4] Bullinger, 340.
[5] Kerr, *ISBE* 4:2973.
[6] Lenski, *John* 1345.

[7] Dods, *ExpGT.* 4:865
[8] Bruce, ibid.
[9] Leon Morris, *John* 850-1.
[10] Lenski, *John* 1381
[11] Bultmann, *TDNT* 6:205.
[12] Lenski, *John* 1379.
[13] Griffith Thomas, *BSac* (125): 318.
[14] Kerr, ibid. Cf. Beasley-Murray, (WBC 36) 369: "a highly individual expression of depressed unbelief that gives way to adoring faith." Calvin disagrees, and describes Thomas as obstinate in his slowness and reluctance to believe: "His dullness of apprehension . . . astonishing and monstrous stupidity (and) shame compelled him to break out into this expression [My Lord and my God!], in order to condemn his own stupidity."
[15] Z. C. Hodges, *BSac* (135), 142.

Eat, Drink and Be Merry, for Tomorrow We Die

Isa 22:13: *Let us eat and drink, for tomorrow we die!*

The Valley of Decision refers to Jerusalem besieged by the Babylonian army. Rather than seek Jehovah's help and obey the call to repentance, to weeping, sackcloth and mourning, Israel turned to what may be called a combination of "jesting laughter and ridicule," and "contemptuous credulity" regarding God's judgment upon them. At the same time there is "a desperate determination" to spend the remainder of their lives—soon to end—in pleasure and dissipation. [1]

There is nothing inherently evil about enjoying the fruits of our labor. [2] However, to remain unrepentant at the threat of divine punishment, indeed, to ignore God's warning and find in the occasion reason for partying is unpardonable; and as the folks in Noah's day discovered, dangerous. They were forewarned of coming judgment, but to no avail, for the antediluvians ate, drank, married, and were given in marriage, until the day that Noah entered the ark, and the flood came and destroyed them all (Luke 17:27). This eating and drinking is called "profane," an attempt to use sensual pleasures to hide from God's righteousness; it is a practice considered a "mark of this-worldly enjoyment, of passing satisfaction, of license and pleasure seeking"; and the prophet attacks "the practical atheism of the ignorant, short-sighted, self-sufficient, hedonistic [pursuit of sensual pleasures] or careless." [3]

You see why the LORD was displeased with Israel's behavior, and led Isaiah to characterize their self-indulgence with the words, *Let us eat and drink, for tomorrow we die!* We Americans may or may not see "the handwriting on the wall" with respect to judgment, but I cannot help but wonder whether our reaction will be similar to that of Israel. In other words, as this country is besieged by natural catastrophes: hurricanes, mud slides, drought, floods, earthquakes, fires, pestilence, "global warming," and disease; and as our moral behavior continues to decline with frightening rapidity as we are besieged with inner corruption: alcoholism, abortion, dope addiction, crime, racism, anti-Semitism, homosexuality, terrorist activity—not to mention fighting in Iraq and Afghanistan—will we go hog-wild with our desire to be entertained, amused, to live luxuriously, leaving God out altogether?

Eat, drink and be merry seems to be a popular saying among us even now. Preaching judgment and worldwide catastrophe is ridiculed; we are called prophets of gloom and doom, attitudes made all the worse when men predict the end of the world (in disobedience to the Bible) and set dates—and the world continues on. But judgment *is* coming. Such predictions stir up rebellious old natures and increase our involvement in materialism, sensuality, amusement, and merry-making. Calvin says, "For wherever God threatens, the greater part of men either vomits out their bitterness or sneeringly ridicule everything that has proceeded from God's holy mouth." Is this kind of reaction more likely in nations which have been blessed abundantly by God? Is the "eat, and drink, for tomorrow we die" philosophy a natural consequence of ingratitude and the abuse of God's providence and mercy? Are "doom and gloom believers" of a coming Tribulation really responsible for triggering the scoffing at divine judgment?

1 Cor 15:32: *If the dead do not rise, "Let us eat and drink, for tomorrow we die!"* Paul cites Isa 22:13 to point out that if the dead are not raised, then Jesus Christ did not rise. What does it profit a Christian to believe in the bodily resurrection of Christ if He did not rise? Why not accept the motto of the Epicureans who taught man's highest good consisted in squeezing all the happiness one can get out of life right now! This devotion to sensuous pleasure philosophizes, "Since die we must, let us meanwhile enjoy the time, and not torment ourselves before the time with empty fears;

53

if death is the end of man, there is nothing better than that he should indulge in pleasure, free from care, so long as life lasts" (Calvin). If there is no resurrection, then there is no judgment, no rewards or punishment. So why not press all the pleasure we can out of life, for tomorrow we die; and when you're dead you're done!

> We sometimes hear Christians say that if this life were all, then they would still rather be Christians. But Paul disagrees with such an idea. If there were no resurrection, we would be better off to make the most of *this* life. We would live for food, clothing, and pleasure. This would be the only heaven we could look forward to. But since there is a resurrection, we dare not spend our lives for these things of passing interest. We must live for 'then' and not for 'now'. (MacDonald, 1807)

Eccl 8:15: *So I commended enjoyment, because a man has nothing better under the sun than to eat, drink, and be merry.* Pleasure is a gift from God. However, it is not God's will that we make idols out of pleasures or pleasure-seeking. The proper attitude is voiced in Eccl 2:24: *Nothing is better for a man than that he should eat and drink, and that his soul should enjoy good in his labor.* [4] Indeed, the person who views pleasure this way is called wise and righteous; he enjoys life and accepts all good gifts as coming from God. On the other hand, the person whose motto is *eat, drink and be merry* but gives no thought to God is called a fool and wicked.

> It is a materialistic point of view, but it kept the writer from despair. Life is out of joint, the rewards of goodness and wickedness are often reversed, no ray of light falls on the future, but make the most of the present; eat, drink and have a good time while one can, perhaps on the ground that God even could not rob one of pleasures actually enjoyed. (Barton, ICC, *Ecclesiastes,* 155)

Solomon did not teach a "pie-in-the-sky-by-and-by-when-you-die" philosophy. And those who say that Christians hold to such a creed need to study the words of the apostle Paul who states our living God "gives us richly all things to enjoy" (1 Tim 6:17).

The point made by the Preacher is (1) pleasure is a reward from God (2) it is to be earned by working (3) enjoy and be content with what He gives (4) recognize your accountability to God. This attitude "under the sun" is a foretaste of the joy we Christians experience "above the sun," reminding us of the saying, "All this and Heaven too."

Luke 12:19: *And I will say to my soul, "Soul, you have many goods laid up for many years: take your ease; eat, drink, and be merry."* A parable is literally something "thrown alongside of," derived from the words *para* (alongside of) and *ballo* (to throw, cast or hurl). The Parable of the Rich Fool is told by our Lord to warn His disciples of the false doctrine and hypocrisy of the Pharisees. We note immediately the egocentrism of this rich farmer by the number of references he makes to himself. Hear him say within his heart, "What shall I do? . . . I have no room . . . I will do . . . I will pull down . . . I will store . . . I will say to my soul."

A sensual life wasted on earthly enjoyment is doomed to perish. [5] Eating, drinking and being happy is "the most to which the worldling who forgets God can aspire, hoping to secure it by his possessions." [6] To center life's dependence upon what one assumes are sufficient tangible assets is spiritual death. This is true for many reasons: (1) Life is more than things. (2) Whatever we do own is only by the grace of God. (3) Hoarding is in itself evidence of greed and selfishness, a failure to think about the needs of others. (4) Life is really dependent upon God, not upon what we possess. (5) Leaving God out of our lives is a fatal omission. (6) Man is ignorant of the future (Prov 27:1).

He has no idea what may happen. He may drop dead at any moment; fire may destroy his possessions; robbers plunder, swindlers defraud, and ill health debilitates, causing him to lose his ability to manage his holdings. (7) Pride of possessions and love of luxury are stumbling blocks to spiritual salvation. "What folly to think that 'all' that a man lives for is to satisfy his sensual appetites; to forget that he has an intellect to be cultivated, a heart to be purified, a soul to be saved!" (Barnes). In other words, he puts human life (*psuche:* psyche) on an animal level; he puts the seat of his feelings, desires, and affections under the dominion of material possessions. He speaks of his soul in such a way as to impress that he is ignorant of his spirit.

If he had said, 'Body, take thine ease, for thou hast goods laid up for many years,' there had been sense in it; but the soul, considered as an immortal spirit, separated from the body, was no way interested in a barn full of corn or a bag full of gold. If he had had the soul of a swine, he might have blessed it with the satisfaction of eating and drinking; but what is this to the soul of a man? (M. Henry).

Thought

Tony Auth

EAT, DRINK & BE MERRY!
FOR YOU'RE PROBABLY DEAD.

NEW ORLEANS

TONY AUTH / The Philadelphia Inquirer tauth@phillynews.com

[1] Calvin (Isa 22:13); Alexander, 385.
[2] Eccl 2:24, 3:13; E.J. Young, 2:103. Nolland, (WBC 35B) 686: "The enjoyment of life here is not the 'last meal before execution' of Isa 22:13, nor is it the modest comfort held out by the Preacher of Ecclesiastes to the toiler in the midst of the vanity of it all."
[3] Goppelt, *TDNT* 6:136; Behm, *TDNT* 2:689; Kleinknecht, *TDNT* 3:120. Watts, (WBC 24) 286: Instead of repenting as God called for, the opposite occurred. "There was celebration of the temporary liberty—all the more precious because it was unlikely to last (v13). The drunken show in the streets reflected the irresponsibility of the leaders."

[4] Cf. Eccl 3:22, 5:18, 9:7; Kaiser, *Hard Sayings* 293-4. Murphy, WBC (23A) 86: "He is not espousing here a vapid [dull, uninteresting] life of joy, but showing an appreciation of the limited day-to-day pleasure that can be one's 'accompaniment' in a God-given life span."
[5] Behm, *TDNT* 2:693; Goppelt, ibid: 6:139-40. Calvin: He swells into pride by relying on his abundance, forgetting he is just a man.
[6] Bultmann, *TDNT* 2:774.

Ethiopia's Stretched-out Hands

Psa 68:31: *Ethiopia will quickly stretch out her hands to God.*

This verse has been used for many years by certain African-American preachers to encourage Black-Americans.[1] Study reveals that the envoys (princes, dignitaries, magnates, or ambassadors) are men of noble rank, and they shall come and acknowledge the God of Israel as the true God. It is the prediction that Ethiopia will quickly stretch out her hands to the Lord in a gesture of supplication (humbleness), a hastening to present peace offerings as "the willing seeker after grace, eagerly desiring and embracing the Christ of God." [2]

Here the region or country represents the inhabitants, and "the hand is also put for a gift to anyone." [3] Thus they shall bring gifts (Pss 68:29; 72:10) in that day with eagerness and haste, for the Hebrew word rendered *stretch* means to cause to run. Hands that had been stretched out *against* Israel (2 Chron 14:9), now stretch out to Israel's God.[4] Here is a picture of the conversion of Ethiopia and Egypt (Isa 19:21, 45:14). The future restoration of Israel will influence other peoples (Rom 11:12). Egypt and Ethiopia are often joined together; they are mentioned here as examples of the nations that will come to Jerusalem to honor the LORD God Jehovah, and to pray, praise and worship the Lord Jesus Christ!

Even Africa—wronged, degraded, oppressed, exploited, injured Africa—will come; and the worship of her children will be as acceptable to God the Father as that of any other of the races of mankind that dwell on the earth (Barnes). We agree with that assessment, but point out that this text is not a prediction of the rising in triumph of the Black race. We reject Adam Clarke's interpretation which makes this a literal final fulfillment under Solomon; he adds, "But as this may be a prophetic declaration of the spread of Christianity, it was literally fulfilled after the resurrection of Christ." No, fulfillment of Psa 68:31 is still future. The emphasis of the verse has nothing to do with a subdued, mistreated, exploited people finally ascending (again?) to places of world prominence. Here is a picture of two nations, former enemies of Israel and part of the Beast's kingdom and sphere of influence (Ezek 38:5; Dan 11:43), who will be converted. In the Kingdom or Millennial age they will join with multitudes from other nations in paying homage to Christ. Indeed, the whole world will fall at the feet of the Lord Jesus Christ.

[1] Growing up in the Black community, I often heard this verse interpreted this way. See Bradford, 44-46.

[2] Spurgeon, *Treasury* (Psa 68:31) 2:146.

[3] Bullinger, 547, 578 and 863: By *Metonymy* (a figure of speech that consists in substituting for the name of a thing an attribute of it or something which it naturally suggests) Ethiopia is first put "for the inhabitants who lift up their hands." Keach, 88: *Prosopopeia* or *Personification* is the technical term for describing Ethiopia as a person, or anything that is not a person (obviously, Ethiopia has no hands) and is figuratively introduced or proposed as a person.

[4] Keach, 89: stretched out in prayer, and in giving gifts of gold to the Lord. Calvin: The hands of Cush will run out to God, meaning Ethiopia "will with great alacrity (eagerness) and delight surrender her power and influence unto God."

Evil Eye: Prov 23:6-7: *Eat thou not the bread of him that hath an evil eye* (KJV). *Do not eat the bread of a miser* (NKJV).

We must ever guard the Eye-Gate, for "the eyes entice to sin." [1] Recall that Eve "saw that the tree was good for food, and that it was pleasant to the eyes;" Lot "lifted up his eyes, and beheld" the well-watered plain of Jordan, and chose the land of Sodom and Gomorrah. While fleeing the wicked city, Lot's wife looked back and was turned into a pillar of salt (Gen 3:6, 13:10; 19:26). Potiphar's wife cast longing eyes upon Joseph, and attempted to seduce him. Samson saw a Philistine woman in Timnath, desired her and married her. He saw a harlot in Gaza and committed fornication with her. He also saw Delilah! David saw a beautiful woman (Bathsheba) washing herself, and sent for her (Gen 39:7;

Jud 14:1, 16:1, 4; 2 Sam 11:2-4). We see, we want, and we attempt to get it, in whatever way possible, hook, crook, or took!

Now the **Evil Eye** is not the "double whammy," the slang expression for a supernatural spell or hex or jinx; a superstitious belief that a gaze or stare could cause material or physical harm. Throughout the centuries it has been held that certain people possess a mysterious power to look at a person and with a glance inflict harm or death. [2] One who has an *evil eye* is a miser (NKJV); stingy (RSV, NIV); niggardly (Moffatt) or churlish; [3] envious; [4] covetous (Gill); or malicious (Barnes). He is avaricious, self-seeking, uncompassionate, mean and hostile. He has a grudging, illiberal spirit (JFB), and is vicious in disposition or temper. An evil eye is the opposite of a bountiful, generous (Prov 22:9), or benevolent eye. In the Gospels (Matt 6:23, 20:15; Mark 7:22; Luke 11:34) using the words "evil eye" the ethical sense prevails, and *envy* is stressed.

When the context is ignored, there is the danger of suggesting that if a man entertains good thoughts he **is** good! He may be good so far as other humans are concerned, but in God's sight "there is none who does good, no, not one." Even the plowing of the wicked is sin (Prov 21:4). Only through faith in the shed blood of the Lord Jesus Christ are we justified, declared righteous in the sight of God.

Here is the situation. You are invited to eat; you accept because you desire his delicacies. He says to you, "Eat and drink! Help yourself! I'm glad to have you come and dine with me." However, he deceives you even as he feeds you. Why? It is because his motive for inviting you is evil, ulterior (Gen 14:21-24). He may be playing politics, seeking your good will or to place you in his debt. He is concerned about the cost of the meal, counting the bucks with each bite; or hoping you will choke with each crumb. You really are not welcome. Imagine wanting to vomit upon realizing you have eaten the bread of deception, and wishing you could take back all of the earlier compliments and thanks you extended.

Thought
Some years ago, I preached a sermon entitled, *An Invitation from the God of the Bible* (Psa 91:1). I mentioned that some places you go, you know you are not wanted. If when you enter the home, the dog growls, the cat hisses and humps up its back, the parrot swears

at you, and the goldfish spit pebbles at you, you know you are not welcome. But at least the animals are above board. The human host may not be.

[1] Michaelis, *TDNT* 5:377. See **As a Man Thinks in His Heart.**
[2] Juan, 89: "dirty look, looking daggers, stare someone down," and "if looks could kill," are remains of belief in the evil eye.
[3] Toy, ICC, *Proverbs*, 430.
[4] Michaelis, ibid, 5:376.

Eye for (an) Eye: Exod 21:24: *eye for eye, tooth for tooth, hand for hand, foot for foot* . . . Lev 24:20: *fracture for fracture, eye for eye, tooth for tooth* . . . Deut 19:21: *life shall be for life, eye for eye, tooth for tooth, hand for hand* . . . Matt 5:38: *You have heard that it was said, 'An eye for an eye and a tooth for a tooth.'*

I. The Law of Moses

The execution of this law belonged to the civil magistrates. Referred to as the *Lex Talionis,* or law of retaliation, it "was based on a sound principle of civil law for the guidance of the judge." [1] OT Scriptures make it plain that the authority for punishment was not vested in private persons, but in the government. This principle holds true in the NT also (Rom 13:1-4; 1 Pet 2:13-14). It was never intended as a basis for authorizing personal revenge or vindictiveness, or what Calvin (Exod 21:24) calls, "man's private passion." Indeed, the desire for vengeance was rebuked by our Lord Jesus. Private vendettas are forbidden: You shall not take vengeance, nor bear any grudge against the children of your people, but you shall love your neighbor as yourself: I am the LORD. The law of retaliation "is a restriction upon unrestrained vengeance." [2]

II. Christ Found No Fault with Moses' Law of Punishment

Our Lord does not condemn the law but rebukes the attempt to use it for personal retaliation. He emphasizes humiliation and self-denial (Matt 16:24). Though it may seem He opposed the Mosaic Law, actually His opposition was to those whose interpretation of the *Lex Talionis* approved of unlimited personal vengeance. Christ insisted that His disciples learn to suffer loss and not resort to personal revenge. [3] The Scribes and the Pharisees are the ones guilty of violating the purpose of the law of retaliation. With their "false gloss," religious leaders applied the law to private vengeance (Gill, Matt 5:38). Unwilling to confine the rule to magistrates, they felt justified making it a rule whereby the offended could get revenge; for them it became a matter of private conduct (Barnes: Matt 5:38-41).

> Thus the scribes and Pharisees deduced that in his dealings with others, every man should likewise retaliate in kind and should in every case insist on his full rights . . . The worst feature of this perversion was the fact that those who insisted on their rights adorned their revengeful and base actions with the very Word of God as though God Himself bade them act as they did. (Lenski, *Matthew* 240)

Christ "radically modified their message," [4] declaring that the Law did not refer to "private revenge, that it was given only to regulate the magistrate, and that private conduct was to be governed by different principles" (Barnes). By taking such matters in their own hands they had violated the injunctions of the OT. [5] The religious leaders emphasized the legal over the ethical. We face this problem today, for in our society are people who believe that what they declare legal is also moral: abortion, gambling, homosexuality, prostitution, etc. Christ did not want the minds of His disciples to dwell on trivialities—deciding how much money should be given for the wounded victim's pain, cure, and loss of time, shame, etc. — but to set their minds on ethical standards established by God. "In taking up this position Jesus was in harmony with the law itself, which contains dissuasives against vindictiveness (Lev 19:18)." [6]

III. Characteristics of This Law

Note that it was **Fair**, "avoiding excessive leniency or extreme severity." [7] It was the duty of the judge to compensate the plaintiffs fairly for their injuries, for all too often personal revenge was carried to the extreme; the punishment the victim desired to inflict was more than the evil that had been suffered. For example: "One could not kill a man because he had caused the loss of one's sight." [8] Sometimes those offended overreacted to the offense, for when properly administered the law actually helped to end feuds. [9]

This law's purpose was to restrict unrestrained vengeance. In many cases (but not for murder) paying a fine or replacing damaged property was sufficient. Understand then that *eye for (an) eye* was not a license for inflicting harm and finding satisfaction in cruelty. [10]

Another characteristic is **Context.** Do not ignore the context of the four passages under study. Read the context "in order to correctly interpret a legal text . . . a law is understood more by the spirit than by the letter;" furthermore, isolating the verse from its context, and not allowing the light of the other verses with which it is connected to shine upon the verse under study obscures the proper interpretation.[11] The importance of context is readily seen in the Sermon on the Mount where the Lord Jesus substitutes for the principle of *an eye for an eye, and a tooth for a tooth,* "the other cheek is to be turned, the cloak is to be added to the coat, the second mile is to be traveled, no goods are to be withheld from him that asks, and enemies are to be loved." [12]

Intentionality: Whether an offense has been committed accidentally or intentionally and deliberately is a matter to be weighed in judging that offense; indemnity is required, whether for curable or incurable wounds. The only unquestionable law of retaliation in the Mosaic code refers to *intentional* murder, for which there is no other retribution but *life-for-life* in the literal sense.[13] Moreover you shall take no ransom for the life of a murderer who is guilty of death, but he shall surely be put to death (Num 35:31; Lev 24:21b).

Literality: Taking a word or phrase literally is our first rule of interpretation (*hermeneutics*). If a literal view conflicts with another passage that is clearly understood, we are cautioned not to interpret the word or phrase literally, but to interpret them in the sense of "proper and full compensation; notwithstanding the wording, the expression cannot literally be *Lex Talionis.*" [14] For example, Lev 24:18: Whosoever kills an animal shall make it good, animal for animal. This verse does not teach that since you killed my goat, I want your goat killed. It teaches restitution of the value of the slain goat; give me a goat of equal value to replace the one you killed. Likewise, for the false witness to suffer the same trouble that he had intended his victim to experience (Deut 19:15-19: *You shall do to him as he thought to have done to his brother*), does not mean raise up false witnesses to tell lies or slander the false accuser so that he suffer what he had hoped his victim would have experienced.

IV. Miscellaneous Thoughts

Well aware of the difficulties and controversy associated with the determination of the place and purpose of the Sermon on the Mount, we offer the following interpretation: Christ directed His teachings here to His disciples, not to unbelievers. He desired that they learn to return good for evil. Inasmuch as they were believers, the message is not seen as offering the lost the way of salvation. Note in the Sermon "the absence of those elements which are distinctly Christian: redemption by the blood of Christ, faith, regeneration, deliverance from judgment, the Person and work of the Holy Spirit." [15] As we learned concerning the Law, so we learn here: "God never expected any man in this world to fulfill its provision." [16] Here is a standard that looks beyond the Church Age (Pentecost to Rapture). Here are laws describing the Kingdom Age—that period on earth after the Tribulation, an age in which Jesus Christ rules the world head-quartered in Jerusalem. "Such laws are guidelines for happiness in this world and rewards in the future world for those who are regenerate believers." [17]

They are rules describing the way of life for true children of the kingdom and give us a "composite picture of the kind of person who will inherit Christ's kingdom." [18] This interpretation does not mean the Sermon is unprofitable for us today (2 Tim 3:16-17). There is a beautiful moral application to and for the Christian. It is a picture of that perfect standard of righteousness demanded by the Law; a portrait of the principles of the kingdom of heaven on earth, that time when the Mosaic law of the theocracy will govern. [19]

> [Literally] it gives the divine constitution for the righteous government of the earth. Whenever the kingdom of heaven is established on earth it will be according to that constitution . . . such a standard as this belongs to another social order other than the present one. It is designed for a day when the King reigns upon His earthly throne . . . The social order in the earth which the kingdom prescribes must be such as shall make possible this supermanner of life. The King Himself must be present and reigning . . . [here] is the

King's own pronouncement on the terms of admission into the yet future earthly kingdom and prescribes the required manner of life in that kingdom . . . the yet future earthly kingdom, which is covenanted to Israel. (Chafer 5:103,107, 113-14; 3:24)

Hammurabi reigned as king of Babylon 1792-1750 BC during which time he codified the laws of Mesopotamia and Sumeria. Whereas the exact date of the Book of Exodus has not been settled, even the earliest dates given fall after the establishment of the Code of Hammurabi. Because the Babylonian legal code existed before Moses was moved by Jehovah to write the Pentateuch (the first five OT Books) there are scholars who caution: "These words did not originate in the OT, as most people believe." [20] I do not believe Moses borrowed anything from Hammurabi's Code. Within a given society with similar racial groups, customs and manners, naturally there would be similar rules concerning retaliation. It is more likely that this concept of retaliation existed very early in human history. Perusal of the Legal Code of Hammurabi reveals some extremely cruel judgments, giving rise to the thought that personal vendettas are justified.

Yet the law was merciful in allowing money compensation in place of the man's life. This is in contrast to the Code of Hammurabi which required like for like, and if a son or daughter were killed so the owner of the ox should forfeit the life of his own son or daughter. (Connell, *NBC* 122) [21]

Other expressions that come to mind: "The modern version would be 'bumper for bumper, fender for fender." [22] A phrase we often hear is *tit for tat*, or *tit for tap*, i.e. blow for blow. This may be the Dutch *dit vor dat* ("this for that") corresponding to Latin, *quid pro quo*.[23] Eye for (an) eye is commonly heard today, used "by those who wish to extract equal revenge for something done against them." [24]

---

[1] Fulghum, 74; AB Bruce, *ExpGT* 111; cf. M. Henry, Matt 5:38-42.
[2] Lev 19:18; ATR, Calvin: Matt 5:38.

[3] Tasker, 67.

[4] Brewer's, 374.

[5] JFB; Pro 20:22: Do not say, "I will recompense evil"; wait for the LORD, and He will save you; cf. Pro 24:29.

[6] A. B. Bruce, *ExpGT* 1:112.

[7] MacDonald, 111.

[8] Borland, *Parallel* 157; the point is: physical injuries are not to be punished with similar physical injuries.

[9] Hindson, *Parallel* 1891.

[10] Nelson, 216.

[11] Mikliszanski, *JBL* 295, 298.

[12] Chafer, 4:220.

[13] Mikliszanski, 296.

[14] Ibid., 295.

[15] Chafer 3:24.

[16] Barnhouse, *Romans: God's Wrath,* 1:280.

[17] H. Morris, *Defender's* 1011.

[18] Nelson, 1583; Pilgrim, 1321.

[19] Sco, Matt 5:3; Chafer 4:224.

[20] Hendrickson, 249.

[21] Elsewhere in Hammurabi's Code: #195: If a son strike his father, his hands shall be hewn off. #196: If a man put out the eye of another man, his eye shall be put out [an eye for an eye]. #197: If he break another man's bone, his bone shall be broken. #200: If a man knock out the teeth of his equal, his teeth shall be knocked out [a tooth for a tooth]: Claude H. W. Johns.

[22] Kaiser, *Hard Sayings* 150.

[23] Hendrickson, 724; Brewer's, 1080.

[24] Freeman, 412.

Feet of Clay: Dan 2:33: . . . *its feet partly of iron and partly of clay.*

Nebuchadnezzar, king of Babylon, dreamed and then required his magicians to tell him the dream *and* interpret it; failure to do so meant death. Their lives were spared when God gave the secret and interpretation of this extraordinary dream to Daniel of a frightening image, a picture of Gentile splendor predicting the four great ruling world empires. The predictions have caused the anti-supernaturalists to deny the date (c. 530 B.C.) and Daniel's authorship.

God gave him then a dream which contained a most remarkable revelation. The great man-image the king beheld is the symbol of the great world empires which were to follow the Babylonian empire. The image had a head of gold; the chest and arms were of silver; the trunk and the thighs of brass; the two legs of iron, and the two feet composed of iron mixed with clay. The LORD made known through the prophet the meaning of this dream. (Gaebelein, *Fundamentals* 2:129)

Four metals are mentioned composing the colossus or great statue, each decreasing in intrinsic value, but increasing in strength. There is also a decrease in purity.[1] Premillennial Dispensationalism makes the following observations and interpretations: (1) Head of fine Gold represents Babylon (Dan 2:38), at the time ruled by Nebuchadnezzar, the golden kingdom of the golden age (c. 606 – 538 B.C.). (2) Breasts and Arms of Silver predict the Medo-Persian Empire that followed the Babylonian rule (c. 538 – 331 B.C.). (3) Belly and Thighs of Brass: This third kingdom is Greece (c. 331 – 168 B.C.). Brass is an alloy of copper and zinc or copper, zinc and tin. Bronze is more accurately an alloy of copper and tin. (4) Legs of Iron: This fourth kingdom is Rome (c. 168 B.C. – A.D. 476). (5) Feet of Iron and part of Clay: Here the kingdom shall be divided (Dan 2:41). The Roman Empire began to disintegrate (c. A. D. 476).

The mixture of the iron with clay points to a trend toward rule by the people, or what is called the Laodicean age.[2] Clay symbolizes mankind, people, and suggests transience and weakness. [3] The metals were the kings or rulers. Dan 2:32-3 represents a kingdom with "many elements of permanency in it . . . yet having such elements of feebleness and decay as to make it liable to be overthrown" (Barnes). Predictions are made of a *Revived Roman Empire* consummated once the true Church is translated. Rapture of the Church marks the beginning of the Tribulation period, a seven-year time span. At the end of this period Christ returns to the earth, smashes all opposition and sets up His kingdom with headquarters in Jerusalem. This will mark the end of what is called the "Times of the Gentiles."

Out of all this has come the expression, *"feet of clay,"* a phrase describing an unexpected flaw, human shortcoming, vulnerable point, or critical fault of one esteemed as a hero, great, admired, revered or idealized.[4] One held in high regard or position who "shows disappointing weaknesses of character" is said to have feet of clay. [5] When a flaw or fundamental weakness in a person otherwise revered is seen, that person is said to have feet of clay; he or she is said "to be vulnerable out of proportion to superficial appearances." [6]

[1] Pilgrim, 1189.
[2] This last Church age [*laodikeia*], predicted in Rev 3:14-19, is the church in its final state of 'falling away,' or apostasy. *Laos* (laity) means "people." *Dike* means "rights, justice, or judgment." *Laodicean* (Rev 3:14) is defined as: "People's rights" (Sale-Harrison, 55); "rule of the people" (democracy, Newell, 75); "mob rule, *the democratic church*" (Seiss, 72); "The judging or rights of the People" (Gaebelein, *Revelation* 42); "the rights of the people, the era of democratization" (Ironside, 74); "the people speak" (Pilgrim).
[3] Job 4:19, 13:12; Goldingay, *Daniel* (WBC 30), 49.
[4] Hendrickson, 256.
[5] Brewer, 411.
[6] Jeffrey, 274.

Fig Leaves: Gen 3:7: *Then the eyes of both of them were opened, and they knew that they were naked; and they sewed fig leaves together and made themselves coverings.*

Here we study the attempt by Adam and Eve to hide their nakedness. Recall that in disobedience they had eaten of the forbidden fruit of the tree of good and evil (Gen 2:16-17; 3:6). Although this is the only tree mentioned by name, it is not generally held that the fruit was a fig; [1] nor is there any proof it was an apple! We attach then no special attention to the use of fig leaves other than to suggest the nearest available tree "just happened to be a fig" tree,[2] and that "the unusual size of fig-leaves played a part in this choice." [3] The verb rendered *sewed* means to connect, to plait; and preferable to the word *aprons* is the word *coverings*; they fashioned some type of primitive *girdle*.

Some scholars see a spiritual significance in their efforts to conceal themselves, suggesting the fig leaves "speak of man's attempt to save himself by a bloodless religion of good works." [4] Prior to the fall they knew they were naked, however they were not ashamed of their nakedness (Gen 2:25). Disobedience changed their awareness. Indeed, the proper fruit of sin is shame. As a result of their fall, their fellowship with God was broken immediately. Because *nakedness* refers also to sin's folly and shame, Adam and Eve experienced both spiritually and physically an ill at ease and a fear; thus their nakedness received a new meaning. [5]

"Their lovely naiveté was now replaced by evil thoughts and they covered themselves with fig leaves;" and their "keen sense of guilt" and new knowledge judged everything from a false standpoint and from a perverted position.[6] It is interesting that proponents of nudism seemingly dismiss the matter of sin, and seek to establish some sort of pre-Fall-return-to-Eden society.[7] They seek on their own that redemption of the human body that only God can and will perform (Rom 8:23). Apparently they prefer being unclothed and to wear the skin of sin rather than be clothed in the righteousness of Christ "that mortality may be swallowed up by life" (2 Cor 5:4).

Queen Victoria reigned in Britain from 1837 to 1901. One of the typical characteristics of the Victorian age is what is called prudery, defined as extreme modesty about sex. The example related to Gen 3:7 is the fact that during her reign statues and paintings of naked men and women in museums were covered with fig leaves. [8] What part of their bodies did they hide? Gill and others state that Adam and Eve desired to conceal only those parts of their bodies involved in reproduction. Keil and Delitzsch point out that sin broke the normal connection between their soul and body, so that their bodies stopped being "the pure abode of a spirit in fellowship with God."

> That the sense of shame should concentrate itself around that portion of the body which is marked by the organs of generation, no doubt has its deeper reason—that man instinctively feels that the very fountain and source of human life is contaminated by sin. The very act of generation is tainted by sin. If this scripturally portrayed origin of the sense of shame be accepted as true, then all contentions of anthropologists that shame is rather the outgrowth of inhibitions and custom fall away as secondary and incidental. The scriptural account goes to the root of the matter. (Leupold, *Genesis* 1:154)

What does the use of fig leaves connote in our society today? Figuratively it signifies a device for insufficient concealing, an ineffective camouflage; an unconvincing or inadequate attempt to conceal something considered shameful, improper, indecorous, wrong, or indecent; a flimsy disguise; "a magnificent symbol for human works of any sort" (Barnhouse, footnote #4, below).

Thought: *Liberia's Taylor fires lawyer at his war trial*: Philadelphia Inquirer, 5 June 07. "Charles G. Taylor, the former president of Liberia and once one of West Africa's most feared men," read in court parts of a letter in which "he complained about lacking the facilities and staff to defend himself." He said, "I cannot participate in a charade that does no justice to the people of Liberia and Sierra Leone. . . . I choose not to be a **fig leaf** of legitimacy for this court."

[1] Youngblood, *TWOT* 2:963.

[2] Leupold, *Genesis* 1:154.

[3] Hunzinger, *TDNT* 7:752n19. Wenham, (WBC 1) 76: The fig leaves "were probably used because they are the biggest leaves available in Canaan, though their heavy indentations have made them less than ideal for a covering." Because of the large size of fig leaves, Barnes believes that Adam and Eve sought to conceal their entire bodies from observation; even so, nothing could cover their souls or hide their sin.

[4] MacDonald, 36; S. Lewis Johnson, *BSac* (128) 340, considers all of our attempts to have good works deliver us from sin's ruin are useless Adamic fig leaves; this includes Christian works— baptism, confirmation, attendance at the Lord's Supper, church membership, etc. Barnhouse, *Romans: God's Glory,* 4:161: "Man sinned and became aware of the loss of his garments of light which were the sign of his holiness. Immediately, on discovering this spiritual nudity, he sought to clothe himself with fig leaves, a magnificent symbol of human works of any sort." Pilgrim Bible agrees that what Adam and Eve did was an attempt to cover up the wickedness in their hearts. Calvin also speaks of the folly of the lengths to which we will go to delude God or hide from His presence. Cf. H. Morris, *Defender's* Gen 3:7.

[5] Bullinger, 567.

[6] Nelson 10; Schrader, *Parallel* 21.

[7] Cf. Kidner, 69.

[8] Hendrickson, 260; Brewer's, 395-6.

Filthy Lucre: I Tim 3:3: *A bishop then must be . . . not greedy of filthy lucre [for money,* NKJV]. I Tim 3:8: *Likewise must the deacons be . . . not greedy of filthy lucre [for money,* NKJV]. Titus 1:7: *For a bishop must be . . . not given to filthy lucre [greedy for money,* NKJV]. I Pet 5:2: *Elders . . . feed the flock of God . . . not for filthy lucre [dishonest gain but eagerly,* NKJV].

Different renderings for the phrase *given to* or *greedy of filthy lucre*: covetous of getting money; not making the Gospel a means of gain, or fond of money-grabbing (JBP): greedy of shameful gain or disgraceful gain, made in shameful ways (ATR); lover of money grasping for riches (Pilgrim); fond of sordid gain (NASB); addicted to pilfering, base end of making money or profit (Moffatt); making money discreditably or in unworthy ways (Lock, ICC, *Pastorals*); using base and unjustifiable methods to raise and increase revenues (Clarke); wickedly desirous, covetous of dishonest, dishonorable gain (Calvin).

> It is a covetous disposition, which is a filthy one, and for the sake of gaining money, and amassing wealth and riches as the false prophets in Isaiah's time, who through covetousness made merchandise of men, and supposed that gain was godliness; whereas there is no such thing as serving God and mammon (Gill).

Money-grubbing is not limited to the NT. "*Yes, they are greedy dogs which never have enough. And they are shepherds who cannot understand; they all look to their own way, everyone for his own gain, from his own territory*" (Isa 56:11) [1] "The accusation of making money out of religion was brought against Samuel," and vigorously rebutted by him (1 Sam 12.3-5). [2] Evidently, the early church elders received some stipend, however small or uncertain the amount may have been. If they received nothing they could not be labeled "hirelings," or be accused of being tempted to fleece the flock. [3] Often I hear people say "*Money* is the root of all evil"; they omit the words "*the love*." There is nothing some men won't do if the price is right. Greed is a hugely influential sin (Barnes); men will betray their oath for money. Note the importance of· this qualification for deacons.

Because they were responsible for collecting and distributing church funds to the poor, it was desirable to discourage any acts of embezzlement or misappropriation.

Titus 1:10-11: *For there are many . . . teaching things which they ought not, for filthy lucre's sake [for the sake of dishonest gain,* NKJV]. We separated this verse from the ones pertaining to bishops and deacons, for here Paul refers to the "contradictors, insubordinate or unruly, idle talkers, deceivers and subverters." *Ekstrepho,* rendered *subvert* means to turn inside out, turn aside, change for the worse, pervert or corrupt. Emphasis is upon unbelievers; *of the circumcision* denotes "dangerous teachers who were Jews who mixed Jewish laws with Christian liberty." [4]

In religious circles there ever remain those guilty of seeking popular applause, honor and glory from men, all the while lining their pockets, wallets and bank accounts with "that which is disgraceful," [5] gained by teaching what they ought not to teach. Fowler calls the phrase 'filthy lucre' a cliché and hackneyed. [6] *Filthy lucre* is one word in the Greek; *lucre* is derived from the Latin word *lucrum* meaning "gain, profit or wages." It becomes filthy when it corrupts the sincerity of the Christian ministry. [7]

When William Tyndale translated the NT from Greek to English in 1525 he **mis**translated the Greek *aiskhron kerdos* ("shameful or dishonorable gain") and rendered it as *filthy lucre.* The words do not mean "dirty money" but the word *lucre* was "tarred for the rest of its existence," for the authors of the 1611 KJV kept the phrase. It "soon entered English as a term for money in general, no matter how honorably earned." [8] Our expression, "filthy rich," means very, extremely rich in money or wealth (RH). All the blame is not put on Tyndale for this pejorative [disparaging, depreciatory] sense of *lucre* . . . for he was merely a link, albeit a strong one, in a process that had begun long before with respect to the ancestor of our word, the Latin word *lucrum,* 'material gain, profit' . . . Tyndale thus merely helped the process along when he gave us the phrase *filthy lucre* (AHD).

Thought: Beware of prestidigitating pulpiteers who pull from their preaching pockets whatever pap they deem profitable and powerful enough to pluck money out of the purses of the people seated in the pews (Banks). "The quickest way to double your money is to fold it and put it back in your pocket" (Will Rogers).

71

[1] E. J. Young, 3:397: "Their own way occupies their interest . . . a way of gain for themselves . . . false shepherds sought for all the gain they could obtain . . . When greedy gain fills the hearts of ministers, disaster is sure to follow . . . usefulness in God's service is at an end."

[2] Selwyn, 230.

[3] Bigg, ICC, *Peter & Jude*, 188; Selwyn, ibid. Hoste, 134: "the exhortation, 'not for filthy lucre,' seems to preclude a stated salary. A servant of the Lord truly looking to Him for his support is not serving for filthy lucre". Mounce, (WBC 46), 177: "The overseers may have controlled the church's finances, so it was especially important that they be above reproach in this area. The minister has the right to be supported by believers, for the workman is worthy of his hire, even as the Lord Jesus taught" (Luke 10:7, 8; cf. I Cor 9:7-14; Grudem, 188).

[4] Pilgrim, 1701.

[5] Bultmann, *TDNT* 1:190; Schlier, *TDNT* 3:673.

[6] Fowler, 91, 235.

[7] H. Morris, *Defender's* 1399.

[8] Hendrickson, 261; Jeffrey, 278-9: "In short, the phrase is attached not to money itself so much as to corrupt motives in acquiring it."

Fire and Brimstone: Gen 19.24: *brimstone and fire on Sodom and Gomorrah.* Psa 11.6: *fire and brimstone and a burning wind.* Ezek 38:22: *great hailstones, fire, and brimstone.* Luke 17:29: *it rained fire and brimstone from heaven.* Rev 9:17: *out of their mouths came fire, smoke, and brimstone*; 14:10: *He shall be tormented with fire and brimstone*; 19:20: *the lake of fire burning with brimstone*; 20:10: *the lake of fire and brimstone*; 21:8: *in the lake which burns with fire and brimstone.*

I. Literal Language

Take literally the phrase *fire and brimstone.* [1] The two words are called a *hendiadys,* literally *one through two,* or *one by means of two,* a figure of speech in which a single complex idea is expressed by two words connected by a conjunction; the connection is used to express a single notion that would normally be expressed by an adjective *and* a substantive [noun]. The term means "burning brimstone" or "fiery brimstone." [2] Sodom, Gomorrah, Admah and Zeboiim were real cities (Deut 29:23). The region where this disaster occurred was abundant with petroleum, bitumen (asphalt), salt, sulfur and sulfurous fumes—natural ingredients and physical agents that are taken literally.

The volcanic eruptions, earthquakes, and lightning strikes involved are to be considered as literal physical agents used by God.[3] *Fire and brimstone* is a phrase that is synonymous (*metonymic*) with Hell, [4] a literal place. Just as *Heaven* is a literal place so *Hell* is a place, one of torment burning with fire and brimstone. There are those who do not believe *Hell* is a literal place, but interpret the word as only symbolic. Some years ago *Ebony Magazine* published "What Happened to Hell?" In this article Martin Luther King, Jr., Gardner Taylor, Howard Thurman, Benjamin Mays and others opined that Hell is not a literal geographic place with a literal burning fire. [5] **To the contrary, Hell is a geographical entity to be inhabited** (Rev 19:20).

II. Judgment

A brief reading of the Gospel of Matthew reveals Christ has much to say about Hell: "in danger of hell fire," "whole body to be cast into hell," "son of hell," "condemnation of hell," "weeping and gnashing of teeth," "outer darkness," "everlasting fire prepared for the devil and his angels," and "everlasting punishment." Keep in mind also that in the Book of Revelation the Lord Jesus Christ made many references to judgment. The one word that describes fire and brimstone is **judgment.** Sodom and Gomorrah's destruction was no random catastrophe, [6] but God's deliberate condemnation of wickedness, the Righteous Judge's judgment upon the unrighteous. It was an event describing the future of the ungodly, a warning to the wicked (2 Pet 2:6). Their condemnation to destruction "exerted a strong influence on subsequent ideas of divine judgment." [7]

> That it is a condition of unspeakable misery is indicated by the figurative terms used to describe its sufferings: [everlasting, unquenchable fire; where their worm does not die; the lake burns with fire and brimstone; a bottomless pit; outer darkness and blackness; weeping and gnashing of teeth; ever ascending smoke of their torment; no rest day nor night.] Hell is a place where the lost (unregenerate, reprobate, unbelievers) experience separation from God. (Chafer, 4:430-1) [8]

73

Even as He caused hail, manna and lightning to fall on other occasions, it is clear the Sovereign Judge of the universe used physical agents to destroy the wicked cities and their inhabitants.

III. Modern Use of the Phrase, *Fire and Brimstone:*

In these instances a figure of speech is not a license to modify the thought which the figure expresses; rather it recognizes that a figure of speech in these passages is a feeble attempt to declare in language that which is beyond the power of words to describe. A figure of speech is not a complete demonstration of truth, but the idea of eternal retribution could be conveyed to the human mind in no other way. (Chafer, ibid)

The phrase *fire and brimstone* also is denotes punishment and destruction, at times signifying a "fiery sermon that threatens transgressors with eternal damnation;" [9] or any severe punishment or trial, angry or violent denunciation or recrimination; fiery or passionate rhetoric; or an ejaculation of 'strong language'.

Thought

AUNT HET

The idea of Hell was a necessity. Mankind hasn't yet advanced enough to be decent without jails or some other punishment to fear.

[1] K&D, Gen 19:24: "The words are to be understood quite literally . . . that brimstone and fire, i.e. burning brimstone, fell from the sky."

[2] Myers, 98; *DBI* 123: 'burning sulfur' is the main element in the destruction of the cities; Bullinger, 659: emphasis is on 'burning'.

[3] Kidner, *Genesis* 135; H. Morris, *Defender's* 43: "The most likely explanation seems to be the sudden release by an earthquake and volcanic explosion of great quantities of gas, sulfur, and bituminous materials that had accumulated from materials trapped beneath the valley floor during the Flood. These were ignited by a simultaneous electrical storm, so that it appeared to Abraham, watching from afar, that 'the smoke of the country went up as the smoke of a furnace." Wenham, (WBC 2) 59: "The Dead Sea area still reeks of sulfurous fumes, and asphalt deposits are found, but what combination of natural or supernatural agents destroyed the town remains speculation. The narrator stresses that 'it was from the LORD.'"

[4] Jeffrey, 279-80. Foerster, *TDNT* 5:580.

[5] *Ebony Magazine,* 47 (Jan, 1961); Schneider, *TDNT* 4:597.

[6] Kidner, ibid.

[7] Lang, *TDNT* 6:936.

[8] Thiessen, 392: [The undying worm] seems to be a quotation from Isa 66:24 and it implies that there will always be something for the worm to feed on and for the fire to consume.

[9] Brewer's, 399.

First Shall Be Last and the Last First: Matt 19:30: *But many who are first will be last, and the last first.* Matt 20:16: *So the last will be first, and the first last. Mark 10:31: But many who are first will be last, and the last first. Luke 13:30: And indeed there are last who will be first, and there are first who will be last.*

Our Lord spoke these words on different occasions.[1] Note the different syntax or word order in the phrases, "first shall be last, and the last first," and "the last shall be first, and the first last." Matt 19:30 and Mark 10:31 use similar phrases; and Matt 20:16 and Luke 13:30 correspond. Why do we have these differences, what is the purpose? What is the emphasis intended?

In the Parable of the Laborers, Matt 20:1-16, a group of men were hired early in the morning for a *denarius*, a Roman silver coin that represents a day's wages. About 9 a.m. another group was hired, and then about noon and again at 3 p.m. more men were put to work. Finally, about 5 p.m. the landowner hired the last group. Whereas he had agreed to pay the first men a *denarius,* to all the others he simply said, "Whatever is right I will give you." At the end of the day, about 6 p.m., the first paid were those who came at 5 p.m.; they received a *denarius.* When those first hired came to be paid last, [2] they received their *denarius,* but immediately complained. They did not think it right that all those who came later and did less work should receive the same wage.

To understand this parable we must connect it with Matt 19:27-30. Unfortunately, chapter 20 separates the *purpose* of the parable from the *telling* of the parable. [3] The point is that the parable is the Lord's response to Simon Peter's question, "Therefore what shall we have?" (Matt 19:27). Simon spoke for all of the disciples, and his question reveals "something of the spirit of the hireling, and it is against this spirit that the parable is directed." [4] Emphasis is **not** on the time or the number of hours the men put in; to stress time negates the point made in the story. [5]

What is important is the attitude of the workers. The *first* laborers complained about the wages the later workers received. When it comes to present blessings and future rewards, the grumbling *first* workers will be last. Their murmuring results in forfeiture; the judgment for rewards will bring many surprises (2 Cor 5:10). Those laborers who came later (*the last*) appreciated the grace of God and gladly accepted their wages. The *first* allowed their concept of work blind them to God's grace—His right to do as He pleases with what He owns! It is on this fundamental assertion concerning God's grace that the Lord ends the parable with the statement that the *last will be first and the first last.*

With these truths in mind consider the following interpretations: (1) that the last will take the place of the first or the first take the place of the last (2) that "many who at first were in the kingdom will finally be out of it; while many who at first were out of it will at last be in it" [6] (3) That the *first* refers to the Jews and the *last* to the Gentiles. [7] (4) That the *first* are not old-line Jewish Christians, while the *last* are Gentile Christians; nor are they Christians who have worked long and faithfully (*first*) or late comers (*last*), Christians who have *not* worked hard or long [8] (5) They are not Pharisees versus Christian disciples [9] (6) We reject the idea that the Disciples are *first* (nearest to the Lord, physically), and therefore "hold pre-eminence or special blessings

76

unavailable to those who came on the scene later," other believers who are considered *last.* [10]

Mark 10:31: Here we learn that *our* evaluation of others does not affect God's judgment. *We* stress wealth, power, nobility, influence, legalism, fame, outward appearance (Jas 2:1-3), skin color, etc., but the God of the Bible alone is capable of rightly judging. He alone knows our motives, values and attitudes.[11] Thus believers are reminded that many who are now first in importance and power will someday be last, while those who lack wealth and standing in society today will someday have it all. We understand then that self-complacency, selfish ambition and pride may so vitiate the quality of service as to make one first in sacrifice last in God's esteem. [12]

Luke 13:30: This is part of the answer Christ gives to the question, "Lord, are there few who are saved?" There were Jewish people privileged to witness the ministry of the Lord who considered that was all they needed in order to enter the Kingdom of God. What awful words to hear the Christ pronounce: "I tell you I do not know you, where you are from. Depart from Me, all you workers of iniquity" (Luke 13:27; cf. Matt 7:21-23). As it was then, so it is today: There are greatly honored preachers and church leaders who love their power and position more than they love the Lord Jesus. Like the Jewish religious leaders of old, they presume their relationship guarantees them a place in the kingdom. They have not learned that "Christian activity must not be equated with salvation." [13] Others, unknown to the world, but having a close relationship with Jesus Christ, will be honored in the kingdom. It is in this sense that there are "last who will be first, and there are first who will be last."

> [He] will assign to me my place in His eternal kingdom on the basis of how I lived after I have known Him as my Savior and named Him as my Lord . . . We will be judged on the percentage of yieldedness in our lives . . . an unknown servant who may have been considered by men as a half-pint capacity may have a much greater reward in Heaven because he or she has surrendered that half pint in a percentage that approaches completeness. In like manner the person that the servant worked for may have been considered by those around him as being of barrel capacity, and yet be poor in the judgment of

believers because there was such a great percentage of unsurrendered self. (Barnhouse, *Romans: God's Heirs*, 3.228-29. Anonymous: *Deeds of merit as we thought them, He will show us were but sin, Little acts we had forgotten, He will show us were for Him*)

[1] A. B. Bruce, *ExpGT* 1:252; Plummer, ICC, *Luke*, 348; Hauck, *TDNT* 5:856.

[2] Literally, the *first* to work were the *last* to be paid. When I was an occupation soldier in Germany after World War II, the Black soldiers were paid last, the White soldiers first. By the time we got to the PX, practically everything we wanted to purchase was out of stock. I went to the Inspector General to protest; within several months we all were paid at the same time.

[3] Another man-made chapter division which breaks continuity is that between Matthew chapters 16 and 17.

[4] Trench, *Parables* 174, (would justly) entitle the parable *On the Nature of Rewards in the Kingdom of God.*

[5] Michaelis, *TDNT* 6:868; Kittel, 2:698. Even if those called in the early days of His Flesh are labeled *first,* they are on equality with those called in the *last* days of the Church age (Hoste, 253). In other words, so far as **rank** is concerned, the last shall be *as* the first, and the first *as* the last; one is not superior or inferior to the other; they "are all set upon the same footing" (Trench, ibid. 189). For this reason use of the word "unworthy" to describe those who are not among the first workers, reveals the mindset of those who murmured. The Lord's point is that *first* or *last* they all are called by the grace of God, so that neither the "worth" of the laborer, nor the number of hours worked is a factor in determining calling or rewards.

[6] Lenski, *Matthew* 762-3.

[7] Cf. Bruce, ibid. 569; MacDonald, 1424; M. Henry.

[8] Mentioned by Eugene-Boring, *NIB* 8:393.

[9] "Pharisaic opponents" suggested by Eugene-Boring, *NIB* 8: 392.

[10] Cf. Ezra P. Gould, *Mark*, ICC 196; Hagner, (WBC 33B) 566: the disciples must not presume upon their special status in the present.

[11] Michel, *TDNT* 4:654: cites Schlatter: "The battle of Jesus against human greatness is seen not only in individual statements and actions like [Matt] 19.14, 30, et al; it is a continually active and visible mark of His whole activity." Cf. Perkins, *NIB* 8:651:

Both in the present and in the future, earthly measures of power and status do not apply in the kingdom of God; C. Evans, (WBC 34B) 103. See F. B. Meyer's (*Joseph* 151) use of "the first become last, and the last first."

[12] Bruce, ibid. 252.

[13] Sco, Luke 13:26.

Fleshpots of Egypt: Exod 16:3: *And the children of Israel said unto them, Would to God we had died by the hand of the LORD in the land of Egypt, when we sat by the flesh pots* [NKJV: *pots of meat*].

How easily we forget yesterday's deliverance; we grumble, complain and murmur because of today's troubles. Delight rapidly turns into despair. "Discontent magnifies what is past, and vilifies what is present, without regard to truth or reason" (M. Henry). The events of our text took place "on the fifteenth day of the second month after" the children of Israel had been delivered from Egypt. Need we marvel how soon we are removed! Imagine the absurdity of miserable murmurers calling Moses and Aaron murderers! (Calvin). Imagine accusing their deliverers of being their destroyers. Is it possible that they preferred slavery in Egypt to their present freedom in the wilderness? Apparently the Egyptian task-masters used large pots or boilers to cook the meals of their slaves. [1] Flesh pots may refer to where the cooking took place as well as to what utensils were used. We assume they were well-fed though harshly treated and despised. They remembered "the fish they ate freely in Egypt, the cucumbers, the melons, the leeks, the onions, and the garlic" (Num 11:5).

Evidently their complaining spirit clouded their memory. They forgot the lashes but remembered the leeks; they recalled the cucumbers but forgot the cruelty; melons dismissed miseries; and in their thoughts fish replaced their freedom. Keep in mind the more serious fact that their complaints against Moses and Aaron were really complaints against Jehovah. How seldom we connect the relationship of God's servant with God Himself. This is because often we do not recognize the spiritual battle that takes place. We see only the flesh and blood wrestling. What makes our distrust of God all the more heinous is the fact He repeatedly and miraculously delivers us from our dilemmas and dangers. [2]

Sin blinds us. God's mercies are forgotten, and in our impatience and ingratitude we begin to foolishly exaggerate—we paint a pretty picture of our former circumstances while at the same time portraying an exaggerated hopelessness of our present situation. Indeed, their complaining against Moses was hyperbole. "It was not the custom in Egypt for slaves to sit around flesh pots and eat all the bread and vegetables that they wanted . . . Often in the wilderness these former slaves acted like foolish and whiny children rather than God's people headed for the Promised Land— much like we often act today." [3]

Today's meaning of *fleshpots* has taken an interesting turn. [4] The love of luxury is an oft-cited constituent in the various definitions of *fleshpots*; and such luxuries or advantages are regarded with regret or envy. Sexual gratification or physical, sensual lascivious entertainments along with unrestrained pleasures or amusements are a part of *fleshpots*. The term also includes the place or establishment where these activities are offered.[5]

[1] The flesh pot was a three-legged vessel of bronze that the Egyptians used for cooking, Freeman, 116.
[2] Gill; Durham, (WBC 3) 219: "An all-too-human exaggeration of the diet in Egypt."
[3] Freeman, ibid.
[4] Fulghum, 85: "In literature the expression now frequently means longing for material things, for luxuries of a sinful kind." Jeffrey, 285: "The term 'flesh pots' came to symbolize high living and self-indulgence".
[5] OED: 5:1047.

Fly in the Ointment: Eccl 10:1: KJV: *Dead flies cause the ointment of the apothecary to send forth a stinking savour: so doth a little folly him that is in reputation for wisdom and honor.* NKJV: *Dead flies putrefy the perfumer's ointment, and cause it to give off a foul odor; so does a little folly to one respected for wisdom and honor.*

An *apothecary*, accurately rendered *a perfumer* is one who is highly skilled in compounding or mixing spices and perfumes. [1] This profession was widely renowned in the ancient near east. [2] Today an apothecary is one who prepares and sells drugs and medicines; a druggist or pharmacist. The word apothecary comes from the Latin (*shopkeeper* or *storehouse*), which in turn is derived from a Greek word meaning, *to put away* (*in a receptacle*). The word *flies* is a plural noun, but the verbs *cause to stink* and *cause to ferment* are singular. This is not because the writer was careless or wrote bad grammar, but implies he thought of each fly as causing the smell (JFB). Use of the singular makes the idea **singular.** [3]

Flies are pests, singular or plural. The body of a dead fly entangled in an ointment begins to decay, causing the perfume to bubble, and give off a malodor rather than a fragrance; in other words, "The more delicate the perfume, the more easily spoiled is the ointment." [4] Eccl 9:18 states, "*But one sinner destroys much good.*" Eccl 10:1 continues the thought. Since the fly is such a small creature, it symbolizes a "little folly." Men would define "littleness" as that which does not take much time to commit, a peccadillo, minor indiscretion or "slip-up." What is scary here is the fact that it does not take much to bring down those respected and honored by many. "A man may commit one sin, and this can destroy a lifetime of virtue." [5]

> The man who would remain in the way of profit must take scrupulous care to keep even the smallest grain of folly from taking root in his life. The little fly who has rested amidst the sweet scent of a costly ointment will ultimately be the cause of the ointment's total corrupttion. The Preacher alludes to an everyday occurrence that has passed into a proverb. Just as the insignificant fetid fly has the power of corrupting a quantity of precious perfume by imparting unto it its offensive smell, so a little folly has often shown itself more weighty and powerful than glorious wisdom. From the disagreeable effect which the presence of dead flies in precious moistures produces in the sultry climate of the East arose the Arabic proverb, 'A fly is nothing, yet it produces loathsomeness.' The toleration of the slightest folly in the life of a man of reputation will soon cause his reputation to have a stinking savor. (Hawkins, *Parallel* 1277)

Here is a warning to all who hold high positions, especially to preachers and pastors! Imagine building a good reputation for thirty years and having all to tumble down because of one little drink, one flirtatious moment, one "little white lie [well-intentioned untruth]," a stolen dollar, an unguarded moment, etc. "Envy fastens upon eminency," magnifying the mistakes of the famous, or any who remain under the microscope of the public—especially "those who make a great profession of religion" (M. Henry). The biblical phrase *a fly in the ointment* is an idiom signifying a trifling cause that spoils everything; [6] a small defect that ruins something valuable, a source of annoyance; [7] a detrimental factor, circumstance or detail, a detraction, drawback; a small thing that lessens the value of something; an impediment, snag, hitch, obstacle or sticking point. Surely Christians need always to heed the exhortations, "Walk circumspectly . . . abstain from every form of evil," remembering "a little leaven leavens the whole lump" (Eph 5:15; 1 Thess 5:22; Gal 5:9).

Thought
A man went into a restaurant and ordered a bowl of soup. The waiter brought the soup and started walking away when the man called, "Waiter, tell me what this fly is doing in my soup?" The waiter looked and replied, "The back stroke, sir."

[1] Patch, *ISBE* 4:2321; 1:207; Nelson; (Exod 30:25, 35), 154.
[2] Wm. White, *TWOT* 2:861.
[3] Barton, ICC, *Ecclesiastes*, footnote168.
[4] JFB; Fulghum, 86. Murphy, (WBC 23A) 100: "A small thing, no matter how apparently insignificant, can spoil one's efforts . . . dead flies will spoil the perfume, an ounce of folly can undo wisdom."
[5] Laurin, *Wycliffe* 592.
[6] Brewer's, 407.
[7] Hendrickson, 268.

Forbidden Fruit: Gen 2:16-17: *And the LORD God commanded the man, saying, "Of every tree of the garden you may freely eat; but of the tree of the knowledge of good and evil you shall not eat, for in the day that you eat of it you shall surely die." Gen 3:3: [Eve speaking to Satan]: But of the fruit of the tree which is in the* *midst of the garden, God has said, "You shall not eat it, nor shall you touch it, lest you die."*

This ancient phrase *Forbidden Fruit* "has its origins in Gen 3:3, although the exact words are not found there," nor does the phrase occur elsewhere in the Bible.[1] Commentators use the words forbidden fruit with respect to the disobedience of Adam and Eve in the Garden of Eden. The word *fruit* is used extensively in the Scriptures in a figurative sense: *Fruit* of the womb, body, loins, prosperity, one's own way or hands, an arrogant heart, one's words, mouth or lips, of wisdom, of lies, thoughts, deeds, labor, of the righteous or of righteousness, of the Spirit, etc. There are those who would explain the Fall of Adam as the "first connubial [marriage] intercourse." However, this interpretation is considered a "willful misreading of the plain meaning of the words." [2] One response to this matter refers to the first pair's awareness of their nakedness:

> They were comfortable in their physical bodies, in their sexuality, in their relationship, and in their work—with no wrongdoing. The wording of vv. 24, 25 suggests the couple experienced sexual relations in the garden as a part of their God-intended experience. At 4:1 we first read of procreation, not necessarily the couple's first sexual experience together. (Nelson, 9)

Because the "expression is often associated with sexual matters," [3] a frequent definition of the figurative use of the term forbidden fruit suggests unlawful pleasure, especially illicit love; [4] an indulgence or a pleasure that is illegal or is believed to be immoral; any unlawful pleasure, especially illicit sexual indulgence. I would maintain the primary meaning of forbidden fruit as describing a tempting but forbidden person or thing; anything that is tempting but potentially dangerous. What we eat becomes a part of us, a part of our very nature. By disobeying and eating the forbidden fruit sin caused the spiritual relationship with Jehovah to be broken. Once communion with God is broken, all kinds of sins may issue forth. [5] Accepting this truth, we understand that the emphasis put on the meaning of the words forbidden fruit as primarily sexual in nature is one that is unwarranted, solely the product of man's imagination and not rooted in the proper interpretation of the Bible.

[1] Hendrickson, 270; Fulghum, 86-87: "Although the phrase 'forbidden fruit' appears nowhere in the Bible, and 'apple' is not mentioned in Genesis, they commonly refer to this passage."
[2] Leupold, *Genesis* 1:145.
[3] Freeman, 2.
[4] WBD; Brewer's, 412.
[5] Traver, *BSac* (120) 252. R. Anderson, *The Fundamentals* 3:45: "As the Epistle of James declares, every sin is the outcome of an evil desire. And eating the forbidden fruit was the result of a desire excited by yielding to the tempter's wiles . . . once our parents lent a willing ear to Satan's gospel . . . their fall was an accomplished fact. The overt act of disobedience, which followed as of course, was but the outward manifestation of it. And, as their ruin was accomplished, not by the corruption of their morals, but by the undermining of their faith in God, it is not, I repeat, in the moral, but in the spiritual sphere, that the ruin is complete and hopeless."

Golden Cow (Calf)
Exod 32:4: *And he (Aaron) received the gold from their hand, and he fashioned it with an engraving tool, and made a molded calf.*

A number of phrases, most of them slang, use the adjective *holy* to express surprise, wonder, astonishment, confusion or annoyance. Holy is used trivially to express intensity, unfavorable implication of piety or sanctimoniousness, or used with a following word as an oath or expletive. [1] Among such terms are: Holy Smoke! Holy Cats! Holy Mackerel! Holy Moly! (*moly* is a coined word to rhyme with holy; this is called *reduplication*); Holy Moses! And Holy Toledo!

Holy Joe is a slang term to describe a chaplain, especially in the U.S. Armed Forces, any clergyman, minister or priest, or an excessively pious, self-righteous, sanctimonious or overwhelming religious person. Holy Willie is a hypocritically pious person. Holy Terror is a person of exasperating habits or manners. Holy Roller is an offensive, disparaging and derogatory term or nickname commonly used in America and applied to various religious groups who express their religious fervor by their shouts, frenetic body movements that include rolling on the floor, trances, and other frenzied excitement. [2] "Holy Cow" is an interjection or exclamation that also expresses surprise, bewilderment, astonishment, annoyance, or consternation. [3]

A sacred cow is a figure of speech that describes "Any institution, long-cherished practice or custom that is treated as immune from criticism, modification or abolition;" [4] things in widespread secrecy, held without question like some inscrutable object of worship (WBD). In Exod 24:18 Moses went up into the mountain to be with the LORD forty days and forty nights. There on Mount Sinai Jehovah gave him detailed instructions regarding how the Israelites should worship God. Repeatedly we read that "the LORD spoke to Moses" (Exod 25:1; 30:11, 17, 22, 34; 31:1, 12); and it is while Moses was there "receiving God's law . . . the people were down in the valley breaking it . . . In rejecting God, they were also rejecting Moses." [5]

It is difficult to fathom the mind of Aaron here. Had he also given up on Moses ever returning? It is conjectured that he thought he would find no response requiring the people to break off their golden earrings and sacrificing them in order to make the idol. Instead, they willingly gave of their possessions; their fanaticism proved Aaron wrong; his "cleverness was put to shame" . . . for when it comes to accomplishing "an act of pure self-will . . . there is no sacrifice that the human heart is not ready to make." Not a word is spoken against idolatry, leading us to believe he "had no backbone to stand against this blatant treason and idolatry." [6]

Because Moses delayed coming down from Mount Sinai, the Israelites gathered together to Aaron, and said to him, "Come, make us gods that shall go before us; for as for this Moses, the man who brought us up out of the land of Egypt, we do not know what has become of him." Aaron responded, "Break off the golden earrings which are in the ears of your wives, your sons, and your daughters, and bring them to me." Sin causes us to turn our tables into traps. Recall the Egyptians were so anxious to get rid of the children of Israel that they granted to them articles of silver and gold, and clothing. Now having arrived at Mt Sinai, the people soon turned their blessings into a curse; having lost patience waiting for Moses to return from his mountain-top appointment with Jehovah, they fell into idolatry. The greater part of the people, that is, of those who wore earrings, broke them off. [7] Portions of the very gold they received from their former slavemasters were fashioned into an idol cow to be worshiped. Aaron's part in all of this was shocking.

Had he so soon forgotten that the LORD had said, "You shall not make anything to be with Me—gods of silver or gods of gold you shall not make for yourselves." [8] The verb rendered to break means to break off, rend, tear apart, deliver, tear away, snatch or rescue. Although it does not appear that he thought of creating a worship that would replace the worship of Jehovah, Aaron demonstrated an unpardonable weakness when he acquiesced to their desire for a visible symbol of Him who had commanded no such thing ever be done (Exod 20:4-6). Jehovah was very angry with Aaron; but the LORD answered Moses' prayer and spared Aaron.

Note the assertion of the people, "We *wot* not what is become of" this Moses! (NKJV: We do not know what has become of him). The word rendered *wot* in the KJV comes from the Hebrew word (*yada*) that means to know, to be acquainted with. [9] One way to keep in mind the meaning of this strange-sounding Old English word is to think of the word *wit*. You cannot *witness* what you do not know or have not seen, so keep your *wits* about you; and you will not have to say, "I wot not" or be called a *nitwit*.

Hear also the "scathing, sarcastic and demeaning tones" and contempt in the words, "as for this man Moses" (Nelson 156). Their ingratitude and impatience were expressed in suspicion, ill thoughts and disparagement of their God-appointed leader; and this scene occurs "only three months after the Exodus." [10] Moses had not told them how long he would be there; God had not told him, nor did Moses have any responsibility to tell the Israelites if he had known.

What thoughts went through their minds? Had Moses deluded them, having no intention of returning? Was this his way of deserting them and returning to Midian? Was he dead, having starved to death, or destroyed by thunder, lightning or the glory of the LORD that was like a consuming fire? Or had he been translated to heaven?

The idol was **not** made of solid gold. It was first carved out of wood; the golden earrings were melted, cast into a flat sheet, hammered out by a goldsmith, and the coating of gold plate was then shaped and fastened around the wooden image. [11] The manner in which the idol was destroyed supports this description of its manufacture. According to Deut 9:21 the wooden center of the image was first of all burned with fire, then the gold covering beaten, rubbed or crushed to pieces, and pounded or ground to powder, fine as dust. Moses scattered the powder on the water and made the children of Israel drink it (Exod 32:20), apparently an "internalizing [of] the greatness of their sin," and "perhaps a suggestion that our sins return to us as a bitter potion." [12]

This answer should satisfy Loewenstamm, and others who contend that Exod 32:20 contradicts verses 4 and 24 because "gold does not burn." The idol was not a large elaborate work, for there had not been enough time for that; it was a rushed job, "an imperfect and diminutive (not life-size) figure of gilded wood hastily prepared to meet the urgency of the occasion" (JFB). Aaron and the people violated God's laws against idolatry! By considering the calf a symbolic representation of God they thus professed to be worshiping the LORD. [13]

Barnes states: "Their sin then lay, not in their adopting another god, but in their pretending to worship a visible symbol of Him whom no symbol could represent." Thus "their sin consisted not in a breach of the first but of the second Commandment" (JFB; Exod 20:4-6). The words "let us make gods" point to what Stephen says in Acts 7:41 that they "rejoiced in the works of their own hands." [14] Here we see the vanity of all idolatry (**well described in Isa 44:6-20**). Their folly is evident when they have no answer to the question, "How can an inanimate thing, man-made, having no life or breath, unable to see, speak, hear or think, newly created—sensibly be given credit for delivering you from the land of Egypt or enabling you to continue your journey to the Promised Land?"

Aaron admits the urgency of the people prevailed. He said to them, "'Whoever has any gold, let them break it off.' So they gave it to me, and I cast it into the fire, and this calf came out." Scholars have expressed great concern with the biblical account, especially with the words, "and there came out this calf." (Exod 32:24).[15]

There is nothing contradictory here. The Hebrew word translated *came out* is derived from the verb (*yatsa*, BDB 423f) meaning to go or come out. When used of inanimate things such as in Gen 2:10: a river went out of Eden; Exod 17:6: there shall come water out of the rock, and here in Exod 32:24, like the molten calf out of fire, we need not give life to the river, or to the water or to the golden calf. Whereas a miracle occurred as a result of striking the rock, the water issuing forth had no life of its own.

So it is here with respect to the Golden Calf. No miracle occurred in this incident with Aaron. The cow did not miraculously appear and walk out of the fire!

Moses destroyed the idol, and about three thousand men were killed; God's disciplinary judgment was calculated to teach Israel the awful danger of idolatry. When Moses interceded, Jehovah had mercy on the nation as a whole; Aaron also was spared. The broken tablets of the Ten Commandments were replaced. "That the Israelites were unspeakably guilty and exposed to the destructive wrath of God is made plain . . . God was gracious to Israel nonetheless, and the nation, despite a purging judgment, was preserved." [16]

Contemporary Use of the Expression Golden Calf

It is used "sometimes proverbially with reference to the 'worship' of wealth;" [17] or "one who sacrifices his or her principles for money or personal gain;" [18] It means "to bow down to money;" [19] or make money or material goods as an object of worship or pursuit (RH); the intense veneration and pursuit of money; and it is 'wealth thought of much too highly' (WBD, AHD).

[1] OED 7:319.
[2] Brewer's 527; Hendrickson, 354.
[3] OED 14:339; Encarta: Dictionary of American Slang, 264.
[4] Brewer's, 941; AHD.
[5] Boice, *Acts* 123.
[6] K&D. Borland, *Parallel* 175.
[7] Bullinger, 614.
[8] Exod 20:23; Jehovah warned Israel earlier, but they violated this command; cf. *DBI* 341.
[9] J. P. Lewis, *TWOT* 1:366
[10] Merrill, *BSac* (138), 249.
[11] Molten means "made by melting and casting into a mold," Freeman, 127-8; cf. M. R. Wilson, *TWOT* 2:582. K&D; Isa 40:19.
[12] Borland, ibid. 176; MacDonald, 125.
[13] Cobern, *ISBE* 1:544, the Golden Calf must have been a representation of a Semitic, not an Egyptian deity. Faur, *JQR* (69), 13: "When considering the worship of images in Israel, it is important to distinguish between *idolatry*—the worship of strange gods—and *iconolatry*, the worship of God with images." Faur calls the worship of the golden calf illegitimate iconolatry,

something that "evolved from the notion that ritual consecration had the intrinsic power to induce the spirit of the gods to dwell in the image and thus identify itself with it." He claims there is "a legitimate form of iconolatry."

[14] Girdlestone 21: When the Israelites made the molten calf out of their golden earrings, they said of it, "These be thy Elohim, O Israel," by which they practically meant "this is thy God," for they regarded the image as a representation of Jehovah; cf. Schultz, *TWOT* 2:644. The same formula is used by Jeroboam (1 Kgs 12:28). Scholars differ in their opinions about the basis for the worship of a molten calf. The Egyptians of course worshiped the cow, calf, ox or bull; all were held sacred, so the Jews were aware of this aspect of Egyptian idolatry. Durham, WBC (3) 421: "The probability that the calf was a symbol of divinity widely used among Israel's neighbors, of course makes Israel's idolatry even worse." Clarke: Aaron intended that the true God should be the object of their worship, though he permitted and even encouraged them to offer this worship through an idolatrous medium, the molten calf.

[15] Loewenstamm, *Biblica* (948), 481-89. Gill: Aaron speaks of it as if the gold became in the form of a calf without any design, or without using any methods to put it in this form; but that it was a matter of chance, or rather something miraculous and supernatural. He speaks of it as if it was alive, and came out of itself . . . What Moses thought of this apology is not said; it could not be satisfactory to him: and it is certain the conduct of Aaron in this affair was displeasing to God; and it seemed as if He would have destroyed him, if Moses had not prayed for him (Deut 9:20). Connell, NBC, 130: "An absurd excuse that the calf made itself." Clarke: "silly and ridiculous subterfuge!" M. Henry: "Childishly insinuates that when he cast the gold into the fire it came out, either by accident or by the magic art of some of the mixed multitude in this shape." Barnes: the words may bear the idea that the idol was "finished in a much shorter time than he had anticipated." K&D, Exod 32:24: This excuse was so contemptible that Moses did not think it worthy of a reply.

[16] Hodges, *BSac* (137), 46.

[17] OED, 2:781

[18] Hendrickson, 783

[19] Brewer's, 1168.

Hair White like Wool, White as Snow: Dan 7:9: *And the Ancient of Days was seated; His garment was white as snow, and the hair of His head was like pure wool.* Rev 1:14: *His head and hair were white like wool, as white as snow.*

What is the connection between Daniel 7:9 and Rev 1:14? The title "Ancient of Days" (Dan 7:9, 13) refers to God the Father, and is equally applicable to Jesus Christ (Dan 7:22; Rev 1:8, 13-18). Both purity and eternality are attributed to God the Father and to God the Son (Nelson, 2165). "The phrase 'white like wool, as white as snow' (Rev 1:14) combines the comparisons with snow and wool used in Dan 7:9" and it is believed that the author speaks of Jesus Christ as "equal to God in essence and appearance." [1]

For human beings (and the nation Israel personified) gray hair signifies old age. [2] Whiteness of hair characterizes venerable age; because such hair stands also for wisdom "the hoary white of old age" was held in high esteem by the Jews. [3] I find it impossible to interpret the passages under study as describing **God as an old Man.** I see no need to picture Him thus. [4]

The God of the Bible is eternal (Deut 33:27), everlasting (Psa 90:2); the Creator of time. Furthermore, the glorified body of our Lord ever remains that of a young Man in His early thirties. It is incongruous (inconsistent) to describe "one just risen from the dead, clothed with immortal youth and vigor, as an old man" (Barnes). Keep in mind then: (1) Emphasize the appearance of white hair as a characteristic of veneration, wisdom and dignity.[5] (2) the impression of majesty is also heightened by the description (3) whiteness also symbolizes spotless purity and holiness (K&D) (4) God's appearance (how He manifests Himself to us) is never one that is the result of decay. [6]

Note that His **head** is included, pointing to a crown of glory; "reference is not to age or length of days," but denotes "the radiance of the heavenly being which makes perceptible the majesty of the upper world." [7] (5) Emphasize then the whiteness as radiance. [8] The "white hair" points to God's eternality and "age-long existence," at the same time claiming "the veneration and respect of the beholder."[9] Proper exegesis reveals a picture of One who is capable of participating in the consummation of all things, an ability He has "because of His part in the origination of the world"—for He is the Alpha and the Omega, the First and the

Last, He who lives, and was dead; and is alive forevermore, possessing the keys of Hades and of Death." [10]

Thought
Years ago when I attended Black Muslim meetings it was all I could do to stomach the mockery made of Rev 1:14. They claimed Black Christians had been brain-washed by Whites, creating in us the desire to become white. Consequently, it was in ignorance that we sang, *Oh! Precious is the flow That makes me white as snow; No other fount I know; Nothing but the blood of Jesus.* However, making me 'white as snow' has nothing to do with my skin color.

The argument that the description stating *His hair was white like wool* teaches that Christ was a Black Man is not acceptable. True, the dictionary definition of a Negro mentions "tightly curled, kinky wooly hair." However, the verse does not stress the material but the color. "White **like** wool" does not emphasize the wooliness, but stresses the whiteness. If I say, "Your shirt is green **like** grass," it does not mean you are wearing a shirt made out of grass. Attention is directed toward the greenness not the grassiness. So here in Rev 1:14 accent is placed upon the whiteness, not the wooliness. Besides, how would you interpret 'white **as** snow'? Would it mean our Lord had icicles hanging on His head? No. The emphasis is placed upon the whiteness.

[1] Michaelis, *TDNT* 4:247
[2] Isa 46:4; Brewer's 488.
[3] Leuring, *ISBE* 2:1321. Pro 16:31, 20:29.
[4] Goldingay, (WBC 30), 165, and Smith-Christopher 7:103 et al mention that the phrase Ancient of Days suggests an old man.
[5] *MCED* 316.
[6] JFB; M. Henry: Hoary hairs indicate the decay of age; but in Him there is no sign of decay.
[7] Michaelis, ibid.
[8] G. C. Luck, *Daniel* 88: At the Transfiguration scene our Lord's "clothes became as white as the light" (Matt 17:2).
[9] Tatford, 112.
[10] R. L. Thomas: *BSac* (122) 247.

Handwriting on the Wall (Excerpts from one of my sermons):
Dan 5:5: *In the same hour the fingers of a man's hand appeared and wrote opposite the lampstand on the plaster of the wall of the king's palace; and the king saw the part of the hand that wrote.*

Why Belshazzar, king of Babylon, held this great feast at this time is not known. He may have thrown the party in honor of one of his gods; at any rate, you get the impression he liked to have a big crowd around him at all times. All the big shots were there, in addition to his wives and concubines. Belshazzar was a desecrater, a profane man, a carouser, partygoer, good-timer, and a wine-bibber. Drinking often leads folks to do stupid things. He showed his utter contempt for the living God by desecrating the vessels which had been taken out of the temple of the house of God in Jerusalem when Nebuchadnezzar's soldiers captured it. Imagine, taking sacred vessels and drinking himself drunk from them—an act of malicious despite, purposeful profanation, a case of flagrant sacrilege, an arrogant misuse of the things of God.

He was an idolater who praised the gods of gold, silver, brass and iron, wood and stone—deities that could not hear, know or see. What a deadly combination, drunkenness and idolatry! In the *same hour* of all this madness, Belshazzar's time ran out. Unexpectedly and suddenly, the wanton, mad revelry of the sin-crazed king and his guests ended. In the very midst of their partying and mockery, at the very height of their evil merry-making, there came forth the fingers of a man's hand. Only the fingers were seen, not the whole hand, and wrote: *Mene, Mene, Tekel, Upharsin* – weighed in the balance and found wanting; tested and proved to be at fault, or a failure.

> The fingers are to the Oriental essential in conversation; their language is frequently very eloquent and expressive [often showing] what the mouth does not dare to utter, especially grave insult and scorn. . . The 'finger of God' like the 'hand of God,' is synonymous with power, omnipotence, sometimes with the additional meaning of the infallible evidence of Divine authorship in all His works. (Luering, *ISBE* 2:1111; cf. Deut 9:10, Col 2:14)

> The supernatural occurrence of a hand suddenly appearing and writing on the light-colored plaster of the

palace wall would be enough to startle any king, and Belshazzar was no exception. He may have suspected that the mysterious communication was connected in some way with his [debauched] conduct and the advances of the Persian army nearby. (Borland, *Parallel* 1641)

Inspired with terror (Calvin), Belshazzar was shocked into sobriety. No man in history sobered up as fast as he did. He was startled out of his stupor; detoxed from his drunkenness. His countenance changed, his face flushed, his knees knocked, his hip joints creaked, his pallor paled, his torso trembled, his loins became loose; and his thoughts troubled. Some scholars believe that Belshazzar alone saw the finger writing, or suggest it is uncertain whether others also saw the writing (Gill). I believe others there observed "the hand of the Unseen One attesting his (Belshazzar's) doom before the eyes of himself and his guilty revelers . . . The invisibility of Him who moved the fingers heightened the awful impressiveness of the scene." [1]

No noise, no thunderclap, no lightning flashes, and no angel with drawn sword—just the written Word of God! Just seeing the fingers made the event scarier; and "immediately awakened the thought that the writing was by a supernatural being, and alarmed the king out of his intoxication" (K&D). The entire feast immediately came to an end. Laughter died out. Guests choked on the wine in their throats. The music stopped. The band took a break. The Master of Ceremonies was at a loss for words; the diners were dumbfounded. Fright froze their feet and framed their faces. The life of the party was pooped, paralyzed with perplexity. And the fingers disappeared as suddenly as they had first appeared. *That very night Belshazzar, king of the Chaldeans, was slain* (Dan 5:30).

From this story of Belshazzar's feast has come the well-known phrase *the handwriting on the wall,* although these exact words do not appear in the Bible. The phrase has come to mean today "a prediction of misfortune," a fore-shadowing of trouble or disaster, "even as the words portended Belshazzar's downfall and that of his kingdom." [2] *Handwriting on the wall* signifies a premonition, or clear indication, especially of failure or disaster. It speaks of danger, so-called "bad luck," "an ominous indication of the course of future events," "a portent of change or doom, the coming to an end."

¹ They all knew this was the work of someone superior to man. From their pagan point of view concerning sacrilegious crime, they may have connected this mysterious appearance with their profanation and desecrating of the vessels of the temple of God (Barnes).

² Fulghum, 1014; Brewer's, 1144, 1170; Bullinger, 774. See Johnson and Johnson, *Spirituals* 2:171: Dere's a Han' Writin' on de Wall; and *The Baptist Standard Hymnal*, 236: Handwriting on the Wall.

Head and Shoulders: 1 Sam 9:2: *From his shoulders upward he was taller (higher, KJV) than any of the people* (NKJV). 1 Sam 10:23: *And when he stood among the people, he was taller (higher, KJV) than any of the people from his shoulders upward* (NKJV).

Samuel was displeased when the elders of Israel gathered together at Ramah, and said to him, "Look, you are old, and your sons do not walk in your ways. Now make us a king to judge us like all the nations" (1 Sam 8:4-5). Samuel prayed to the LORD and God spoke to him, "Heed the voice of the people in all that they say to you; for they have not rejected you, but they have rejected Me, that I should not reign over them" (v7). As directed by the LORD, Samuel warned Israel about having a king rule over them; however, the people refused to obey Samuel's voice. ¹ Jehovah then again ordered Samuel to "Heed their voice, and make them a king" (1 Sam 8:22).

While in acquiescence to their will, God maintained His sovereign oversight of Israel, and the king they chose never wielded dictatorial power or authority. Indeed, "God's permissive will is active behind the scenes." ² Nations of that day were much influenced by the outward appearance of those chosen to lead them. "The nations commonly chose **portly** men for their kings;" "size and beauty were highly valued in rulers, as signs of manly strength," and "in all ancient times great respect was paid to personal appearance." ³

The picture painted of Saul is not that of an "ugly duckling" ⁴ or "rags to riches." He came from a proper, prestigious, and influential family (1 Sam 9:1). From a human perspective he was considered highly favored by God. ⁵ Thought to be about 40 or 45 years old (K&D), Saul was handsome, well built and proportional, in the prime of manhood. "A better physical specimen could scarcely be found in all Israel;" a head taller than anyone else; estimates are he was "close to seven feet tall," "a little under seven feet high"—a magnificent physical creature. [6] However, a description of his spiritual qualities is lacking. Nothing is said of his godliness, wisdom, virtue, courage, learning, accomplishments, piety, etc. Only his outward physical appearance is emphasized, a point that reminds us of Jehovah's advice to Samuel in the selection of someone to replace Saul: "Do not look at his appearance or at his physical stature (that of Eliab, oldest son of Jesse, and brother of David), because I have refused him. For the LORD does not see as man sees; for man looks at the outward appearance, but the LORD looks at the heart" (1 Sam 16:7).

How do we use the phrase *head and shoulders* today? There remains the literal measurement of comparing a person's height, as taller by a head. There is, however, the idiom (an expression or phrase whose meaning cannot be understood from the ordinary meanings of the words in it: WBD) that means considerably, very much (WBD). Figuratively, the phrase means far superior to (AHD); far better, more qualified (RH); greatly superior; [7] as a metaphor referring to intellectual or moral stature, it means considerably, by far (OED 7:40).

[1] They repeatedly insisted having *their* will and desire be done.
[2] Chapman, *Parallel* 547.
[3] M. Henry; WBD: Portly means stately, dignified; AHD: *archaic,* Majestic, imposing. "In stricter application portly refers to a person whose bulk is combined with a stately or imposing bearing," under synonym for "Fat." Today, *portly* is commonly used to describe one who is corpulent, stout, having a large body.
[4] Birch, *NIB* 2:1037.
[5] Chapman, ibid; Klein, (WBC 10) 86.
[6] Nelson, 464; MacDonald, 304; G. C. Luck, *BSac* (123) 62; JFB.
[7] Brewer's, 503.

Help Meet: Gen 2:18, 20: *And the LORD God said, "It is not good that man should be alone; I will make him (an help meet for him, KJV) a helper comparable to him . . . But for Adam there was not found a helper comparable to him (an help meet for him, KJV).*

There are those who ignore the fact that God created Adam first, put him in charge, and held him responsible for sin's entrance— "through one man sin entered the world." [1] They rebel against the teaching that the woman is not to usurp authority over the man in the church, ignoring God's establishment of the division of labor that teaches woman's subordination. To ignore such points suggests one does not hold to the verbal inspiration of the Bible [2] and fails to distinguish between *Position* and *Condition* (*Standing* and *State*). Male and female believers maintain the same salvation position or standing, but our condition varies, our roles differ (1 Tim 2:12; 1 Cor 11:3; Gal 3:28). "Woman's subordination does not mean inferiority. Man is not superior in being to woman.

Eve came from Adam, and each man born in the world comes from a woman's womb." [3] Kennedy's allegory of Genesis chapters 2-3 ignores the biblical historical context, creating a picture of a "peasant society under the patriarchal control of the Israelite monarchy" with respect to the Genesis account of Eve's creation. He fails to accept the literal meaning of the key words used in Gen 2:18, 20; and disregards scriptures that do not support his allegorizing (figurative speech, story-telling). [4] The words *help meet* reveal the noun "help" (*ezer*) is derived from the verb to help, succor; used concretely, it is one who literally helps. The word "meet" (*neged*), comes from a verb meaning to be conspicuous. As a noun it is *what is conspicuous* or *in front*.

So Eve is a help according to him who is in front of her, corresponding to Adam, i.e. equal and adequate to himself. No animal could fulfill this position, a counterpart, or a helper matching him. When Adam saw Eve he exclaimed, "This is now bone of my bones and flesh of my flesh; she shall be called Woman because she was taken out of Man" (Gen 2:23). As a perfect help in a complementary relationship, she would participate intelligently in his pursuits and purposes; share his thoughts, experience his affections, bear his children, assist him to live well, dress his food; and she would complete him and bring him glory. [5] "God did not create man an unsocial being." He knew that it was not good to signify incompleteness by living alone. Celibacy in general is a thing that is not good (Clarke). Supplying Adam's deficiency lay in the original purpose of the Creator. [6] The word ***helpmate***, apparently an alteration of *help meet*, [7] speaks of a companion or helper, a wife or husband. ***Helpmeet*** is a misreading of the two separate words (***help meet***) in Gen 2:18. [8] The words *help* and *meet* are separate; and the word translated *meet* means likeness and correspondence in nature. ⁹

Thought

AUNT HET

When you hear one brag that she can do anything as well as a man, it means there's a lot o' things she can't do as well as a woman.

¹ Rom 5:12, 17, 19. True, the word *anthropos* is used rather than the Greek word (*aner, andros,* signifying *male*; Andrew), thus referring to "the genus or nature, without distinction of sex, *a human being, whether male or female*": Thayer; BAGD: "as a physical being, subject to death." Eve's part in the first transgression is not denied; Shedd, 121 makes this clear. He cites Augustine: "But Enos [one] means man in so restricted a sense, that Hebrew linguists tell us it cannot be applied to woman." **The basic point in this matter:** Emphasis is placed upon Adam's responsibility. He was created first, put in authority, and told God's will. (Gen 2:7, 15-17; 1 Tim 2:12-14).

² For example: Fretheim, *NIB* 1:352. Cf. Kaiser, *Hard Sayings,* 93, suggesting that Eve was even to be Adam's 'equal,' and that the LORD never intended for her to be 'an assistant' or 'helpmate' to man.

³ D. K. Lowery, *BSac* (143): 158.

⁴ J. M. Kennedy, JSOT (47) 8; Barr, JSOT (44) 3-17.

[5] Wenham, (WBC 1) 68; Barnes; Calvin; Gill; KT Wilson, *BSac* (148) 452; Schrader, *Parallel* 18; Ross, 126-27; Orr, *ISBE* 2:1374; Clarke, et al. who describe what Eve's companionship supplies.

[6] Leupold, *Genesis,* 1:129.

[7] Hendrickson, 342; WBD.

[8] Helpmeet is a compound absurdly formed by taking the two words *help meet* (in Gen 2:18, 20) as one word (OED 7:128). AHD, 840-41: In 1673 the poet John Dryden used the phrase 'help-meet for man,' with a hyphen between help and meet. Thus improperly hyphened, in time *help meet* became *helpmeet,* one step on the way toward the establishment of the phrase 'help meet' as an independent word. Omission of the words "for him" (KJV) is part of the cause of the trouble. In 'a comedy of errors' the two words helpmeet and helpmate (first recorded 1715) came to mean the same.

[9] Orr, ibid: Suitability or fittingness is implied, but likeness and correspondence in nature are better descriptions; "One like himself, as taken from him, the woman would be an aid and companion to the man in his tasks." Ross, 126-7: "corresponding completely . . . The woman fits the man and completes him in his desperate situation."

Holier than Thou: Isaiah 65:5: *Which say, Stand by thyself, come not near to me; for I am holier than thou* (KJV). *Who say, "Keep to yourself, do not come near me, for I am holier than you!"* (NKJV).

I heard this expression many times before discovering that the exact words *holier than thou* are in the Bible. They are the words of a self-righteous person; one who is pharisaic, exhibiting an attitude of superior virtue, obnoxiously pious and sanctimonious, characterized by an attitude of superior sanctity. [1] The Hebrew word (*Kadash*) means to be set apart, consecrated, or hallowed. [2] Many words in different forms are derived from it, but all represent the idea of being separated or set apart. "Perhaps the English word sacred represents the idea more than holy." [3] That which is used by God or has a position of relationship with Him, or is consecrated to Him is holy or sanctified.

We see then that the words, "I am set apart from you" are based on this verb to be holy. [4] Calvin suggests that since the literal translation is "approach to thyself," implying removal from the speaker, our common English versions of "Stand by thyself," or "Keep by thyself" are not the best renderings. "The Hebrew phrase is the act of standing away from the speaker," or "Keep **to** thyself." [5] One danger of the attitude expressed by these words is that the false claim to holiness makes it difficult to hearken to warnings or accept reproofs. Failure to obey the prophets leads to a lack of repentance that further increases puffed-up-ness. They continue to "swell with insolent pretensions" and to think of themselves more highly than they ought to think (Rom 12:3).

Isaiah informs us that those who speak such words are guilty of rebellion, heathenism, waywardness, and sacrificing and burning incense in worship to idols. They boldly vex Jehovah by consulting the dead and eating the flesh of swine. How could people who engaged in such filthy practices speak to God in this manner? E. J. Young teaches the text is addressed to Jehovah! This is not to deny that folks who are "hypocritical self-justifiers" look down their noses at other men and women, but understand the text suggests the Jews were telling God they no longer wanted *His* "nearness." [6] *"Stop! come not too near me; for I am holy to thee"* (K&D).

Having participated in certain sacrificial rites, they feel that their degree of sanctity forbids them to touch or be touched by those who have not had similar experiences. Still today we encounter men who belong to "secret societies" and allow their spiritual pride to cause them to look down their collective nose at the uninitiated. It is not difficult to tie in this Scripture with the Pharisees and other religious leaders who lived in NT times. Recall that they regarded themselves better than others (Luke 18:11); yet Christ called them "children of the Devil" (John 8:44). Isaiah's language aptly fits the Pharisees who despised the Lord Jesus Christ, the Son of God.

At a Baptist Convention in upstate New York a Jewish man who had a concession across from me noticed one of my pamphlets entitled, "The Chosen People." Within moments he angrily stated that the concept of the Jews as the "chosen people of God" was the very root-cause of anti-Semitism, and **all** of Israel's troubles. However, God did not choose His covenant people based on their own achievements (Deut 7:7-8); and for the Christian it remains ever true that we are not saved by works (Eph 2:8-9; Titus 3:5). Israel failed to see that its election was not to privilege but to responsibility. [7] "They arrogate to themselves a certain superiority, believing that through their practices they have become holy, that is, set apart from others." [8]

Perverted minds take the next step of thinking their holiness is above God's holiness, thus violating that "higher holiness that is spiritual and ethical." Holier-than-thou people shall not escape punishment (Isa 65:6-7, 11-15; Jer 17:4). "Nothing in men is more odious and offensive to God than a proud conceit of themselves and contempt of others; for commonly those are most unholy of all that think themselves holier than any" (M. Henry).

As soul-winners our zeal is guided with "holy wisdom and prudence," enabling us to vigilantly yet compassionately and cautiously deal with those steeped in sin. "Christians cannot be merely indifferent to such men nor avoid them with a holier-than-thou attitude." [9] Pastors must be careful not to handle both hostility and inferiority with a pseudo-sanctification holier-than-thou attitude. [10] The pulpit prophet is separated as one whose motivation is Godward. [11]

Aunt Het

Thought

He never moves a man to say,
'Thank God, I am so good,'
But turns his eye another way—
To Jesus and His blood. [12]

The three things that folks are most proud of are money and family and righteousness, and the hatefulest are the ones proud o' being' so righteous.

[1] OED 7:319.

[2] Girdlestone 175; Lambert, *ISBE* 3:1404: "Nothing is holy in itself, but anything becomes holy by its consecration to Him."

[3] Watts, (WBC 25) 343.

[4] Calvin, (Isa 65:5) 382, footnote #3.

[5] Seitz, *NIB* 6:533: "Who say, 'Keep away; don't come near me, for I am too sacred for you!'" (NIV)

[6] Barnes: "It was a characteristic of a large part of the Jewish nation, and especially of the Pharisees, to be self-righteous and proud." JFB: Such words are "Applicable to the hypocritical self-justifiers of our Lord's time." M. Henry: "The most provoking iniquity of the Jews in our Savior's time was their pride and hypocrisy, that sin of the scribes and Pharisees against which Christ denounced so many woes".

[7] Hindson, *Parallel* 1420.

[8] E. J. Young, 3:504.

[9] D. E. Hiebert, *BSac* (142) 365.

[10] B. Jackson, *BSac* (132) 111.

[11] Ayer, *BSac* (124) 295-6.

[12] Hart, cited by Thomas Spurgeon, *Fundamentals* 3:122.

I Am Black: Jer 8:21: (NKJV: *I am mourning*).

I Am Black but Comely: Song 1:5 (NKJV: *I am dark, but lovely*).

Here are seven Hebrew words translated *black* in the OT (KJV): [1] (1) Esth 1:6 speaks of a black marble stone used in paving. (2) A second word (Joel 2:6), the meaning of which is unclear to Hebrew scholars, probably means to glow, illuminate with anxiety or dread. (3) In Prov 7:9 the word is literally "pupil of the eye." (4) The word rendered *black* means to grow warm and tender, to be or grow hot; [2] Lam 5:10: Our skin was black (hot: NKJV) like an oven because of the terrible famine (KJV). (5) Be or grow dark is the verb used in Lam 4:8: Their visage is blacker than a coal. The context shows that the dark countenance depicts misery and calamity and not some racial characteristic. (6) In the above mentioned Lam 4:8 the word *coal* is derived from a verb meaning to be black. [3] The verse could be rendered: Their visage is darker than blackness.

Two oft-quoted verses using this word are studied here. First: Job: 30:30: My skin is black upon me, and my bones are burned with heat (KJV). My skin grows black and falls from me; my bones burn with fever (NKJV). Job chapters 29-30 support the claim that the primary purpose of the statement, "My skin is black upon me" is to describe a strong feeling of despondency; the Hebrew idiom "I am black" describes misery, calamity and sorrow. [4] Second: Song 1:5-6: I am black, but comely . . . Look not upon me, because I am black (KJV). The NKJV substitutes the word dark for black. It is not Solomon but the Shulamite, a Bedouin woman who is described as black and beautiful. She compares herself with the women who live in the cities; and explains her swarthiness or darkness is due to the sun which beat upon her while working in the vineyards, a task forced upon her by her lazy brothers. She laments that while working there she failed to take care of her own complexion or vineyard.

It has been suggested that the slogan of pride, "Black is Beautiful", for Black Americans since the late 1960s may derive from the Song of Solomon. [5] Controversy has arisen over whether the verse says, "I am black, **but** comely," or "I am black **and** comely." K&D render the statement: "I am black **yet** comely," as if to suggest a contrast, comely in spite of blackness; they add: "These words express humility without abjectness. She calls herself 'black,' although she is not so dark and unchangeably black as an 'Ethiopian' (Jer 13.23)." Clarke says: This is literally true of many of the Asiatic women; though black or brown, they are exquisitely beautiful: "Though black or swarthy in my complexion, yet am I comely, well proportioned in every part." M. Henry apparently looks down upon this blackness; he describes her natural state as "fair and comely," whiteness being her proper color. Is it possible that a bit of racism mixed with the mis-treatment by her brothers, the hard work under the scorching sun—all combine to make "tan" undesirable? Today there are those who desire a "sun tan", but only temporarily!

[As an alternative in Hebrew poetry (Song 1:5) should read]: I am dark as the tents of Kedar, but comely as the curtains of Solomon. The Shulamite's complexion is deeply sun burnt (v6) from the open life of the country. Kedar refers to a nomadic tribe that roamed the deserts of Northwest Arabia. Their tents were made of skins that were very dark in color and were rather unsightly. In contrast, the curtains of Solomon were lavishly beautiful. Our country maiden expresses with frankness the difference in appearance which the sun has wrought upon her. (Hankins, *Parallel* 1286) [6]

This interpretation continues: Moffatt: I am dark, *but* I am a beauty. NIV: dark am I, *yet* lovely. MacDonald translates: she is tanned and dark, but lovely. His endnote (4) reads: "The little [Hebrew] word translated 'but' can be (and more often is) translated 'and.' Then a literal translation would be 'black and beautiful.'" NRSV: I am black *and* beautiful. Septuagint: "black am I *and* beautiful." In favor of black *and* beautiful:

> The Hebrew word she uses to describe her complexion (*sehora*) is unambiguous, despite the numerous efforts by translators to render it more euphemistically and palatably as "dark," "very dark," "swarthy," "blackish," [dark-hued: Barnes] and so on . . . the color "black" is the undisputable meaning . . . Although there is no mistaking the defensive tone in her words, there is no reason to believe that the protagonist is apologetic about her color. (Weems, *NIB* 5:382-3)

(7) Our seventh word means to be dark. [7] At times it is used of clouds, skies, the sun and the moon. Study of the 17 verses containing this word reveals it primarily signifies mourning, sadness and lament; and brings to mind someone dressed in sordid, dirty clothing, neglected and in mourning. Job 30:28: I go about mourning, but not in the sun. RSV: I go about blackened but not by the sun. Here we find Jer 8:21: I am black, rendered by Barnes: I go mourning; and by M. Henry: I go in black as mourners do. [8]

JFB: I am black means: Sad in visage with grief (Joel 2:6: all faces shall gather blackness). Gill: I am black; with grief and sorrow. Moffatt: I go a-mourning, seized with dire dismay. The context shows that Jeremiah expresses near hopelessness and despair. [9] Our study concludes that the OT scriptures do not support the belief that the phrase "I am black" indicates that Job, Solomon, Jeremiah or the Shulamite woman were members of the Negro race. A sovereign God of grace, who is no respecter of faces or races, chooses whom He pleases; and we do well to remember that "no flesh should glory in His presence" (1 Cor 1:29).

[1] Patch, *ISBE* 2:675, eight different words are translated "black."
[2] Pratt, *ISBE* 1:485: Terms rarely used but of special significance in picturing the fearful gloom and blackness of moral darkness and calamity. Job 3:5: May the blackness of the day terrify it. Here Job curses the day of his birth such have been his troubles—loss of his servants, possessions, children, health, etc.
[3] In Exod 10:15 it describes the land that was *darkened.*
[4] We use the word *blue(s)* to express a mood or state of depression, despair or rejection: Brewer's 133, Hendrickson 87.
[5] Hendrickson, 79: the word 'but' in the song casts doubt upon such a derivation.
[6] Watchman Nee's interpretation (*Song* 22) is unacceptable. He allegorizes (suggests the literal sense has a deeper symbolic, figurative meaning). By making "blackness the adamic nature" and rendering the verse, "Black by nature, but comely in Christ," Nee makes blackness symbolize evil.
[7] Coppes, *TWOT* 2:786.
[8] H. Morris, *Defender's* 788: Because of his nation's unrepentant sin, Jeremiah was not merely to don black mourning garments, but actually to become the very personification of mourning. K&D: the verb is "used of wearing mourning, in other words, to be in mourning" (cf. Pss 35:14, 38:6).
[9] Freeman, 369; Craigie et al: (WBC 26) 140: "Because of the suffering coming upon his people, Jeremiah is gripped with dismay." OED: 2:239: Blackness describes Jeremiah as clouded with sorrow or melancholy; dismal, gloomy, sad.

I Come Quickly: Rev 3:11; 22:7, 12, 20.

The word *quickly* may be defined as rapidly, with haste or speed; describing the rate of progress in a motion, action, or process, without consideration of the time at which it begins and ends; [1] something done or made or happening with speed or without delay; promptness of response or action, practically instantaneous, swift, rapid, fast. The Greek lexicons also teach that the word translated *quickly* may be defined as suddenly, swiftly (Thayer) or at a rapid rate (BAGD).

Unfortunately, there are Bible translations, versions and paraphrases which translate *quickly* to read "right away" or "soon." By ignoring the equally valid translation of the word *tachu*, and disregarding the context critics have been moved to say, "It has been nearly 2000 years since Christ left and He has not returned yet." They *quickly* suggest the Bible is unreliable, or cast scorn on the doctrine of the Second Coming of Christ. To interpret the words to mean "right away" leads some people to think God's program has gone haywire, and even to deny any literal, physical return of Christ.

With this problem in mind, consider the following: NIV: "Behold, I am coming soon!" TEV: "Listen!" says Jesus, "I am coming soon." LB repeats the error but adds the footnote stating that the word may be rendered "suddenly" or "unexpectedly." To this list we add: Moffatt: I am coming very soon. I am coming quickly (NASB, Montg). I am coming soon (RSV, NEB). JBP gives us: See I come quickly (Rev 22:7) Yes, I am coming very quickly! (Rev 22:16). Clarke offers: These things will shortly take place.

MacDonald (Rev 22:7) says the Lord "assures us that He will come quickly. This may mean either soon or suddenly, but soon is preferred." This commentator believes that the word *soon* strengthens our hope—our living in the hope of His coming! He states (Rev 22:20): "The hope of a *sudden* return would not excite the same anticipation or watchfulness as the hope of a *soon* return." I do not think this is true. Nelson (2170) puts it correctly: "Christ's return with expected suddenness is an incentive to persevere in faithful service."

Rowland calls the words "I am coming soon" ambiguous. [2] He confuses the words of the angel in Rev 22:10 with the words of our Lord in 22:12. The angel said to John, "Do not seal the words of the prophecy of this book, for the time is at hand." *Chronos* which expresses time in terms of minutes, days, weeks, months, and years is not used here. Instead we have *kairos* which suggests a fixed, definite, appointed, limited season or opportunity, with the added notion of suitableness (Thayer). "The biblical term 'at hand' or 'near' is never a positive affirmation that the person or thing said to be at hand will immediately appear, but only that that person or thing has the quality of imminency." [3]

Tachu does mean **suddenly**. The idea is: "When I come my coming will be sudden!" Once the return button is pushed all of the events predicted will take place without delay. We can rest assured "that when the time arrives the events will follow one another in rapid succession." [4] The Lord may tarry another ten years or a century. We do not know. But whenever He comes, the coming will be in a flash, in a moment, instantaneous. Through the centuries Christians have believed the Lord's coming is imminent. We stay on our toes, expecting, yearning, looking, and anticipating that shout or trumpet blast that signals His return for His Church.

"By **quickly** (Rev 22:12) is not meant that the Second Advent would occur soon after John completed the writing of this book. Rather, it means that the events of the Second Coming will occur so fast, one event quickly following another that many will be taken completely by surprise." [5] Beasley-Murray disagrees, stating there is no warrant for translating Greek *tachy* as 'suddenly.' [6] He fails to see the important difference between "*shortly* take place" in Rev 22:6 and "coming *quickly*" in Rev 22:7.

In verse 6 the verb rendered "take place" or "be done" [KJV] is a tense (aorist infinitive: *genesthai*) which means that the "things which must shortly take place" are 'punctiliar,' action condensed to a **point**, seen simply as an event, indefinite, an action in its entirety. [7] On the other hand, *I am coming quickly* is present tense (*erchomai tachu*). [8] In other words, within the things that must shortly take place, one of them is the coming of the Lord— His coming will occur speedily, without delay at that proper moment. Do not then confuse what the angel said to John with what the Lord Jesus said of Himself. The angel spoke of many things put together, a composite or combination of events seen as one (pointed); the Lord Jesus spoke of one of the events in that complex, namely, His (present tense) return.

[1] OED: 13:15.

[2] Rowland, *NIB* 12:585. Lenski (*Revelation* 659) states it is the angel, and **not** Jesus Christ who speaks in vv 6 and 12; and that the angel refers to himself as the "coming one." Cf. Moffatt, *ExpGT* 5:488: "The epilogue (6-21) is a series of loose ejaculations, which it is not easy to assign to the various speakers . . . indefinite whether God or Christ or an angel is speaking."

[3] *Imminence* has a Latin root meaning to "overhang, jut," suggesting the quality or condition of being about to occur, but like the word *impending* meaning something hanging over one, often indefinitely, and keeping him in suspense (WBD). Sco (Matt

4:17); Brunk, *BSac* (126) 245: It is not uncommon for the Scripture to place side by side events widely separated in time, or to speak of events which were at the time of writing far distant in the future as near at hand. Barnes (Rev 22:20) makes the statement that "the development of these events will soon begin—though their consummation may extend into far distant ages or into eternity." *MCED* 556: the point that "the promise still stands" may suggest that when the promise is fulfilled the coming will be quickly.

[4] Barnhouse, *Revelation* 411.

[5] Wilbur Smith, *Wycliffe* 1525.

[6] Beasley-Murray, NBC 1198.

[7] The words *must shortly take place* are also used in Rev 1:1, and the tense (time) is the same (aorist infinitive), teaching us that coming events are seen as an indefinite point (punctiliar). Burton, *Syntax* (sect 109), 50: "The Aorist Infinitive conceives of an action simply as an event without thought of its continuance . . . without reference to its progress" (sect 105) 49); Dana & Mantey, 199: "The aorist infinitive denotes that which is eventual or particular." Cf. Machen (sect 299) 137; on Rev 22:7 ATR offers this solution: "We must recall that *tachu* and *en tachei* are according to God's time, not ours (2 Pet 3:8)."

[8] Dana & Mantey, ibid: "The present infinitive indicates a condition or process." Burton, (sect 108) 50: "refers to action in progress."

Itching Ears: 2 Tim 4:3: *For the time will come when they will not endure sound doctrine, but according to their own desires, because they have itching ears, they will heap up for themselves teachers.*

Paul predicts that the church will experience apostasy in the last days. An example of this falling away is the failure of self-satisfied professed Christians to endure sound doctrine. Giving in to the desires of their hearts, church members abandon faithful preachers of the gospel and teachers of the Bible and replace them with false preachers-teachers. Their eagerness to gratify delighting their ears is vividly described by the words "they heap up" for themselves such teachers.

The compound verb (used only here) means to accumulate in piles, overwhelm, load in heaps or great numbers, suggesting "a confused crowd of teachers, each teaching different things, so becoming a burden too heavy for the mind to bear." [1] They "collect teachers in masses," accumulate them in piles; and ironically, heaping together "stresses the superficiality of their desire for knowledge" [2] Their desire for pleasure is impossible to satisfy, and indulgence serves only to increase or aggravate their desire, "hence the heaping up of those who may minister to" it. [3]

The purpose of securing such teachers is described as a remedy for *itching ears*. The word translated *itching* (*knetho*) used only here in the NT means (actively) to scratch, (passively) to itch, tickle, titillate, or rub.[4] Figuratively, to itch is to experience curiosity; it is a restless desire or craving for something; an insatiable desire of variety. Calvin defines this "elegant metaphor" as "excessively desirous of novelty." It is "a well-known image for the curiosity that can be relieved only by scratching them with interesting and spicy bits of information." [5] They enjoy scandal-mongering, hearing news or current gossip; [6] their desire to hear whatever is spectacular or sensational is an attempt to satisfy or conform to their lusts.

Ears tired of hearing the truth long for new teachings even if what they hear is false; "they will refuse to listen to the simple truth, they will turn aside to listen to all those empty legends." [7] Even today there are church-members who do not want to hear things that convict or reprove them, but desire to hear that which will make them feel good about themselves. [8] Itching ears are theater-loving ears that delight in being entertained. Itching ears are those that "have become tired of the sound of oft-repeated truth and that long for new though deceitful teaching." [9] Itching ears are ears that desire to be "'tickled' by preachers who do not preach the Bible. Many pastors bow to the wishes of ungodly congregations who only want to hear what pleases them."[10]

Thought: Give us a nice liberal preacher who will tell us more and more about nothing until we know less and less about everything. Give us a psychological politician-preacher who will puff us up with the purpose-driven profundity of his philosophical platitudes. Give us a slick-haired Dapper Dan, a happiness huckster, a guarantee guru, a wellness wizard, a prosperity prophet, who will meet our material needs, who will preach the pie out of the sky so we can eat it now! And then by and by, when we die, we will be carried through the sky in the chariot of our choice—a Rolls Royce! (W. L. Banks)

[1] Lock, ICC *Pastorals*, 113.

[2] U. Luck, *TDNT* 7:1096.

[3] N. J. D. White, *ExpGT* 4:177: Unfortunately, their concept of a teacher is one who gratifies their aesthetic sense, but does not instruct their mind or guide their conduct.

[4] Mounce, (WBC 46) 575; JFB: "Itch in the ears is as bad as in any other part of the body, and perhaps worse." I wonder what it feels like to have a cast on your leg, and feel an itching under the cast!

[5] Dunn, *NIB*, 11:855.

[6] Brewer's 563; Hendrickson 117.

[7] Lock, ibid. 111.

[8] Pilgrim, 1697; Nelson, 2060; Gill: They want to hear what is pleasant, comfortable . . . such things as the purity of human nature, the power of man's free will, the excellence of his righteousness, and the merit of his works.

[9] Leuring, *ISBE* 2:886; Acts 17:19-21; Isa 30:9-11; Wallis, *Wycliffe* 1389.

[10] Wemp, *Parallel* 2516; their preaching is not Christ-centered.

Jacob's Ladder: Gen 28:12: *Then he dreamed, and behold, a ladder was set up on the earth, and its top reached to heaven; and there the angels of God were ascending and descending on it.* John 1:51: *And He said to him, "Most assuredly, I say to you, hereafter you shall see heaven open, and the angels of God ascending and descending upon the Son of Man."*

With the aid of his mother Rebekah, Jacob stole the blessing due his older brother, Esau. Fearful for Jacob's life, Rebekah prevailed upon Jacob to flee to Haran where her brother Laban lived. This would be the last time she would ever see Jacob. Ostensibly the motive for his departure was to make sure he would not marry one of the daughters of Canaan, but one of the daughters of his uncle. And so Isaac sent Jacob away to "Padan Aram, to Laban the son of Bethuel the Syrian, the brother of Rebekah, the mother of Jacob and Esau" (Gen 28:5).

At a certain place along his journey, Jacob stopped to sleep. With a stone as a pillow, he lay down and fell asleep. "Then he dreamed, and behold, a ladder was set up on the earth, and its top reached to heaven; and there the angels of God were ascending and descending on it." For many years this order—ascending and descending—bothered me. I would have written descending and ascending. The answer that satisfies my heart is the awareness that the angels were right there with Jacob. [1] You could say they were Jacob's invisible bodyguards. [2]

Considering the fears and apprehension of this lonely fugitive, and "the inward tumult of his mind," this dream was a blessing, for it "was intended primarily to intimate the divine care of Jacob and his interests as an individual." [3] Jacob recognized in that place that God was by his side, promising him guidance through life, and future greatness. [4] Despite the deceit Jacob practiced, here was the assurance of divine protection and the blessings of God's Covenant with Abraham. [5] He was encouraged that Jehovah would work things out for Jacob's own good and for his descendants. [6]

Heaven was busy on his behalf. Many commentators agree that the ladder signifies communication between heaven and earth; a visible symbol of the real and uninterrupted fellowship between God in heaven and His people upon earth (K&D). Attempts to describe the duties of these angels stretch beyond "sanctified imagination" when we are told they (1) passed to and fro on "benevolent errands" of mercy (Barnes, JFB); (2) they received commissions from heaven and descended to carry them out. Continually going back and forth, they brought fresh messages, and performed miraculous operations, as if the whole host of them were constantly employed in such services (Gill); (3) they ascended with the prayers and praises of believers, and descended with the answers. (4) God's messengers ascended to Him with their reports and petitions, and returned with His replies; [7] (5) The divine messengers first hear the prayer to God before they bring down the answer from Him (6) angels upon the ladder carry up the wants of men to God, and bring down the assistance and protection of God to men (K&D). These are some suggested angelic "duties".

In John 1:51, the Lord Jesus Christ takes the place of the ladder in Jacob's dream. Through Him the blessed works of God would be accomplished, proving He is the Messiah. Nathanael would have evidence that angels come to his aid, and that he has the kind of protection and assistance from God which would show 'more fully that he was the Messiah' (Barnes; JFB). He was made to see that 'communication between heaven and earth opened wide and the Son of Man to be the real Ladder of this conversation.' [8]

Through Christ there is fellowship, communication between heaven and earth—He is indeed the bridge, the link, the point of contact, the ladder! As the Son of Man (God Incarnate, John 3:13) He is the locus or center-place of 'traffic' that brings heaven's blessings to mankind, [9] "the place where the earthly and the heavenly, divine and human, temporal and eternal meet." [10] Jesus Christ is the "grand connecting medium," the bond of fellowship between heaven and earth, and between God and man, for He is both 'the Son of God' as Nathanael said, and 'the Son of Man' as the Lord Jesus said Himself. God and man meet in Christ.

He is the true Jacob's ladder (ATR). In Christ God came down to man; through Christ we have man ascending to God. Calvin: "It is Christ alone, therefore, who connects heaven and earth: he is the only Mediator who reaches from heaven down to earth: he is the medium through which the fullness of all celestial blessings flows down to us, and through which we, in turn, ascend to God." [11] The expression "climbing Jacob's ladder" is sometimes used to denote climbing the ladder of success. [12] In the Negro Spiritual, *We Are Climbing Jacob's Ladder,* Lovell says that Jacob's name is not the main issue:

> Jacob's experience has been chosen because it is the most available, the most dramatic, the most impressive and acceptable simile. His life story is used as a point of departure to expand the really important thrust of the spiritual, namely, the determination to ascend 'round by round, step by step' from the low estate of slavery. The ladder was that of a new Jacob who felt it extremely important to rise, for he had been kept down for too long. He must climb up the material and spiritual ladder; indeed, he is challenged to climb to 'heav'm' with the fortitude of a 'soldier of the cross.' And to the sinner comes the question, 'Do you love my Jesus?' The next stanza inquires, 'If you love him, why not serve him?' (Lovell, *Black Song:* 119, 214, 245, 322, 371) [13]

[1] Leon Morris, *John* 170: "spoken of as ascending first . . . may imply their presence on earth already."
[2] Wenham, (WBC 2) 225.

[3] JFB; Clarke: God prepared Jacob to meet all occurrences with the conviction that all was working together for his own good.

[4] Yates, *Wycliffe* 32. Jacob could now sing, "Precious promise God hath given, To the weary passerby, On the way from earth to heaven, 'I will guide thee with Mine eye'" (N. Niles).

[5] Freeman 49; Tenney: *BSac* (120) 305: By this vision God transmitted to Jacob His renewed promise to his forefathers and a fresh promise of blessing for Jacob.

[6] Hendrickson, 389.

[7] Tenney, ibid.

[8] Calvin: The ladder was a symbol of Christ. In John 1:51 the word 'you' in "I say to you" is plural in the original. This is why the KJV says "I say unto you," not "I say unto thee." Furthermore, in the phrase "you shall see," the verb is also plural, so that the KJV says "ye [plural] shall see" instead of 'thou [singular] shalt see." The point is: Though He speaks to Nathanael "he uses the plural as a reference to all six disciples present. This was necessary, for they all 'shall see' what is here promised" (Lenski, *John* 174).

[9] Beasley-Murray, (WBC 36) 28.

[10] O'Day, *NIB* 9:533.

[11] Keach, 975; cf. Tenney, *BSac* (121) 21; (132) 146-7. Gill (John 1:51).

[12] Freeman, 49-50.

[13] Cf. Johnson and Johnson, book 1:59; Chenu, 123.

Jehovah's Witnesses: Isa 43:10, 12; 44:8: *You are My witnesses.*

I. Definition

The Hebrew word translated *witness* is found 69 times; it means testimony, evidence, and probably is derived from the idea of reiterating, hence emphatically affirming. "The semantic [study of words] development apparently is that a witness is one, who by reiteration emphatically affirms his testimony." [1] In the NT the verb *martureo* (see our word, martyr) means to testify, i.e. to affirm that one has seen or heard or experienced something, or that he knows it because taught by divine revelation or inspiration; it is to give testimony, declare, confirm. Used emphatically, it is to utter honorable testimony, give a good report, speak well (of), or approve. [2]

II. Inability of Gentile (Pagan) Nations

"The things which the Gentiles sacrifice they sacrifice to demons and not to God" (1 Cor 10:20). Paul said: "that you, once Gentiles in the flesh . . . that at that time you were without Christ, being aliens from the commonwealth of Israel and strangers from the covenants of promise, having no hope and without God (*atheoi*: atheists) in the world" (Eph 2:11-12). This truth—"salvation is of the Jews" (John 4:22)—hated by the world, is used by Satan to spread anti-Semitism. Gentiles who heard of Israel's God denied what they heard was true. Others entirely ignorant of Jehovah could not attest to the veracity and power of their own gods and goddesses. Pagan beliefs were false, unfounded, and unverifiable. Man-invented religion can never produce a record of fulfilled predictions as a testimony of divine authority. [3]

III. Israel Testifies of Jehovah

No other nation can truthfully claim the relationship that Israel has with the true and living God (Deut 7:6-8). Israel has much to testify, including predictions made by Jehovah concerning enslavement in Egypt; deliverance from Pharaoh; wandering in the wilderness; and settling in Canaan. They were literally fulfilled, enabling Israel to testify that Jehovah is able to predict events with one hundred percent accuracy. [4] The fact that predictions were carried out means that by their own knowledge and experience Israel was certain of God's dealings with them. He enabled them to experience and to perceive His goodness and power. [5]

Jehovah repeatedly admonished, "You shall remember that you were a slave in the land of Egypt, and the LORD your God redeemed you" (Deut 15:15). God had called this nation to be His servant and qualify as a witness to the pagan Gentile world. How could they forget their victories over nations that sought to prevent their possession of the Promised Land? How could they forget their bountiful food supply (manna, quail, water), or the pillar of cloud by day and of fire by night, the preservation of clothing, shoes and health? And what of leaders like Moses, Joshua, Samuel, David and Solomon whom God raised up, to say nothing of the wonderful prophets the LORD commissioned and sent forth!

> At Sinai Israel in its totality was to be constituted into a nation or kingdom of priests to mediate between God and the nations because all the earth is the LORD's. What

the tribe of Levi was to the people of Israel, Israel as a nation was to be to the nations of the world, mediated through the people of Israel to the world of mankind. Israel's calling was of world significance and for a world ministry. 'Ye are my witnesses, saith the LORD, and my servant whom I have chosen'—this was the LORD's charge to Israel. Thrice He called Israel 'witnesses' and twenty-one times in Isaiah 40-54 He spoke of 'servants.' Israel was not an end in itself; God had the world in mind. (Peters, *BSac* (136), 8) [6]

IV. Fulfillment of Israel's Role as a Witness

We understand then that the term *Jehovah's Witnesses* describes the nation Israel commissioned by Jehovah to make known to the world the only true God. No other nation, no man-made organization has a right to this phrase. Faith demands that the redeemed of the LORD say so—willingly! God in mercy assures Israel that He would demonstrate His sovereign power by casting down the Babylonian Empire, and returning the Jews to Palestine. Because of disobedience and unbelief, Israel failed to carry out its assignment; "actually, the historical Israel never fulfilled this high ideal." [7] The servant-nation will eventually be saved by the Servant-Messiah, for as Paul points out in Romans 11:25, "Israel's blindness is only 'in part'." It is our belief that the 144,000 (Rev 7:4-8, and 14:1) constitute the true Israel that will fulfill its "Witnessing Purpose." "On the basis of the guidance, deliverance and revelation which is grounded in its election and which it has experienced, [Israel] will declare to the nations of the world the uniqueness, reality, and deity of God." [8]

---

[1] Schultz, *TWOT* 2:648: the word appears some 67 times in the OT, and is derived from the root meaning 'return, repeat, do again.'

[2] One may testify in a (1) legal sense, of testimony in court before a judge (2) in an historical sense, of the testimony or attestation of an historian (3) in an ethical sense, of testimony concerning one's character, and (4) in a predominantly dogmatic sense respecting matters relating to the truth of Christianity. A person who is put to death or made to suffer greatly because of his refusal to renounce religious principles or other beliefs is called a martyr. In the persecuted early church the Greek word *martus* came to mean one

who witnessed unto death. It is first used in Acts 22:20 referring to the blood of Stephen who was "rocked to sleep" (Acts 7:59-60).

[3] Archer, *Wycliffe* 640; Young, 3:151: Israel is a witness not only to the utter impotence of the idols but also to the truthfulness of what their God has spoken. Strathmann, *TDNT* 4:484: For these witnesses or deities have nothing whereof to testify. They see nothing and hear nothing. The makers of idols are impotent. Their favored gods are of no use to them. In this trial they will be put to shame. In contrast, Israel is told three times: "You are My witnesses."

[4] Hindson, *Parallel* 1371.

[5] M. Henry: The power of His grace, the sweetness of His comforts, the tenderness of His providence, and the truth of his promise. MacRae, *BSac* (121) 222: In Isa 43:10 the thought is stressed that the outstanding reason they can be sure God will deliver them is the fact that he has chosen them for a special task.

[6] Cf. Hindson, ibid 1369: God announces His purpose for redeemed Israel that all the nations should be gathered unto Him for salvation. The servant as a nation is to function as the LORD's witnesses. Young, 3:151: The last words do not constitute the object of witness, as though the LORD had said, 'Ye are my witnesses that I am the LORD.' It is better, because more in keeping with the grammar, to render, 'Ye are my witnesses, and therefore I am God.' The thought is that 'Ye who witness for me must witness to the truthfulness of what I have said and done, and thus, it is evident that I am God, the One who is absolutely powerful."

[7] Young, 3:149; Seitz, *NIB* 6:377: Israel's testimony has the capacity to reconnect it to God in the most basic sense, a sense undone in Isaiah's day, leading to Israel's death and destruction. Pilgrim 988: Israel has yet to be a good servant to God, but the time will come when the nation will turn in faithfulness to her Master and King.

[8] Strathmann, ibid.

Job's Comforters: Job 16:2: *I have heard many such things; miserable comforters are you all!*

In the phrase "such things," Job refers to the speeches of Eliphaz, Bildad, and Zophar, although his "sarcastic response" [1] follows the speech made by Eliphaz in chapter 15. After hearing of his adversity, the men "made an appointment together to come and mourn with him, and to comfort him" (2:11). For seven days and seven nights they sat in silence with him. Job broke the silence with his lament, cursing the day he was born; then began the dialogues with his friends (chapters 3-31). Consistently they accused Job of having committed some terrible secret sin; indeed, they called him a hypocrite, insisting that the grief he suffered was self-inflicted; unless he repented and changed his evil ways, his situation would not improve but continue to worsen. Repeatedly Job was told, "God don't like ugly!" [2]

Job says in the first place that he has often heard such things and further they are tiresome comforters, even to address themselves to him with such boring words. In saying that he had often heard such things, he indicates that they must not bring him common, ordinary remedies, since his sickness was so great and so extreme. [3] It seems that "these things" are the conventional picture of the fate of the wicked that Job often heard even before the dialogues began. [4] Their rebukes served only to disappoint, and distress, irritate and grieve Job. He knew that their accusations were untrue, their counsel irrelevant.

Often we find that self-righteous counselors betray "their ignorance of the comfort of redemptive righteousness." Gill states they sent Job to "a convicting, condemning, and cursing law, for relief." They assume they speak for God. Legalistic, self-righteous folks are not very helpful to those suffering. I have heard Christians callously quote: "Well, you know, God makes all things work together for good!" (Rom 8:28). A minister friend of mine, barely able to make ends meet and provide food for his family, was told by certain brethren, "Well, we're praying for you." They never contributed one cent to help him! Miserable super-dupers! No wonder Job compares his friends to broken cisterns and deceitful brooks that disappoint when any expectations of comfort are raised upon them. [5]

Consider more closely what Job says about them. He belittles them as *Miserable Comforters*. The word for miserable (*amal*) involves labor, toil, trouble, mischief, sorrow, travail, pain, grief, iniquity, misery, perverseness, weariness, wickedness, a burden and annoyance. "A perusal of the varied synonyms used in the KJV to render this word suggests its negative overtones. Such are the categories of grievance expressed by this noun." [6] The word for comforter (*nacham;* Nahum means Comforter) means to be sorry, console oneself, repent, or regret. "The origin of the root seems to reflect the idea of 'breathing deeply,' hence the physical display of one's feelings, usually sorrow, compassion, or comfort." [7] Now put the two words together: **Miserable Comforters.** This phrase is called an *oxymoron;* [8] they are comforters of trouble; or troublesome comforters. [9]

> Job expects of comforters that they will take his part; how can there be sympathy if they position themselves theologically over against him? . . . A professed comforter who will not share one's point of view but sits in judgment on it is indeed a comfortless comforter, or rather, a comforter who increases the sufferer's distress, a torturer of a comforter. To speak concretely, inasmuch as they have found in Job's suffering proof of guilt, they have only magnified his suffering. The thought is closely similar to that of 13:4, where the shape of the line is parallel: "healers of worthlessness, all of you." (Clines, [WBC 17] 378) [10]

The term *Job's Comforter* is applied to any one who, like Job's friends, under the guise of admonishing comfort, aggravate distress; [11] it is a proverbial phrase for one who intends or professes to comfort, but does the opposite. [12] Often such people have good intentions but are awkward in carrying them out. Rather than alleviate they "grieviate." Instead of giving relief they cause grief. The medicine they offer is toxic; they are diseased physicians. Their words are "Monotony without matter, mouthings without mercy."[13] Such a person is "one who unwittingly or maliciously discourages, saddens, or increases the misery of the person he seemingly offers consolation, sympathy or comfort." [14] To paraphrase Job: "Speaking of trouble, rather than comforting me in my troubles as a good counselor should, you have increased my trouble despite your claims to the contrary" (Nelson 844).

[1] Kline, *Wycliffe* 474.
[2] Brewer's 577; Jeffrey 404-5; Hendrickson 396: "the scolding lectures they delivered to him now known as Jobations."
[3] Calvin, *Sermons* #7: "When Will Windy Words End?" 92.
[4] Clines, (WBC 17) 378.

[5] Nelson, 833; Pilgrim, 742: "Job likened his friends ('my brethren') to the little brooks that are rushing torrents in the winter but that dry up under the summer sun, cheating the hopes of travelers who look for water there and perish in the desert."

[6] Allen, *TWOT* 2:675. The use of the verb *amal* along with its noun and adjective derivatives is in keeping with the terrible afflictions of Job. Elsewhere in Job the word is rendered: *sorrow* (3:10): *misery* (3:20; 11:16; 20:22: *wicked* KJV). Allen, ibid; 'misery' is preferable to 'wicked'. *Trouble* (4:8: *wickedness* KJV; 5:6-7); *wearisome* (7:3): *mischief* (KJV, 15:35; NKJV *trouble*).

[7] Girdlestone, 87: *Nacham*: "The original meaning of this word is generally understood to be *to draw a deep breath,* and this is taken as the physical mode of giving expression to a deep feeling, either of relief or sorrow."

[8] A figure of speech in which words of opposite meaning or suggestion are used together: *a wise fool; cruel kindness* (WBD); incongruous or contradictory terms are combined: *a deafening silence; a mournful optimist* (AHD).

[9] Clines, ibid 367, 369, 378; Moffatt: "plaguy [or *plaguey*] comforters." Calvin: ibid, 94: They are tiresome comforters because they do not bring him suitable remedies at all . . . they jump to conclusions. Driver & Gray, ICC *Job*, 142: Eliphaz and his friends "add to his trouble by forcing upon him conventional words of comfort, not springing from their hearts."

[10] Job 13:4: KJV: "Ye are all physicians of no value;" NKJV: "you are all worthless physicians."

[11] OED 8:248. Gill; Stevenson, 1271: "One who, pretending to comfort, aggravates the distress of somebody."

[12] OED: 3:535; Stahlin, *TDNT* 5:788.

[13] MacBeath, 51; M. Henry: "When we are under convictions of sin, terrors of conscience, and the arrests of death, it is only the blessed Spirit that can comfort effectually; all others, with out him, do it miserably, and sing songs to a heavy heart, to no purpose."

[14] Jeffrey, 404-5.

Judge Not: Matt 7:1: *Judge not, that you be not judged.*
Luke 6:37: *Judge not, and you shall not be judged.*

I. Judgment Defined:

To judge is to distinguish, separate, discriminate, discern, form an opinion, estimate, or make up one's mind. "When we judge, we discriminate between good and evil, right and wrong, truth and falsehood, innocence and guilt, sheep and goats." [1] By itself the word *judge* is neutral as to the verdict. In other words, it may indicate condemnation or an unfavorable sense; but it may also be favorable, honorific, or commendatory. [2] Both aspects (negative and positive) are true of the Greek word, *krino*. However, when the word *kata* is prefixed and we have *katakrino*, the judgment is negative, unfavorable, and condemnatory. In this very common proverb among the Jews, "Judge not refers to an unfavorable and condemnatory judgment." [3] Context helps us here, and we note that the tense of the verb teaches that the judging is habitual; we are dealing with "the habit of censoriousness, sharp, unjust" personal criticism. [4]

II. This Text Is Often Misinterpreted:

From the lips of both Christians and non-Christians we hear the words "Judge not that you be not judged" taken out of context, as if to suggest it is wrong to judge anybody at any time whatever! This text "should not be taken as a prohibition of all judging or discerning of right and wrong." [5] Rushdoony says Matt 7:1 is "far more generally known" and "certainly heard more frequently" then John 3:16:

> One can hear it quoted by everyone from politicians to talk show hosts as well as in letters to the editors, editorials, and the like. America's most famous advice columnist will not shy away from calling people busybodies, losers, or mentally ill on the basis of a letter, but should anyone bring up anything resembling Biblical morality she tells them to 'judge not'. . .The injunction to 'judge not' is not to be used as a universal principle to justify everything under the sun. To do so is to say 'these two words are my escape clause from everything else the Bible says.' To do so would be to say that God made a mistake, that after all those specific injunctions He put two words together in a sentence that not only forbid us to apply His injunctions but makes us tolerate everything He condemns . . . It is not judgment that is condemned, but *hypocritical* judgment. (Rushdoony) [6]

From the fact that God's judgment threatens man it is often deduced that no man has the right to judge another. This does not imply flabby indifference to the moral condition of others nor the blind renunciation of attempts at a true and serious appraisal of those with whom we have to live. What is unconditionally demanded is that such evaluations should be subject to the certainty that God's judgment falls also on those who judge, so that superiority, hardness and blindness to one's own faults are excluded, and a readiness to forgive and to intercede is safeguarded. (Buchsel, *TDNT* 3:939)

III. Permissible Judgments

We acknowledge the presupposition of the necessity of making judgments, for God has enabled us and ordered us to make value-judgments on "*specific* occasions . . . and to choose between different policies and plans of action." [7] There are situations and conditions in which judgments are allowed, indeed, ordered:

1. Church Discipline: Matt 18:15-17; 1 Cor 5:9-13 [8]
2. Trouble-makers: Rom 16:17-18
3. Qualifications of church officers: 1 Tim 3
4. False teachers: 2 Tim 3:5; Matt 7:15-20; Eph 5:7, 11; 1 John 4:1
5. Magistrates, courts, judges, those in authority over us: Rom 13:4 [9]
6. Unequally yoked with unbelievers: 2 Cor 6:14
7. Teaching false Doctrine: 1 Tim 6:3-5
8. Ourselves: 1 Cor 11:31
9. Other scriptures ordering judgment: John 7:24; Matt 7:6

We cannot suppress "our faculty of judgment." It is impossible both psychologically and morally to close our eyes to all distinction between good and evil. We automatically apply our own standards of conduct on people we meet; and whether only in thought or in action also, it is a part of our nature. What kind of judgment we make is another matter, and is a major point of our exposition of Matt 7:1. [10]

IV. Forbidden Personal Judgments (many overlapping)

1. The judgment of motives [11]
2. Judgments based on prejudiced information
3. Judgments based on appearance: John 7:24; Jas 2:1-4 or "according to the flesh" John 8:15 [12]
4. Pride: saints who have forsaken all may judge wealthy Christians [13]
5. Character assassination
6. Censoriousness. This word appeared often in our research. It means "highly critical" (AHD); "too ready to find fault" (WBD) [14]
7. Contemptuous and supercilious attitude
8. Carping criticism and fault-finding
9. Lack of compassion and love [15]
10. Hasty, ill-conceived, unjust, rash
11. Undue and depraved eagerness to judge—to put in Hell! [16]
12. Ambitious desire for honor
13. Inquiry into the actions of others that is influenced by curiosity
14. Harsh and uncharitable, unmerciful
15. Spirit of revenge and a desire to do mischief
16. Hypocritical, self-righteous, pharisaical [17]
17. Conscientious scruples: "about matters that are not in themselves right or wrong," Rom 14:1-5
18. Service of other Christians: 1 Cor 4:1-5; Rom 14:1-13 [18]

> [This person] goes around looking for faults and judges everything and everybody harshly. He sets himself up as an authority for saying the last word about others. He speaks with a finality which no one is to challenge. His verdict allows for no errors in his judgment or weaknesses in the other person. All that can be known is known—or ignored. The criticism is without feeling and unfair. It is often a judgment of motives which are neither known nor understood." (Chilvers, 8)

V. We Should Not Practice This Dangerous Kind of Judgment

1. We are all sinners, unworthy to condemn others personally
2. God, as well as people will judge us by the standards we use to judge others [19]

3. We have no business attempting to usurp God's prerogative, acting like we are God

4. We are ignorant of all the facts. Only God has full knowledge of our deeds, motives, etc; He alone has the right and the ability to judge righteously, Jas 4:11-12 [20]

5. We judge falsely, wrongly

6. The consequences are indeed, serious:

    a. Those wrongly judged are depressed (Clarke)

    b. Moral fiber is weakened

    c. The self-righteousness of such critics is increased

    d. Retaliation or revenge is fostered (vengeance belongs to God)

    e. Divisiveness is intensified

    f. Hypocrisy fails to call forth divine judgment upon itself

    g. An assumption of power and capacities we do not have

7. Self-righteousness, pride and conceit of the one who judges

8. Oftentimes snap judgments are wrong, causing serious injury to the one judged

9. Jealousy and envy often at the root of finding nothing good to say about others

10. We violate the law of love [21]

11. Lack of mercy: Luke 6:36-37

12. Our judgment may be "fleshly," cf. IV: 3.

13. Shows lack of faith in God's judging. It is a failure to rely completely upon His judgments. We see much evil going on in the world, and seemingly there is no justice. We may then be led to think that if we do not judge evildoers they will escape with impunity.

14. Defeat the possibility of reconciliation. [22]

[1]   Hendry, (*ThTo* 40) 122.

[2]   Eugene-Boring, *NIB* 8:211.

[3]   Bullinger 341; Hindson, *Parallel* 1901.

[4]   ATR; Tasker 79; Kent, *Wycliffe* 940.

[5]   Hagner, (WBC 33A) 169.

[6]   Calvin: These words of Christ do not contain an absolute prohibition from *judging* but are intended to cure a disease, which appears to be natural to us all . . . pretence for setting aside all distinction between good and evil. Tasker, 80: In Matt 7:6 the

Greek "makes it clear that it is not every kind of judging that comes under the ban expressed in verse 1."

[7] Hagner, ibid; Tasker, ibid.

[8] Buchsel, ibid. These include disputes between believers, as well as serious sins of members; but not "with merciless severity."

[9] Hendry, ibid, 121: We are forbidden to take the law into our own hands. Yet we are mindful of the imperfection of human judgment by virtue of the "graduated series of courts and the possibility of appeal, from lower to higher to highest." Even the "Justices" of the Supreme Court fall short with their divided decisions.

[10] Hendry, ibid: 113, 121, 124; Barnes: It is impossible *not* to form an opinion of conduct that we know to be evil.

[11] Rice, 114: "One is not to pass Judgment on people's motives and hearts, since one does not know them. We can never tell definitely what people think, how they feel, or the desires of their hearts. We cannot tell whether or not people are saved. Only God who knows the heart can do so. The particular reason given here for not judging others is 'that ye be not judged.' Do you want others judging your heart, your motives, your deeds, condemning you when they cannot have all the evidence?"

[12] Hendry, ibid: 116-17: "Flesh" is used here metaphorically or figuratively for "human or worldly." In a literal sense we look at the beauty of face, shape of body, length of hair (or color or absence), biceps, broad shoulders, breasts, clothing styles, etc. and "much of our judgment of people is influenced by their physical appearance," skin color or race, credentials, etc.

[13] MacDonald, 1227.

[14] *Censor* and *censure* have the same Latin root meaning to appraise. *Censor* stresses more the idea of examining for the purpose of expurgation (purging out), removal, suppressing, what is considered objectionable morally, politically, or otherwise. *Censure* expresses disapproval of, find fault with; blame, or criticize harshly (*critic*: *kritikos*) derived from *krino*, the main verb in Matt 7:1 and Luke 6:37.

[15] Lindsay: *St Luke* 107: "Christian love is the principle of all good judgment and actions. It makes men refrain from passing judgment, and be patient in thinking well of others . . . Love restrains from hasty judgment of our neighbors, from pitiless condemnation, and from withholding pardon." JFB: When we exercise a censorious disposition, we violate the law of love.

[16] M. Henry: we must not judge of their eternal state; calling them hypocrites, reprobates, and castaways is stretching beyond our line.

[17] Scholars repeatedly remind us that this "scathing rebuke for those who assume to judge others when self-judgment has been neglected" (Chafer: 5:110) is directed at the religious rulers, the scribes and Pharisees (A. B. Bruce, *ExpGT* 1:128). Lenski, *Matthew* 289; *Luke* 373, says this kind of judging was the "Vicious fault of the scribes and Pharisees who set themselves up as judges over all others, gloried in their own false holiness, and despised all others (John 7:49); they acquitted each other and condemned the rest; they were wrong in both their verdicts. . . . [doing] just what the natural man always loves to do," in order to acquit themselves.

[18] Walvoord, *BSac* (123) 100: "We should not judge each other, but rather should give our principal attention to fulfilling our own stewardship in such a way that we will have a good report when we must render account."

[19] Freeman, 417.

[20] Cf. H. Morris, *Defender's* 1015; Hindson, *Parallel* 2026.

[21] Plummer, ICC, *Luke* 189: "Censoriousness is a transgression of the royal law of love, and an invasion of the divine prerogatives."

[22] Hendry, 122: "God's purpose in judgment is reconciliation and reunion . . . with God, judgment is subservient to reconciliation." I would add that because of God's holiness the matter of retribution and punishment broaden the concept of God's purpose in judgment.

Keep Silence before Him: Hab 2:20: *But the LORD is in His holy temple; let all the earth keep silence before Him.*

We forthwith dismiss the idea of using this text as a call to worship. For many years, in my first pastorate, I heard it sung at the beginning of the Sunday morning church services. [1] Habakkuk's purpose was **not** to have this scripture set to music and then used to quiet the congregation in order to begin services or help the worshipers attend to the sermon. This command to keep silence is not a call to believers to gather to worship.

The context reveals that Habakkuk is well aware of Israel's miserable spiritual plight; but he is much dismayed that Jehovah would use a wicked nation like Babylon to chasten Israel.

However, Israel must know that the idol-worshipping, pagan Babylonians shall be punished also. The true and living God, ever ready to help His own, pronounces woes upon the Chaldeans for their many evils, especially the delusion of worshiping idols.

The Hebrew word rendered *keep silence* "is probably onomatopoeic" Onomatopoeia means literally to make or do a word or name. Such words as *boo, buzz, cuckoo, hiss, murmur, ping-pong, quack, slap,* are spelled like they sound; they imitate the sound associated with the action or object referred to; they seem "suggestive of its quality" [2] In Hab 2:20, the Hebrew word used sounds like the interjection, *hush!* [3]

When will this exhortation be obeyed? One interpretation states the silence of which Habakkuk speaks comes at the end of the Tribulation age, and that it marks that time when the Lord Jesus Christ enters the rebuilt Temple at Jerusalem. [4] Inasmuch as only believers enter the Kingdom age, the Millennium, all the earth will indeed be hushed in awe of His Presence and Majesty. [5] Calvin states calling the holy temple heaven is "an unsuitable interpretation." [6]

I accept the interpretation that the reference is to God's heavenly temple, [7] supported by the following Scriptures: Zeph 1:7: Be silent in the presence of the LORD God; for the day of the LORD is at hand; Zech 2:13: Be silent, all flesh, before the LORD, for He is aroused from His holy habitation. Psa 11:4: The LORD is in His holy temple, the LORD's throne is in heaven. Temple of His holiness describes heaven; from His holy habitation is heard "the thunderous call of an outraged God against a world that has too long mocked Him. Now comes the appointed day. Now the principles of judgment shall be executed in the sight of all." [8]

Though the forces of evil still rage, and multitudes serve their dumb, lifeless, useless idol-gods, the silence in heaven portends tremendous judgment is about to take place. [9] When Jehovah God speaks in judgment it is most appropriate for humanity to keep silent. Indeed, the world is commanded to reverence Him! When He judges, the human race on earth is to be still before Him, and know that He is God (Psa 46:10). "He is the invisible God inhabiting His heavenly temple and all-powerful, therefore it behooves all nations to be solemnly and humbly reverent before Him . . . The nations do well, as well as individuals, to submit silently to Him waiting for His judgment." [10]

[1] *The New National Baptist Hymnal*, 531. Pilgrim 1267: This does not have direct reference to the fact that God meets His people in churches today, although He certainly does do that: Nelson, (Hab 2:20) 1523; (Zeph 1:7) 1527; (Zech 2:13) 1540. The call to silence is not an invitation anticipating worship, but the demand for awesome or respectful silence as God announces His impending judgment.

[2] Fowler, 420.

[3] Weber, *TWOT* 1:221: The verb means to keep silence, be still, hold peace, tongue; it is an interjection with imperative force commanding people to 'hush,' refrain from speaking (Amos 6:10) or weeping (Neh 8:11) or in grief for the dead (Amos 8:3).

[4] Pilgrim (1267): "It is a part of the vision Habakkuk saw of the time when the Lord Jesus Christ will enter the rebuilt temple at Jerusalem."

[5] Rev 8:1: *When He opened the seventh seal there was silence in heaven for about half an hour*. Jehovah contemplates showing His power in judgment upon the earth, upon those described as "earth dwellers" (Rev 3:10, 6:10, 11:10, 13:8, 14; 14:6, 17:8). The Church has been snatched up, and six seals of judgment have been broken already. From the one unbroken seal a new series of judgments comes, unleashing still more increasingly severe judgments. Having opened this last seal, there is silence in Heaven for about half an hour.

[6] Calvin, Hab 2:20

[7] H. Morris, *Defender's* 972.

[8] Barnhouse, *Romans:* God's Wrath (Rom 2:16) 108.

[9] Smith, Ralph L. (WBC 32) 109-10.

[10] Feinberg, *Habakkuk* 29.

Kwanzaa and First Fruits

The words *first fruits* occur approximately 34 times in 32 verses of the KJV of the Bible. *First fruits* in the OT are animals (domesticated and wild), tree fruits or grapes, or grain cut at harvest offered by the Hebrews to Jehovah God. It is a sacrificial technical term designating that which is holy to God and consecrated to Him before the remainder is used for other purposes. In the OT two different Hebrew words are used.

One seems generally to mean what is prepared by human labor (Lev 23:9-11; Num 15:17-21); the other refers to "the direct product of Nature," "especially to things sown" (Exod 23:16; Lev 2:14-16). There is no absolute distinction made between the two words. "In acknowledgment of the fact that the land and all its products were the gift of Jehovah to Israel, and in thankfulness for His bounty, all the first-fruits were offered to Him." [1]

In the NT the Greek word *aparche* is used eight times. In Rom 11:16 the *first fruit* is the nation Israel; in Rom 8:23 and 16:5 reference is to the *first fruits* of the Spirit, and of Achaia unto Christ. In 1 Cor 15:20, 23, the risen Christ is the *first fruits* of them that slept; in 16:15 the household of Stephanas is called the *first fruits* of Achaia. In Jas 1:18 God has made us a kind of *first fruits* of His creatures. In Rev 14:4 the redeemed 144,000 are described as the redeemed *first fruits* to God and to the Lamb. John Wycliffe in 1382 mentions *first fruits* (Num 18:12) in the first translation into English of the whole Bible. Over two centuries passed before the expression was used figuratively to mean "the first product of one's efforts." [2]

The concept of *first fruits* is a religious one; it teaches that all belongs to God. We acknowledge His ownership and demonstrate it by our willingness to give Him the *first fruits*. "Because everything belongs ultimately to God, the first ripening of the harvest was ritually offered to Him." [3] In 1966, Dr. Maulana Karenga (Ronald Everett), an African-American activist scholar and Black Studies professor, founded *Kwanzaa,* a secular (?) festival to celebrate culture, community, and family from 26 Dec to 1 Jan. **Kwanzaa** means *first-fruits* and is derived from Swahili, a language widely used as a medium of communication between peoples of different languages living along the East Coast of Africa, from Somalia to Mozambique. *Swahili* means "coast people," although most African Americans trace their ancestry to the West Coast of Africa.

Unfortunately, celebrators insist "Kwanzaa is a cultural and not a religious holiday," and they are adamant in rejecting the religious nature of their celebration! Why? Karenga answers: "We wanted to keep it cultural . . . [so] that it would be available for celebration by all different tendencies in the Black community: Christian, Muslim, Yoruba people, traditionalists, people that don't believe can celebrate Kwanzaa because it's out of our cultural heritage and because it does not challenge these other people's religion."

However, it is recorded that Karenga said that the seven principles came "from African religion" (*Kawaida Theory,* 25). It is suggested celebration of Kwanzaa "can produce psychological benefits to the Black man's growth in America." Kwanzaa will "help to solidify and raise the level of pride and dignity of the Black man as it helps to broaden the knowledge of his positive contributions." On another occasion, Karenga stated Kwanzaa was created to introduce to Black people new values, "which, if practiced, would give them a set of priorities and lead to their liberation and a higher level of human life." Compare the seven principles taught by Kwanzaa with the teachings of the Bible:

Kwanzaa	The Bible
1. Unity – *Umoja*	Eph 4:3-6
2. Self-determination - *Kujichagulia*	Phil 2:12
3. Collective work and Responsibility - *Ujima*	Acts ch(s) 2-3; 2 Thess 3:10
4. Cooperative Economics - *Ujamaa*	Acts 4:32
5. Purpose - *Nia*	1 Cor 10:31
6. Creativity – *Kuumba*	Eccl 9:10
7. Faith – *Imani*	Heb 11:6

Despite the protests to the contrary Kwanzaa is a religious celebration. All the talk about principles of life: unity, creator, behavior, and faith—point to a system of belief and acknowledgment of a superhuman power. Without faith in the shed blood of Jesus Christ man's highest level of attainment is but one more step into the pit of Hell. Note what is called "specificity." Of all the languages and dialects in the continent of Africa, who gave any American Black the authority to select one word from Swahili to speak for all Black Americans? By what authority is December 26th through January 1st established as the time for observance? By whose authority were the rules for celebration set up—the fasting from sunup to sunset; prayers, thanksgiving, lighting of candles, family feast, exchanging of gifts, use of symbols, etc.? The Kwanzaa principles of Blackness run smack dab into God's Word: "No flesh shall glory in His presence" (1 Cor 1:29). God is no respecter of faces or races.[4]

Knowledge is not necessarily power. We may be told what to do but not have the power to do what we are told. Race pride provides very little energy needed to successfully carry out the principles espoused by Kwanzaa. And whatever is accomplished comes solely by the energy of man. There is no fear that Kwanzaa is "a legitimate competitor or threat to Christianity." Christ has no competitor; He is God. How sad that Black Americans are so gullible, so ready to swallow race gimmicks without a heart change by Christ. Kwanzaa remains no more than the religion of secular humanism; Kwanzaa is kwakery!

Thought

"Don't bother me with Scripture,
I know what I want to believe."

ETERNITY

[1] Levertoff, *ISBE* 2:1114; D. J. Williams, 48 (note 67): "The offering of a portion as first fruits was deemed to consecrate the whole."
[2] Hendrickson, 263.
[3] *DBI*: "First fruits" 310. *MCED* 255: "God expects His share from the first, not from the scraps of leftovers at the end."
[4] Acts 10:34, 35; I Pet 1:17; Deut 10:17; 2 Chron 19:7; Col 3:25.

Let Your Conscience Be Your Guide

Our purpose in studying the often-heard admonition or cautionary advice, "Let your conscience be your guide," is to properly answer the question, *"Is the Conscience an Infallible Guide?"* The word conscience (*suneidesis*) is literally, *with knowledge, joint-knowledge.* It is an inner sense, a knowing within oneself, the exercising of a consciousness or awareness of what is moral or ethical—the rightness or wrongness—of our conduct and motives—that "part of our being that tells us we ought to do the right thing personally." [1]

Human conscience is the result of the Fall of Adam and Eve (Gen 2:17, 3:1-7), at which time there came the awareness of right and wrong.[2] All human beings have a conscience,[3] so the expressions "unconscionable" or "he has no conscience" must be limited to some specific issue or deed, and not the totality of human nature. Note the adjectives modifying the word *conscience*:

(1) Good: [4] Acts 23:1; 1 Tim 1:5, 19; Heb 13:18; 1 Pet 3:16, 21.
(2) Weak: this is the conscience that seemingly cannot come to a decision, 1 Cor 8:7, 10, 12.
(3) Pure: 1 Tim 3:9; 2 Tim 1:3.
(4) Seared: [5] 1 Tim 4:2.
(5) Defiled: Titus 1:15; 1 Cor 8:7.
(6) Evil: Heb 10:22.
(7) Without Offense: Acts 24:16, literally, undamaged, blameless, clear, or giving no offense. [6]
(8) Cleansed, purged: Heb 9:14. [7]

Consider now what the conscience does: it

(1) Judges. [8]
(2) Accuses: reproaches (*kategoreo*) a major task, Rom 2:15.
(3) Excuses (*apologeomai*), to talk oneself off of a charge, defend oneself, Rom 2:15.
(4) Convicts: John 8:9; cf. Rom 2:15.
(5) Witnesses: Rom 2:15, 9:1; 2 Cor 1:12 (*marturion*), 4:2, 5:11. [9]

> We can and should listen to our conscience, but it is not an infallible guide to right conduct. It tells us that we should not do what is wrong and that we should do what is right, but by itself cannot tell us what *is* right or what *is* wrong. Only God's written Word, the Bible, can teach us that. When the Holy Spirit shines on its pages, teaching us what we do, then conscience will tell us that we ought to do it. But without the Word of God, even though conscience will tell us to do the right thing, we

will not know what the right thing is and we will err, as Paul had done. (Boice, *Acts* 375; my paraphrase)

Conscience is neither a fool-proof standard nor an infallibly safe guide; it may be weak, seared, defiled, or evil. It works with what it has—influenced by fear, egotism, education, culture, social customs, self-interest, etc.—so that a man may commit a terrible act and his conscience not accuse him or make him feel guilty of wrongdoing. Paul is an example of a "conscientious wrongdoer," one whose "spirit and character were commendable, while his conduct was reprehensible." [10] Disobey your conscience—enlightened or unenlightened—and you commit a self-destructive act, a sin. Thus we give an ambiguous reply to the question, "Shall I always obey my conscience?" Yes, but remember sin has perverted the conscience, forcing us to state, "The conscience is **not** an infallible guide!" Enlightened by the Word of God we are enabled to follow it safely, "relying on its truthfulness and proper balance." [11] Only when the conscience is illumined by God is it reliable. [12] Only when it judges according to the Word of God is its verdict absolutely infallible.

Thought

Dennis the Menace

"YOUR CONSCIENCE, JOEY, IS SOMETHING THAT MAKES YOU TAKE ONLY ONE COOKIE, WHEN YOU COULD HAVE TAKEN *TWO.*"

[1] Boice, *Romans* 1:239; cf. Girdlestone, 72.

[2] Barnhouse, *Romans: God's Discipline* 4:118-19: Innocent Adam and Eve "knew nothing about evil, and had no thought of making choices." Their failure to trust God led to their disobedience, and "the consequence was the curse of conscience."

[3] Pilgrim, 1580: *Man's Conscience*, Rom 2:14-15; Chafer 7:92.

[4] Girdlestone, 74: A good conscience, according to Scripture, is not only a sense of freedom from past guilt, but also a consciousness of purposing and doing that which is good in God's sight; it implies purity of motive and action; it is inconsistent with a deliberate course of sin, or with departure from the living God, and it is closely connected with faith in Christ. Cf. Bullinger, 550, Rom 13:5. Many verses containing the word *conscience* refer merely to man's awareness or consciousness of right and wrong: Rom 13:5; 1 Cor 8:7; 10:25, 27-29; Heb 9:9, 10:2; 1 Pet 2:19.

[5] Our word *cauterize* comes from the Greek word here rendered *seared*. Refusal to listen to the voice or word of God hardens the heart; continued refusal increases the hardening until it reaches the point of no return—considered "past feeling, reprobate." Thiessen, 162: But "nowhere does it intimate that conscience can be destroyed."

[6] Girdlestone, 72: Paul "evidently signified that he was not conscious of living or aiming to live in any course which was wrong in the sight of God or really offensive to man."

[7] The Holy Spirit cleanses the conscience from dead works by the blood of the Lord Jesus Christ (Heb 9:14). We must have our hearts sprinkled from an evil conscience (Heb 10:22) in order to eliminate the sin that built a wall between God and man.

[8] Thiessen, 10: "It judges whether a proposed course of action or an attitude is in harmony with our moral standard or not and urges us to do that which is in harmony with it and to refrain from that which is contrary to it." Conscience has thoughts: calculations, reflections, reasoning; its self-judging voice groans and cries out or remains silent.

[9] The Holy Spirit works in and through human conscience (Rom 9:1); cf. Chafer, 7:93.

[10] Thiessen, 163; 1 Tim 1:13.

[11] Byatt, 182.

[12] Barnhouse, *Romans:God's Discipline,* 4:119.

Like People, Like Priest

Hos 4:9: *And it shall be: like people, like priest.*

Priests acted as intermediaries between God and man. As representatives of Jehovah they held high positions in their society. Their relationship with the LORD required they live holy (separated), and dedicated to the LORD's work. Duly authorized to serve in sacred things, "particularly to offer sacrifices at the altar," they acted as middle men between worshipers and God. [1] The priests with whom Hosea dealt were tragically guilty of leading their people astray, and along with the political leaders of the time were primarily responsible for Jehovah's rejection of the nation. [2]

They failed to teach the people about the LORD, and this resulted in a lack of knowledge that caused the people to go to ruin, be destroyed. Jehovah threatened to reject them from being priests for Him (v. 6), for they had forgotten His law. Their corruption included abusing their office in order to stuff their own bellies. Here's the way it worked: The more the people sinned, the more sin offerings were received by the greedy priests. "They had a vested interest in the continued sin of Israel." [3]

> They eat up the sin of My people – Feeding could be meant figuratively, i.e. a corrupt parasitical relationship between the priests and the people's sin. The priests, who should lead the people away from sin toward Yahweh, subsist off the people's iniquity instead. The verse could be read literally: The priests gain their livelihood from (the people's) 'unorthodox' religious practices. (Hosea 4:8: Yee, *NIB* 7:239)

What is the meaning of "like people, like priest"? Despite their authority and relationship with Jehovah, the priests "having abused the honor conferred on them" (Calvin), disqualified themselves by their corruption. Rather than reprimand the people they encouraged them in their wickedness. Such behavior calls for condemnation and judgment, the very thing to which the phrase "like people, like priest" alludes. In other words, emphasis is **not** upon the idea that the people have become like the priests. [4] Admittedly, both aspects are true in our society today: Preachers and priests become like the members of the congregation; and the members become like their religious leaders. They corrupt each other. [5] Paul stresses the role of the people in 2 Tim 4:3.

We live in the Laodicean (people rule) Church Age (Rev 3:14-19); increasingly church members call "pastors who will be like them, rather than call pastors who will help them to be like Christ." [6] Like people, like priests means both groups will be judged; what happens to one happens to the other; sharers in sin must expect to be sharers in ruin (M. Henry); and it shall be: As with the people, so with the priest. [7] It is not denied that there are degrees of punishment for evildoers (Luke 12:47-48) just as there are degrees of rewards for believers (2 Cor 5:10). "The punishment will be appropriate to the crimes. The evildoers will get exactly what they deserve;" no one will be exempt from the coming punishment. [8]

Thought

Aunt Het

Of course the rest of us should be as good as preachers but we despise preachers who are not better than the rest of us.

[1] Moorehead, *ISBE* 4:2439.
[2] H. Morris, *Defender's* 933. Wyrtzen, *BSac* (141), 324.
[3] Feinberg, *Hosea* 38. Reeve, *ISBE* 4:2644-45: The sin offering was the most holy, and the priest alone might eat what was left of the ram, pigeon or flour, in the holy place. Lev 6:26: The priest

who offers it for sin shall eat it. The guilt offering (trespass) was a special kind of sin offering . . . certain classes of sin required a guilt offering "with reparation in money" (shekels of silver), Lev 5:14—6:7.

[4] Harper, ICC, *Amos & Hosea* 258.

[5] Feinberg, ibid: 38-39: "The people were no less culpable than the priest, nor was he less blameworthy than they. He conformed his life to their ways and they, viewing the godless conduct of their teachers, found an example they delighted to follow as well as confirmation for their own deeds." M. Henry: They harden one another in sin.

[6] Fink, *Parallel* 1671-72

[7] Isa 24:2. Bullinger: 730: Sometimes the word 'as' is followed by the word 'so,' to strengthen and heighten the comparison, and make it clearer. Young, 2:150-51: "Here we are given a picture of anarchy. When all the distinctions of class are completely obliterated, then anarchy follows . . . Hosea apparently places his principal emphasis upon the priests' failure to impart the knowledge of Yahweh, whereas in the present passage the emphasis is not restricted to the religious sphere." K&D: "Therefore it will happen as to the people so to the priest." Moffatt: "Priests shall fare like people." Cheyne, 66: priest shall fare no better than the people. His official 'nearness' to Jehovah shall be no safeguard to him; M. Henry.

[8] Stuart, (WBC 31) 80; Eidevall, 235.

A Little Child Shall Lead Them

Isa 11:6: *The wolf also shall dwell with the lamb, the leopard shall lie down with the young goat, the calf and the young lion and the fatling together; and a little child shall lead them.*

The prophet had four perspectives: (1) his own time (2) captivity or exile (3) the coming of the Messiah, and (4) the Millennium or 1,000 years. There is additionally a three-fold emphasis: (1) cursing (2) blessing (3) restoration. Study of the prophets becomes even more difficult when you factor in such matters as (a) whether they served before, during or after the Captivity (Exile) (b) the four perspectives may not be in chronological order (c) nor their treatments proportionate, for some events may be missing—such as the destruction of Jerusalem, the birth of the Messiah, His crucifixion, second coming, or description of the Kingdom age.

135

Isaiah 11 is a prophetic picture of the glory of the Millennial Kingdom set up when David's Son returns in glory. During this thousand-year period, paradise comes to all animal creation as the entire world rejoices in redemption. It is not a scene enjoyed only by the Jewish people. Although Israel will be the paradisiacal center of the earth, the redemption is not so localized. [1] Put simplistically, the biblical scheme is *Israel—Church—Israel.* Once the Church is removed the spotlight of history once again falls upon the tiny nation of Israel.

All nature is transformed. "They shall not hurt nor destroy in all My holy mountain, for the earth shall be full of the knowledge of the LORD as the waters cover the sea" (Isa 11:9). The golden age of the past returns, and wild beasts will no longer prey on others. [2] The overall picture is one of great fruitfulness (Amos 9:13), abundant water, peace—between the nations, between animals, and between men and animals—longevity of life, no disease; and Christ ruling with a rod of iron. A miraculous change takes place! Two longstanding enemies—the wolf, fierce, killing—the lamb, meek, helpless, defenseless—are now perfectly reconciled. [3] The leopard shall lie down with the young goat and not devour it. The calf and the young lion and the fatling (a young lamb or calf, fattened for slaughter) shall feed together. The cow (heifer) and the bear shall feed; their young ones shall lie down together side by side in the pasture. The lion shall eat chopped straw like the ox (Isa 65.25), no longer thirsting for blood or flesh—this ruthless, almost unstoppable killer with its fearful roar, ferocious, destructive power, irresistible strength, bold stealth, and savagery, now a purring kitten! [4]

I reject "spiritualized" interpretations that make men who were like savage wild beasts now meek lambs willingly submitting and appearing like little children. [5] The wild and the domestic shall dwell together in peace. They will cease to be what they became, like man after the flood, to become as they were when first created. "In that day I will make a covenant for them with the beasts of the field, with the birds of the air, and with the creeping things of the ground. Bow and sword of battle I will shatter from the earth, to make them lie down safely" (Hos 2:18: cf. Ezek 34:25-6).

Two phrases often heard: (1) **the lion and the lamb shall lie down together** [6] (2) **a little child shall lead them.** [7] I have heard these latter words often taken out of context, and used in the following manner: A young person comes to Christ, returns home, and with talk backed up by a changed life, the Holy Spirit uses the youngster to win over the parents—sometimes to get them to attend church where they hear the Gospel and are saved.

In the context we have the picture of a young, inexperienced boy, "who can scarcely be trusted with tame animals, but like a shepherd that drives his flock, he leads these without fear and in perfect safety." [8] This beautiful picture of peace and prosperity continues (v8). The child just weaned (two or three years old), a suckling, [9] plays with delight and immunity, boldly stretching out its hand over the hole of a beast formerly considered one of the most dangerous. [10]

> [Cruel beasts are miraculously regenerated]. This can only be realized in the return of the Messiah to establish the kingdom of God (65:17-25). In God's peaceful kingdom, carnivores will become herbivores; natural enemies will become companions; and little children will play safely near the dwellings of formerly venomous snakes. In the coming kingdom, a youngster will be able to lead formerly wild animals . . . emphasizing the end of terror, fright, and danger in the coming kingdom. (Nelson, 1132)

[1] Alexander, 1:253; Hesse, *TDNT* 9:508: "When the Messiah begins his reign, the whole world achieves the state that God originally planned for it." [paradisaical optional spelling].
[2] G. B. Gray, ICC, *Isaiah* 218-19; H. Morris, *Defender's* 729: "In the original creation, all animals were herbivorous (Gen 1.30), and these conditions will be restored in the coming kingdom age when Christ returns." Sco, Rom 8:21-22: Even the animal and material creation, cursed for man's sake, will be delivered by Christ.
[3] Bullinger, 688-89.
[4] *DBI* 514: "The lion is the quintessential carnivore, but the messianic kingdom will differ so much from the familiar world that its lions will be vegetarian and lie down with the lamb. This kingdom will be ruled by a lion-like lamb." Michaelis (*TDNT* 4:253) claims that "the promise that lions will be peaceful in the last time finds no echo in the eschatological statements of the NT," but see Rom 8:19-22; Rev 5:5: Christ, the "Lion of the tribe of Judah."

[5] **I believe the following interpretations are** *incorrect*: JFB: "These may be figures for men of corresponding animal-like characters. . . . But more likely a literal change in the relations of animals to man and each other." K&D: "such commentators as Luther, Calvin, have taken all these figures from the animal world as symbolical." Barnes: It is not a reference to any literal change in the nature of animals. "It does not appear how the gospel has any tendency to change the nature of [animals]; it acts on men, not on brutes; on human hearts, not on the organization of wild animals. . . . The fair interpretation of this passage is, therefore, that revolutions will be produced in the wild and evil passions of men—the only thing with which the gospel has to do."

Gill: not to be understood of the savage creatures, as if they should lose their nature, and be restored, as it is said, to their paradisiacal estate . . . but figuratively of men, comparable to wild creatures . . . not to be understood literally . . . but in a parabolical and enigmatical sense; and interprets them of the Israelites dwelling safely among the wicked of the nations of the world, comparable to the wild beasts of the field."

Contrary to the above statements: These beasts are **not** human beings or symbols of human beings; they are literal animals. Hindson, *Parallel* 1321: The dangerous predatory animals, wolf, leopard, lion, bear, are to be taken as literal, and not symbolic of various types of hostile people. Archer, *Wycliffe* 621: The references to the little child (v6) and the sucking child (v8) clearly preclude construing the beasts as various types of men. Young, 1:388: "All enmity will disappear, not only from among men, but even from among beasts, and even between men and beasts all will be in harmony."

[6] *USN & WR* (Mar 06) 63, headline: *Inflation Lion and Job-Market Lamb Lie Down Together*. The article deals with that "fallacy that strong job markets create inflation . . . [there is] plenty of evidence in this economy that 5 percent unemployment and virtual price stability coexisted for long periods of time."

[7] *Chosen People* (Mar 07) 7, headline: *A Little Child Shall Lead Them*. A little Russian Jewish boy received the Lord at a *Chosen People Ministries* service. He became greatly concerned for his immediate family. Staff members learned from the boy's mother that he could not travel in their family car because they did not

have a car seat. God provided a secondhand one that they gave to his mother. Over-whelmed with their attention and love, she called and asked to meet to talk about their organization and their faith. After almost four hours of questions and answers, she gave her life to Christ.

[8] Young, 1:388-9. Gray, ibid.

[9] Tucker, *NIB* 6:141: "represent[s] children generally, human beings at their most vulnerable stages."

[10] Watts, (WBC 24) 173: "the innocence of the child-herder, the suckling, and the toddler accent a world without harm or danger."

[11] Nelson, 1132.

A Little Leaven Leavens the Whole Lump

I. The word leaven does *not* always refer to evil

First consider this negative argument [with which I do **not** agree]. Many scholars teach that leaven is used in a "good sense *and* an evil sense." Most believe that in 1 Cor 5:6 and Gal 5:9, leaven symbolizes *evil*. However, with respect to Luke 13:20-21: And again He said, "To what shall I liken the kingdom of God? It is like leaven, which a woman took and hid in three measures of meal till it was all leavened," we find scholars teaching the leaven represents *good*. We are told that the emphasis is upon the kingdom of God, insignificant in the beginning, but in time filling the entire earth. [1]

As for Matt 13:33: "The kingdom of heaven is like leaven, which a woman took and hid in three measures of meal till it was all leavened," even more scholars believe leaven signifies a positive image, portraying the spread of the Gospel, worldwide evangelism, and the conversion of multitudes. The gates of Hell shall not prevail against God's kingdom! [2] In support of this interpretation we are told we must not stereotype figurative language in the Bible, for one figure does not always "stand for one and the same thing." [3] God's Kingdom starts small, as a mustard seed, but in time grows and fills the entire earth. This growth is not the result of human ingenuity, powerful armies, skilled administrative organization or political alliances.

It is the work of the Holy Spirit Who will not allow false doctrine and moral corruption to impede the dynamic growth effectuated by "an internal dynamic." Leaven spreads its influence silently and strongly, altering and transforming all that it contacts, clearly for good, emphasizing its "pervasive power." [4] In the parables leaven is likened to the preaching of the Gospel that causes the small group of believers to grow into a world-wide organization filling all the nations with righteousness and true holiness.

II. Leaven *always* refers to evil, never to good
This is the position I hold. The word leaven *never* refers to good, but always to evil. In Luke 13:21 leaven symbolizes evil, not a picture of good spreading world-wide by way of the Church. Rather, it portrays "the externalism, unbelief, evil doctrine, and worldliness which tend to inflate the church." [5] In Matt 13:33 "the leaven is not just false profession of unsaved church members but false doctrine which they will attempt to bring into the church." [6] Throughout the parables of our Lord in Matt 13 it is His intention to show that evil continues to exist and grow; it is Christendom, where Christ is professed but not possessed. **Consistency requires that we do not interpret any one of these parables contrary to the theme projected by our Lord**. [7]

The argument put forth by Trench (*Parables*) and ATR ignores context. Illustrations of the figurative use of words like lion and dove must be interpreted within their context, a principle that is not as AT Robertson calls it, "exegetical jugglery." The parable of the leaven must "fit with the other parables in picturing the evil course of this evil age," so that this age is characterized as one in which wickedness and false doctrines slowly spread until the whole world is contaminated. [8] "Both the growing mustard seed and spreading leaven indicate that, as the outward kingdom grows, both its membership and doctrine will increasingly become corrupted." [9] Leaven **always** symbolizes impurity, evil, corruption, malice and wickedness, throughout the entire Bible. [10] Doctrinally, leaven expresses itself in (1) Pharisaism, externalism in religion (2) Sadduceeism, skepticism as to the supernatural and as to the Scriptures (3) Herodianism, worldliness. [11] Leaven is always used in a bad sense. [12]

> Leaven, which brings about fermentation, is uniformly regarded in Scripture as typifying the presence of impurity or evil . . . The teaching that leaven in this parable represents the beneficent influence of the Gospel pervading the world has no Scriptural justification.

Nowhere in Scripture does leaven represent good; the idea of a converted world at the end of the age is contradicted by the presence of tares among the wheat and bad fish among the good in the kingdom itself. Although biblical truth has a beneficial moral influence on the world, the mingling of leaven is not the method of divine salvation or enlargement of the kingdom. Tares never become wheat. The parable is, therefore, a warning that true doctrine, represented by the flour, would be corrupted by false doctrine. (Sco, Matt 13:33)

If the leaven in Luke 13:20-21 and Matt 13:33 symbolizes the optimistic, positive growth of God's kingdom, what is the historical point in which this takes place? What is the time reference? Currently statistics do not support the belief that such growth is occurring. The period from Pentecost to the Rapture is described as perilous (1 Tim 4:1-3; 2 Tim 3:1-7); evil men and impostors will grow worse and worse (2 Tim 3:13). Apostasy within Christendom is growing! Is this "good leaven" to spread *after* the Church is translated? No. Dispensationalists find no scriptural evidence of leavening for good in the Tribulation era, that time immediately following the translation of the Church.

In fact, when all the Christians are translated their Holy Spirit "salty" influence is taken away [the Holy Spirit is not removed, for He is omnipresent], and it is this removal that helps precipitate the awfulness of the Tribulation. From this perspective there is no scripturally valid chronology or time period in which leaven represents beneficial growth. "When the Son of Man comes, will He really find faith on the earth?" (Luke 18:8). Any attempt to make leaven represent the remarkable growth of the church is a mistaken interpretation.

III. 1 Cor 5:6: *Your glorying is not good. Do you not know that a little leaven leavens the whole lump?* Here the problem is the permission of sexual sin in the life of the church. One of the men in the assembly was sleeping with his stepmother (his father's wife); note the present tense, "a man *has* his father's wife." There were those in the church who knew about it, but said nothing, did nothing. It is interesting how we can boast of our evildoing. [13] Paul said, "Your vaunting is not good; your puffed-up-ness is not seemly (proper)." Some members may have argued, "Well, it's just the sin of one member. Why generalize on the strength of just one case? How can this single incident affect the whole church?"

This is a specious (seemingly reasonable) excuse for negligence (ATR), but the truth is, "One sinner destroys much good" (Eccl 9:18). In the original the word *little* is emphasized by placing it first in the sentence. The argument (called *a fortiori*: to the stronger) implies that if a little leaven has such an effect, what will it be like when the whole lump is leavened? If even one immoral act has a septic (rotten, poisonous) influence in an assembly, how much more must a scandal of this magnitude (an incestuous relationship) corrupt the whole life of the church! They failed to see their "whole-lump-ness," and the fact that "no sin can be considered an isolated event." [14]

Just one drop of poison is all that is needed. Let one wicked man in the church do as he pleases, and in time the entire congregation becomes contaminated. [15] Indeed, such laxity may cause new believers to fall into sexual immorality. Such pervasive perversion is true even if the members are not aware of the man's bad living. Where it is known among the members and nothing is done about it, the deterioration is more deeply seated and serious. Note the implicit guilt taught in Rom 1:32. Indifference to grave misbehavior in the church makes every member partly responsible for it. [16] Failure to hold the evildoer accountable not only involves the conscience of all of the members, but fails to maintain purity in the local church. [17] Because sin is like a cancer, the immediate remedy is drastic surgery! Allow leaven to remain and it will spread its defilement. [18]

IV. Gal 5:9: *A little leaven leavens the whole lump.*

As in 1 Cor 5:6 these words constitute a proverbial saying, "referring to the tendency of an influence seemingly small to spread until it dominates the whole situation." [19] The poison of false doctrine had not yet spread widely in the church in Galatia. While the fermentation process was moving, [20] it had not permeated the assembly. [21] Barnes suggests that false teachers with their few doctrines had pervaded the assembly already. It appears, however, that Paul was alarmed more by the insidious nature of such leaven, its potential to corrupt, than by the actual extent the church had been affected. The leaven here is false doctrine.

Recall that the Lord Jesus had warned the disciples to beware of the teachings of the Pharisees and Sadducees, which doctrine He called leaven (Matt 16:11-12). Because the false teachers *are* what they teach, you may include them as leaven also. These purveyors of falsehood are called legalizers or Judaizers; they sought to discredit Paul, and taught that the Galatians should be circumcised and keep the Mosaic Law, observing certain dietary rituals, worship on special days, etc. [22] Paul called this a re-enslavement, a return to the bondage of the law.

Objectors argued (similar to the objections mentioned at Corinth), "Why let such a small thing be made a subject of serious controversy? After all, only a few people held to some one ritual (or even a few rituals) as essential, and weakly held to it at that! So why make such a big fuss?" Some protested, "I'm not hurting anybody but myself." This is simply not true; no sin is an isolated event. Furthermore, if you put yourself under the law system you are obligated to keep the whole law. [23]

Paul would not entertain the idea that small errors—though not thought of as such by the legalizers—cause little or no trouble. No, said the apostle; small errors have a devastating effect upon the church (which is considered as a singular unity). In time, false doctrine increases and infects many. Avoid at all costs mixing law with faith. Understand then that Paul uses the word *leaven* figuratively here; it represents "corruption of salvation doctrine by legalism, especially the insistence on circumcision." [24]

---

[1] Nelson, 1725: "in this parable, it is positive;" Lenski, *Luke* 743: "Leaven pictures the good power of Christ's rule"; Caird, 149; *DBI* 498; AB Bruce, *ExpGT* 1:567; Nolland, (WBC 35B) 730: because of this small-scale beginning, the whole world will be transformed; Allis, *EvQ* (19) 254-273.

[2] M. Henry; Barnes; Windisch, *TDNT* 2:905: leaven represents something good; Lenski, *Corinthians*, 220: "good sense"; Trench, *Parables* 118: in its "obvious sense . . . it prophesies the diffusion, and not the corruption of the Gospel"; Eager, *ISBE* 3:1862: "clearly the hidden, silent, mysterious, but all-pervading and transforming action of the leaven in measures of flour that is the point of the comparison"; Bruce, ibid 1:201: "Jesus had the courage to use it as an emblem of . . . the Kingdom of God coming into the heart of the individual and the community." Burton, ICC,

Galatians 283: "On leaven as a symbol of good see Matt 13:33 and Luke 13:20-21."

[3] Trench, *Parables* 117.

[4] ATR; Freeman, 437: "Jesus used leaven to illustrate the pervasive growth of the kingdom of God."

[5] Borland, *Parallel* 2045; Hoste & Rodgers, 74-75; 270-71; MacDonald, 1424: This evil doctrine with its insidious power to spread has been introduced into the pure food of the people of God.

[6] Hindson, *Parallel* 1919; MacDonald, 1257: leaven is evil doctrine.

[7] Kent, *Wycliffe* 953: "evil existing till the end of the age."

[8] Rice, 202.

[9] H. Morris, *Defender's* 1027.

[10] Walvoord, *BSac* (124) 198; Pilgrim, 1341: reference is to the great ecumenical movement of the world.

[11] Sco, Matt 13:33.

[12] Bullinger, 765.

[13] Phil 3:19: whose glory is in their shame; Findlay, *ExpGT* 2:809.

[14] Mitchell, *Parallel* 2292.

[15] Sampley, *NIB* 10:847; D. J. Williams, 96.

[16] Robertson & Plummer, ICC, *1 Cor* 101: "To be indifferent to grave misbehavior is to become partly responsible for it . . . The leaven that was infecting the Corinthian church was a vitiated public opinion."

[17] Quine, *BSac* (149) 62; Kitchens, *BSac* (148) 211-13: Four problem areas in the Church: (1) Private and Personal Offenses That Violate Christian Love (2) Divisiveness and Factions That Destroy Christian Unity (3) Moral and Ethical Divisions That Break Christian Standards (4) Teaching False Doctrine.

[18] Pilgrim, 1608; Hays, *NIB* 11:315: Expel the "flagrant sexual offender from the church . . . take action to preserve its integrity by excising the cancer before it can spread." Quine, ibid. Church discipline is to maintain purity in the local church; remove him!

[19] Burton, ibid; Calvin.

[20] Action in progress; MacDonald: evil is never static.

[21] Rendall, *ExpGT* 3:185. Roustio, *Parallel,* 2397.

[22] Byatt, 85.

[23] Mitchell, ibid. Josh 7:11-12; cf. Gal 3:10; Deut 27:26.

[24] H. Morris, ibid. 1299.

A Living Dog Is Better Than a Dead Lion

Eccl 9:4: *But for him who is joined to all the living there is hope, for a living dog is better than a dead lion.*

I. Context

This commonly used wayside-saying, with its wide application and broadness of meaning, easily has become accepted as a proverb. [1] The phrase "a living dog is better than a dead lion" appears only here in the Bible. As far as man can determine— "under the sun"—we can be confident that to be alive and conscious is superior to being dead. For the Christian whose perspective is *above* the sun, to be absent from the body is to be present with the Lord; this is far better (2 Cor 5:8; Phil 1:23). From the writer's point of view, "when you're dead, you're done!" and in the grave there is no awareness of any thing. "The meanest thing with life in it is better than the noblest without." [2] The belief that death reduces you to a state of nothingness, and "consciousness on any terms is preferable to non-existence," [3] is the thrust of this proverb that teaches "the uselessness of the dead." [4]

The context teaches that life of any kind is preferable to and superior to Death, mankind's inveterate enemy that shows no respect of persons. "While one is alive, there is a hope of finding meaning to life and the possibility of attaining success in life that carries beyond the grave." [5] Such is the hope the living may have; however, death destroys all such dreams! The Preacher expresses the desire that men repent before they die, and indicates that there is "hope of doing something to the glory of God" while they are still alive.

II. Dogs

Nothing good is said in the Bible about dogs; they simply were not held in esteem. In America, for the most part, dogs are looked upon as "man's best friend," in spite of recent news about gambling on dog fights, and torture of the dogs. Their fantastic sense of smell has made them valuable assets in detecting bombs, dope and even certain diseases; their aid to the blind is well-known. We spend millions of dollars on dog food each year; and many dog owners pay dearly at the veterinarian's office. This is a far cry from their value or regard in Hebrew society in Bible days.

There are four basic categories for the symbolic description of dogs: (1) **Self-Abnegation**: self-denial, renunciation or "put-down." This is usually expressed in the presence of nobility. David before King Saul calls himself "a dead dog" (1 Sam 24:14). [6] (2) **Sodomite**: "The price of a dog" (Deut 23:18) refers to the wages from male prostitution. (3) **Contempt**: Goliath asks David with contempt, "Am I a dog that you come to me with sticks?" (1 Sam 17:43). Our text, Eccl 9:4, belongs in this section, so do the phrases "dumb dog," one that cannot bark, and "greedy dogs." Shimei is called a "dead dog" by Abishai. [7] The enemies of the Suffering Savior are called dogs. [8]

Similarly, Exod 11:7 (a dog move its tongue) expresses the idea of angry growling," [9] and means "to sharpen the tongue," evidently connoting speaking against another with hostility. (4) **Voracious** (greedy, ravenous, or rapacious): They are snarling "canine garbage disposals," street scavengers, running wild through the streets. [10] Dogs licked the blood of Naboth, Ahab, and of Jezebel and ate her flesh (1 Kgs 21:19, 23; 2 Kgs 9:36). Even in Job 30:1, where sheep-dogs, held in a higher regard mainly because they are owned and trained to work with sheep are still linked with the dogs of Exod 22:31 in an implied inferiority.

Flesh torn by animals was not to be eaten by humans, but given to the dogs. Sheep-dogs are included here as flesh-eaters, along with the voracious street scavengers roaming about without a master. [11] The words "dog, dog's, or dogs" are found 41 times in the KJV of the Bible. In the NT the word dog occurs nine times. [12] In the OT the word *keleb* (Caleb) is used thirty-two times; [13] of this number I have mentioned eighteen as examples covering the four basic categories in which the word "dog" is used.

III. Lions

Not only does the word lion (lions, lioness, etc.) occur more often than the word dog, but there are at least six Hebrew words used with renderings like: lion, young lion, fierce lion, old lion, lioness, and whelp. [14] Literal references deal with the lions slain by Samson, David, and Benaiah; and humans slain by lions. [15] The majority of the references to lions are figurative. Two main categories are: (1) Symbolizing Royalty and Leadership.[16] Israel's leadership is described in Num 24:9; Judah's in Gen 49:9-10. [17] (2) Lion is also a figure of God and His power. [18] He is likened unto a bone-breaking lion (Isa 38.13); a lion in ambush (Lam

3.10); a tearing lion (Hos 5:14), and a lurking lion (Hos 13:7). Just as the "king's wrath is like the roaring of a lion," so God in His wrath and judgment will roar. [19]

IV. Conclusion: What is expressed here in Eccl 9:4 is the mind of man "under the sun," as far as the human eye can see, and the human mind determine. The contrast between dog and lion is one that reinforces the point that the *living* lowest of the low is better off than the greatest of the *dead*, that life is superior to death. When the lion dies he is reduced to a state of nothingness. [20] He is king no more; he has lost his dignity and strength.

So it is also with human beings. Hope is associated with human activity, but lacking in those who are dead; the dreams of the living are shattered in death; hope exists only where there is life. [21] Looked at from the standpoint of size the *living* mouse is superior to the *dead* elephant. "The vilest, as long as they have life, have hope; the noblest who die unconverted have none" (JFB). In other words, a living despicable creature is preferable to a dead highly respected creature. Death reduces the royal beast to a state of uselessness. Transferring the concept to human beings, we establish that the living beggar is preferred to a dead Rockefeller or Howard Hughes. A poor peasant who is alive is preferable to the formerly powerful potentate who is dead. As harsh as this sounds, may the truth be used to "exhort the wise and pious to cheerful confidence in God, whatever their condition in life" (M. Henry). Death closes the door of opportunity to obtain blessings in this present life or rewards in the next life. For all who love the Lord Jesus Christ, death is a gate to Heaven where we shall live eternally with Him who cleansed us in His own blood!

[1] Bullinger, 761-62.
[2] Brewer's, 642.
[3] Towner, *NIB* 5:340.
[4] Macalister, *ISBE* 2:801.
[5] Davis, *BSac* (148) 301; Hawkins, *Parallel* 1275; Nelson 1092.
[6] Mephibosheth calls himself a "dead dog" (2 Sam 9:8).
[7] Isa 56:10-11; "Dead dog" is a title used contemptuously of someone considered vile and mean (2 Sam 16:9; Brewer's 293). Oswalt, *TWOT* 1:438: To treat someone like a dog is to deal with one considered utterly worthless.

[8] Spurgeon, *Treasury* (Psa 22:16, 20) 1:329, they hound Him, and thirst to devour Him. Psa 59:6: KJV: "they make a noise (NKJV: growl) like a dog"; Oswalt, ibid: their barking is compared to the sniping of an enemy. Spurgeon, *Treasury* (Psa 59:6) 2:15 adds: "David compares his foes to Eastern dogs, despised, unowned, loathsome, degraded, lean, and hungry, and represents them as howling with disappointment, because they cannot find the food they seek."

[9] *TWOT* 1:326.

[10] MacDonald, 916, endnote #32.

[11] Jer 15:3: "the dogs to tear" (KJV); "the dogs to drag" (NKJV) is the figure of sheep dragged off to be eaten.

[12] *Kuon,* five times; *kunarion,* little or domesticated dog, four times.

[13] Oswalt, *TWOT* 1:439.

[14] A whelp is a young offspring of a mammal. Cf. Day, *ISBE* 2:1895-96. Adjectives describing the lion are: old, young, great, and strong (Judg 14:18), roaring or growling (Job 4:10, Psa 104:21; Isa 31:4), fierce, tearing (Psa 7:2), ravenous, bold (2 Sam 17:10), waiting secretly, lurking (Psa 10:9), greedy of prey (Psa 17:12), mighty (Prov 30:30), destroying, and devouring. Satan is described as "like a roaring lion," (1 Pet 5:8).

[15] Judg 14:6; 1 Sam 17:34-37; 2 Sam 23:20 [1 Chr 11:22]; 1 Kgs 13:24; 20:36; 2 Kgs 17:25; Dan 6:24.

[16] Towner, ibid.

[17] Varner, 44-45: "The kingly character of Judah, as mentioned in [Gen 49:10], is appropriately symbolized by the lion who is often called the king of beasts. This theme is carried through the Scriptures, even into the NT. Rev 5:5 describes a scene in the throne room of Heaven in which the lion of the tribe of Judah is the main character. This is a messianic reference to the Lord Jesus Christ who, by descent, was a member of this tribe."

Sco, Gen 49:10: "Rule in Judah will not depart until He comes, when that sovereignty will be heightened to include the world." It was of the tribe of Judah "that King David, and all the rightful Jewish kings, and *the* King, the Lord Jesus Christ, were born. Shiloh, meaning *Peace-bringer* refers to the Lord Jesus Christ. He is the One who will gather the Jewish people together out of all the countries of the earth, and His rule will bring peace to all the peoples of the earth" (Pilgrim, Gen 49:10).

[18] Barton, ICC, *Ecclesiastes* 159: "The lion was a symbol of regal power, and is used metaphorically . . . of God."
[19] Prov 19:12; Jer 25:30; Hos 11:10; Joel 3:16; Amos 1:2.
[20] Barton, ibid 160; Jeffrey, 457: "Death is a great leveler." Fulghum, 159: "Death brings all to the same level."
[21] Murphy, (WBC 23A) 92; Bultmann: *TDNT* 2:522.

Lo! Matt 28:20: *"and lo, I am with you always, even to the end of the age."* Amen.

This word, called a particle, is found usually at the beginning but sometimes in the middle of a sentence (John 5:14: behold, see). The word *behold* may be placed in the "midst of a sentence in such a way that the words which precede it serve to render the more evident the strangeness of what follows" (Thayer: John 3:26). Note the purpose and use of the words, "Lo!", "See" and "Behold":

(1) The speaker desires to draw attention to something; "take notice"
(2) When introducing something unexpected
(3) To enliven a narrative by marking a scenery change or transition
(4) To emphasize the importance of what follows
(5) To inform of the basis of a conclusion or action taken
(6) To indicate the person spoken to is ready to listen or obey
(7) To point to a truth newly recognized or asserted
(8) To emphasize here and now
(9) To call attention to detail

In the OT various Hebrew words rendered "lo" are also translated "ha, behold, though, look, see" and sometimes in context, "if." The traditional translation *behold* is outdated in modern English and fails to convey the full meaning carried by this particle. *Behold* may be rendered, "I'm ready now," "here I am," or more colloquially, "at your service." Gen 22:1 "Behold, here I am" (KJV) is translated, simply, "Here I am" (NKJV). Abraham's unqualified availability and unhesitating readiness to obey are implicit in his simple response. [1] In the NT the words (*ide, idou*) translated "lo" are derived from the verb *to see.* Imitating the Hebrew words used above, we may substitute "remember, be

149

assured, surely, consider, look, suddenly, now, here, there, see, or behold." Combined, these Hebrew and Greek words are found more than a thousand times. Try substituting the various definitions cited above, and attempt to ascertain the purpose of the writer. Though particles are indeed small words, never under-estimate their importance or their value as part of God's inspired Word.

Thought

An avid pilot finally convinced his pastor, who had never flown before, to take a ride with him. The preacher was afraid of heights, so the pilot attempted to comfort him. "Didn't the Lord say, 'I am with you always'?" (Matt 28:20), he asked. The minister answered, "Sir, the correct quote is, 'Lo, I am with you always.'"

[1] Practico & Van Pelt: Tim Laniak, 148-49.

Lord, Have Mercy

I. Mercy Defined

What does it mean to have mercy? Mercy is defined as com-passion, pity, kindness, favor, goodness, and loving-kindness.[1] Mercy suggests clemency, sympathy, leniency, forgiveness, charity, mildness, forbearance, tenderness and indulgence. To have mercy is to console, alleviate misery, succor the afflicted and feel sympathy for the distraught. Since we deal with the phrase "Lord, have mercy!" we must describe what is meant by *His* mercy. It signifies "not merely His pardon of offenders, but His attitude to man, and to the world generally, from which His pardoning mercy proceeds."[2] Mercy is God's goodness exercised in behalf of the need of His creatures.[3] This main characteristic of God contemplates man "as one who is bearing the consequences of sin, who is in a pitiable condition, and who therefore needs divine help. It may be defined as the goodness or love of God shown to those who are in misery or distress, irrespective of their deserts."[4]

II. Mercy Already Given

The God of the Bible supremely manifested His mercy when He gave His Son as the perfect Substitute for sinners. If we keep in mind that God the Father provided the sin-bearer, His Son the

Lord Jesus Christ, that all our sins might be forgiven, then there is no need for us to ask for this mercy. Why should Christians ask God for that which He has given to us already! [5] The expression, "Lord, have mercy!" is often found in the Gospels. From Matthew's Gospel alone we have the following: **Matt 9:27**: Two blind men followed the Lord Jesus, crying out, "Son of David, have mercy on us." **Matt 15:22**: A woman of Canaan cried out to the Lord saying, "Have mercy on me, O Lord, Son of David!" **Matt 17:15**: A man came to Christ, kneeling down to Him and saying, "Lord, have mercy on my son."

Matt 20:30-1: Two blind men sitting by the road, when they heard that Jesus was passing by, insisted upon crying out, "Have mercy on us, O Lord, Son of David." [6] In the examples from the Gospels are those who ask for mercy either for themselves or for others; and they ask because of their desire to be healed of blindness, epilepsy, leprosy, lameness; or to be delivered from demon-possession, or torment in Hades.

I have limited this study basically to the NT because the OT phrase, "LORD, have mercy!" is much more involved with respect to different verbs and nouns, doctrinal aspects, frequency of the words translated mercy, etc. [7] After the resurrection of Christ we do not find anyone asking for mercy. Paul thanks the Lord for His mercy shown to him and to the ill Epaphroditus (Phil 2:27); he is grateful for God's mercy that encouraged him in his ministry (2 Cor 4:1); and he thanks Christ that he obtained mercy because the evil things he did before conversion were done ignorantly in unbelief (1 Tim 1:13, 16).

In 2 Tim 1:16, 18, the apostle said, "The Lord grant mercy to the household of Onesiphorus . . . The Lord grant to him that he may find mercy from the Lord in that Day." Here the word mercy is used in the sense of reward. Because they extended such kindnesses to Paul, he prays that the Lord will bless them now, and reward Onesiphorus "in the coming day of divine reward" (2 Cor 5:10).

No one *after the resurrection* of Christ says, "Lord, have mercy" **with eternal salvation in mind.** Instead we read that those once disobedient to God have now obtained mercy (Rom 11:30; 2 Cor 4:1); according to His mercy He saved us (Titus 3:5); according to His abundant mercy has begotten us again (1 Pet 1:3, 2:10); looking for the mercy of our Lord Jesus Christ unto eternal life (Jude 21). [8] We add that the use of the word mercy in the salutations does not invalidate our point that after Christ rose from the grave we have no examples of anyone praying, "Lord, have mercy!"

> When Jesus Christ died on the cross, all of the work of God for man's salvation passed out of the realm of prophecy and became historical fact. God has now had mercy on us. For anyone to pray, "God have mercy on me," is the equivalent of asking Him to repeat the sacrifice of Christ. All the mercy that God ever will have on man, He has had already when Christ died. This is the totality of mercy. There *could* not be anymore. (Barnhouse, *Romans: God's Discipline:* 4:2)

III. Mercy Distorted?

Consider now use of the phrase "Lord, have mercy!" as it is commonly used in Black Society in America. Through the years I have heard it applied in a number of different ways, and have concluded that the interpretation of the speaker's intent has to be determined by the situation then unfolding and to some degree by the inflection [volume, pitch or tone] of the speaker's voice. I have often wondered whether the idiomatic or particular manner in which we use the phrase is an example of taking the Lord's name in vain.

Some time ago when Bernard Hopkins was middleweight champion, he got into a scuffle with some of the backers of William Joppy, an opponent of Hopkins. "The brother's got smoke coming out of his ears," (Don) King said after Hopkins had charged into the Joppy supporters. "I'm scared to death. Lord, have mercy!" What did King mean? (1) Sarcasm is often one thing detected in this use of the phrase "Lord, have mercy!" (2) It may be uttered because of something said that is regarded as outlandish or stupid, suggesting, "Now ain't that dumb!" (3) At times it expresses mock fear, feigning fright at what was just said or done (4) Its use may express a desire for God to open eyes blinded by a determination not to see, or to shut a mouth that has been running too long.

(5) Preachers may use the phrase to emphasize some point made in the sermon: (a) expressing the wonder of his statement (b) or his desire for his audience to perceive what has been said (c) or when repeated (at least three times?) may indicate time out to find

his place on his manuscript (6) Oddly enough, when something fortunate or "lucky" happens, one may be heard to say, "Lord, have mercy!" in such a way as if to say, "I can't believe it! What a surprise! Talk about luck!" Perhaps we all would do well to remember Lam 3:22: Through the LORD's mercies we are not consumed, because His compassions fail not.

[1] Girdlestone, 113.
[2] Walker, *ISBE* 3:2035.
[3] Chafer, 7:235.
[4] Berkhof, 72; cf. Thiessen, 86-87.
[5] Luke 1:78-9; Rom 9:23, 15:9; Eph 2:4; Titus 3:5; 1 Pet 1:3, 2:10; Bultmann, *TDNT* 2:484.
[6] Cf. Mark 10:47-48; Luke 16:24, 17:13, 18:38-39.
[7] Girdlestone, 111-116. Study of the term in the OT does not help concerning the current use of the phrase among Afro-Americans.
[8] Trench, *Synonyms* 171: "In the Divine mind, and in the order of our salvation as conceived therein, the *eleos* (mercy) precedes the *charis* (grace). God so *loved* the world with a pitying love (herein was the *eleos* [mercy]), that He *gave* his only begotten Son (herein the *charis* [grace]), that the world through Him might be saved (cf. Eph. 2:4; Luke 1:78-79). But in the order of the manifestation of God's purposes of salvation the grace must go before the mercy; the *charis* (grace) must go before and make way for the *eleos* (mercy)."

Man Proposes, and God Disposes: Prov 16:1, 9, 33.

Prov 16:1: *The preparations of the heart belong to man, but the answer of the tongue is from the LORD.*

The three verses from Proverbs 16 are interrelated, and all drive home the point that the God of the Bible is sovereign. The saying *Man proposes, but God disposes* is "in general agreement with biblical thought, but it does not fully express the determinism that is intrinsic to this saying. Human beings are totally dependent upon Him, even though they are at the same time morally responsible." [1] Literally Prov 16:1 reads: "To man are the dispositions of the heart; but from the LORD is the answer of the tongue." Ordinarily, we express our plans in action or speech, both areas in which humans feel they are most in control. Man plans but God "disaplans". We propose our wishes, but God responds as He thinks proper. He does as He pleases. He is not answerable to any of us, nor is He subject to "our manipulations and theological demands." [2]

Preparations are the dispositions, plans, schemes, or arrangements of man's mind, but the answer of the tongue is the LORD's. There may be a thousand schemes and arrangements ruminating in our heart, which we may earnestly desire God to bring to full effect; however, they may not be for our good or God's glory. It is therefore in our interest that God has the answer in his own power. At the same time, there is no suggestion that we can prepare our own heart to wait upon, or pray to the Lord; or that without divine guidance anything good can come from our heart (Mark 7:21-23). We may have many schemes and projects which we may beg God to accomplish, that are not of God. Indeed, we leave God out of our plans, failing to say in our heart, "If the Lord wills." (Jas 4:15). Finally, this interesting interpretation is suggested: Although persecuted Christians often plan ahead what to say in their defense at trial, the Lord will give them the proper words to speak at the time needed. [3]

Unscriptural Sayings: "God helps those who help themselves," and "If you take the first step, God will take the second step" are sayings I often hear. [4] Such phrases smack of humanism, and should not be used by Christians for a number of reasons. **First:** Jer 10:23: O LORD, I know the way of man is not in himself; it is not in man who walks to direct his own steps. This verse teaches that man cannot find the way alone, no matter how intelligent, educated, strong, rich, or determined he is.

Second: Phil 2.13: For it is God who works in you both to will and to do for (of: KJV) His good pleasure. This scripture is not directed to unbelievers but to Christians. The Sovereign God of the Bible is in absolute control, so that whatever we do that is good it is because He takes the first step. Whatever good steps we take it is because of His ordering, motivation and strength.

Keep in mind that we were dead in trespasses and sin until the Holy Spirit touched us and gave us new life in Christ. Prior to this new birth we were totally unable to please God. Now He works (energizes) in us to be "Willers" (present infinitive), and "Doers" (present infinitive) of His good will. We cannot produce in ourselves the power to will and to do. He gives us the ability so that we might "work out our own salvation," that is, solve our own problems. We are then left without excuse if we fail.

"Name it and claim it" is another spurious and trite saying. It is not biblical. With its humanist twist, it would bypass the sovereignty of God. We cannot claim anything, nor do we deserve anything in and of ourselves. So why pretend we are super spiritual? Furthermore, such language feeds on the materialistic prosperity push of our times. What counts here is "His good pleasure." We repeat: what we name and claim may not be His will or for our good.

Prov 16:9: *A man's heart plans (deviseth: KJV) his way, but the* LORD *directs his steps.*

The conditional promises of Prov 11:14 and 15:22 teach that wise guidance (good steering) and many-sided advice lead to the successful fulfillment of a plan. However, the use of human counselors is counteracted by the unconditional promise of the warning that man does *not* have the last say—God does.[5] Distinguish therefore between the human plan [6] and the divine direction.[7] The journey involves many decisions, but there is consolation in the belief that the LORD's direction brings success along the way.[8]

Does the writer in Proverbs speak of evildoers, or of the righteous, or of all people? Gill believes the verse does not deal with the wicked, for their hearts are froward (willful), continually devising mischief and evil imaginations (Prov 6:14, 18); God does not direct their goings, or prosper them. We are told that only a good or righteous person, one influenced by the Holy Spirit by God's grace is considered; only the steps of a good man are ordered by the LORD (Ps 37:23). I believe that Prov 16:9 describes all humankind, believers and unbelievers.

The old nature in all of us ever devises and thinks its own way; we are short-sighted, and cannot see what God sees. Our pride, self-confidence, arrogance, lack of spirituality all blind us to the will of God, so that God's all-ordering providence must overrule our plans. In contrast to man's anxious devising of his own way stands the LORD's sovereign disposal of his steps (JBF). "The LORD is directing both the righteous and the unrighteous. He is leading the righteous toward eternal blessing, and the wicked He is leading inexorably toward their appointment with divine judgment." [9]

Some Thoughts on Free Will: [Our will] "is free in the sense that we are not conscious of any necessity being imposed upon us. All human action is included in this conception." In order to judge us God *causes* (stronger than *permits*) blindness or strong delusion. God does not create the evil heart, "but rather brings out into overt action that which is latent within the heart to the end that it may be judged." [10] The Lord made our wills as instruments whereby he might accomplish His sovereign purpose. It is inconceivable therefore that the will of the creature should ever thwart God's ultimate purpose.

When exercising his will, man is conscious only of his freedom of action. He determines his course by circumstances, but God is the author of circumstances [11] and controls emotions, thoughts, determinations, situations, and all combinations of such. Whether or not we grasp the theology involved here—for there is an "I, yet not I" (Gal 2:20) involved for the Christian—rest assured of this major point: It is not biblical to teach (1) "if you take the first step, God will take the second," or (2) that "God helps those who help themselves." [12] God helps, period. "When we do anything at all it is really God doing it. In one sense He does it all . . . God is the One who energizes in you both the impulse and the energy to carry out the impulse. This is the mystery of grace and the cause of his energizing is his good pleasure in accomplishing salvation for His people." [13]

Prov 16:33: *The lot is cast into the lap, but its every decision is from the LORD.*

The Use of Lots: The Arabic word for *pebble* is probably related to the Hebrew word for *lot*. Little stones were used in casting lots. Since the OT does not explain or describe what a lot is or how lots were cast, it is best to assume different methods and techniques were used at different times, places and purposes. "Apparently common in various contexts in which human power of discrimination and decisions were inadequate," [14] casting lots "was probably universal in the ancient world; the deity was supposed to direct the throws," for He controls all human affairs. The people believed that "the lot did not fall indiscriminately," but was a method whereby they could determine the will of God. [15]

We must not let the use of *lots* cause us to think there is such a thing as chance, or events by chance; those events which seem most fortuitous or contingent are all disposed, ordered, and governed, by the sovereign will of God. The use of lots is to be seen as an appeal to the omniscient, omnipresent, and omnipotent God (Gill), and the decision taken as coming immediately from the Lord, so it was for them not a matter of "luck" or blind chance.

Lots were used to determine the will of God in such varied matters as having to decide boundaries, divide inheritances, allot land or territory, or slaves; select soldiers, discover evildoers and troublemakers, settle disputes, keep strong opponents apart, end contentions, choose a scapegoat; position gatekeepers, assign priests to their courses, designate persons (singers, musicians and porters) to their duties or for service, or for punishment; determine guilty persons, make decisions in important public and private affairs, distribute booty, answer questions, ascertain the future, even the dividing of our Lord's garments at Calvary. Choosing Matthias to take the place of Judas is the last instance in the NT of the use of a lot. [16]

There are differences of opinion about the rightness of using lots. One point of view asserts "this is not a special sanction of lots to determine matters, much less to determine the divine will. It is merely a declaration that the lot—the most capricious of human acts—is controlled by the all-powerful God." [17] Another commentator sees God's "tacit approval" of the use of lots, and states, "The use of the lot as a means of ascertaining the will of Deity is referred to at least without expressed censure." [18]

I agree with MacDonald who points out that in the OT and even up to the time of Pentecost the casting of the lot was a legitimate way of determining the will of God. The whole process seemed very much a matter of chance, but the Lord overruled to reveal His guidance. "Today the complete Word of God gives us a general outline of God's will. When we need specific guidance in matters not covered in the Word, we learn His will through waiting on Him in prayer. There we find that every decision is from the Lord" [19]

Examples of God's Super-ruling: Super-rule is the literal meaning of the word sovereignty. [20] God not only has created all things, and preserves them, but also exercises sovereign control over His creation, including control over human affairs. We call this sovereign control providence. [21] Some examples: (1) Balaam blessed, rather than curse Israel (Num 22:6; 23:7-12). (2) Caiaphas, high priest among those who plotted to kill the Lord Jesus, "prophesied that Jesus would die for the nation" (John 11:49-52). (3) Daniel's enemies were thrown into the den of lions from which Daniel was freed (Dan 6:24). (4) Haman hanged on the gallows he prepared for Mordecai (Esth 7:9-10). [22] (5) Herod and Pilate, Gentiles and Jews gathered together to do God's predetermined purpose (Acts 4:27-28) (6) Jezebel sought Elijah's life, but was slain (1 Kgs 19:2; 2 Kgs 9:33) (7) Jonah: ran away from Nineveh, but ended up preaching there. (8) Sold into slavery by his brothers, Joseph saves them from starvation (Gen 45:7). (9) Onesimus planned to leave Philemon forever, returns (Phlm 12). (10) Saul of Tarsus on his way to imprison Christians is arrested by the Lord (Acts 9) (11) Simon Peter having returned to the fishing business, is reminded he is to be a fisher of men (John 21; Matt 4:19).

Thought: There was a church member who would arise each morning and open up the Bible, stick a finger in it, and whatever verse it pointed to would consider that God's will for him for that day. This particular morning he got stuck in the New Testament. The first time he turned to Matt 27:5, which said, Judas "went and hanged himself." Perturbed, he tried again and turned to Luke 10:37, "Go, and do likewise." Exasperated, he tried a third time, and his finger pointed to John 13:27: "What you do, do quickly."

[1] Murphy, (WBC 22) 119-20.
[2] Van Leeuwen, *NIB* 5:163; Hawkins, *Parallel* 1226: "Man's limited ability to plan his life is the subject of verse 1"; Nelson, 1054: "Our loving Lord is in control of our seemingly chaotic situations."
[3] MacDonald, 831; Matt 10:19-20.
[4] Aeschylus (525?-456 BC), Greek dramatist, wrote (*The Seven Against Thebes*), "God loves to help him who strives to help himself." Hendrickson, 465: This universal proverb is found in Hebrew, Greek, Latin, and English (since the 15th century), and many other languages; Brewer's, 671: "The germ of the maxim lies in Prov 16:9."

[5] Parsons, *BSac* (150) 160-61.

[6] Man's devising; Wood, *TWOT* 1:329-30

[7] Oswalt, *TWOT* 1:964-65

[8] Murphy, ibid 121.

[9] Hawkins, ibid: Whatever man may intend, that which actually eventuates is decided by God.

[10] Chafer 1:240-41.

[11] Ibid., 241.

[12] To this a wag has added, "But God help those who are caught helping themselves." See note 4 above.

[13] ATR, *Paul's Joy in Christ* 82.

[14] Kalland, *TWOT* 1:171-72; Van Leeuwen, ibid; probably stones were put into the bosom-fold of a garment, or into a vessel, and shaken until one sprang out.

[15] Toy, ICC, *Proverbs* 334. Hawkins, *Parallel* 1228; Nelson, 1055.

[16] Acts 1:26. The Hebrew word is found 77 times, and the first mention of casting lots is found in Lev 16:8; Freeman, 333-4.

[17] Harris, *Wycliffe* 571.

[18] T. Davies, *ISBE* 2:861-2.

[19] MacDonald, 831, 834.

[20] Culver, *TWOT* 2:949: "Sovereignty, the legal foundation of government in the sense of ultimate authority or right. Men today are accustomed to finding this in constitutions and the nature of man, but in the Hebrew Scriptures *all authority is God's* and it is this authority which is [named] *mishpat"* (judging, disposing).

[21] Thiessen, 122.

[22] Kalland, ibid: "Throughout the book of Esther the providential timing of events decisively favors the Jews against Haman."

Mizpah: Gen 31:49: *May the LORD watch between you and me when we are absent one from another.*

Recall that for fear of Esau (Gen 27:41-46), and encouraged by his mother Rebekah, Jacob left home and fled to his uncle Laban. There he fell in love with Rachel, and served his uncle seven years for her. At the wedding Laban secretly substituted his older daughter, Leah. Jacob protested, and after Leah's week, he also married Rachel, but had to work seven more years for Laban for free. Jacob's family grew (with four wives: Leah and her handmaid, Zilpah; Rachel and her handmaid, Bilhah), and he prospered. Twelve sons and one daughter were born.

He desired to leave, but Laban knew he had been blessed by Jacob's God, and wanted him to remain. When Jehovah multiplied Jacob's cattle, Laban's children complained that Jacob had stolen everything that belonged to their father. Finally God told Jacob to leave. Laban was beginning to look at Jacob cross-eyed anyway. As Jacob told Rachel and Leah, "Your father's face is against me. But the God of my father has been with me. You know I served your father well. He has deceived me and changed my wages ten times. But the LORD protected me with him" (Gen 31.4-7).

Jacob stole away with all of his family and possessions, but when Laban was informed three days later, he pursued Jacob for seven days before catching up with him. Earlier, God had visited Laban in a dream and warned him not to touch Jacob. When he caught up with Jacob, all he could do was accuse him of sneaking away his daughters as if they were captives taken with the sword. Unknown to Jacob, Rachel had stolen the idol gods of her father to take with her, so that Laban's complaint continued: "You didn't even allow me to give you a farewell feast, or kiss my daughters and grandchildren goodbye! Besides you stole my gods!"

Jacob permitted a search, not knowing that Rachel had hidden the idols. She was not searched, for she claimed "the custom of women is upon me" (monthly period), as she sat upon the camel-saddle hiding the images. Jacob became angry because Laban had chased after him, accused him of theft, searched his property, and slowed up his journey. Laban agreed to make a covenant, [1] and a stone for a pillar was set up as a memorial. Laban gave the pillar an Aramaic name; Jacob named the pillar in Hebrew, both titles meaning, "The heap of witness." [2] They both called the pillar, Mizpah, literally, *watchtower*. [3] The heap of stones would witness Laban's request that Jacob treat Leah and Rachel well, and take no other wives. Neither one would pass over the pile of stones to do the other harm when they are "hidden one from another." Mizpah speaks of suspicion, and the lack of trust between Jacob and Laban. [4]

How did Mizpah become a benediction? Through most of my years in the church I heard the Mizpah used as a blessing. In spite of all I taught against this practice, it remained popular. I understand our desire for the Lord to watch over us after we leave church. But we must learn not to take phrases out of context in order to prove or back up some point that *is* valid, and which has better contextual support in other scriptures. The following

160

comments call for abandoning the use of Mizpah for a benediction:

> It is unfortunate that this unkind word, full of suspicion, should in our day so often be used as a benediction at parting. This almost amounts to a wicked perversion of Scripture. . . Mizpah was not originally the pleasant term that uninstructed Christian sentiment has made it to become. It is a sinister word containing an implicit threat . . . The use of the name [Mispah] in Gen 31:49 . . . originally . . . was far from a benediction. It was a sign of a kind of boundary between Jacob and his hostile father-in-law. Both parties here promised to keep the peace . . . Often used incorrectly as a benediction, in their original context these words were rather, a malediction. Laban and Jacob distrusted one another. (Leupold, *Genesis* 2:856) [5]

[1] Schrader, *Parallel* 83, calls it "a mutual non-aggression pact"; MacDonald, 67, "a nonaggression treaty."

[2] Yates, *Wycliffe* 35: 'Outlook Point,' where a watcher could see the entire country in both directions; OED 9:922. Adventist groups have used the interpretation 'watchtower' as a motto.

[3] Ewing, *ISBE* 3:2068-9. Hartley, *TWOT* 2:773 (Mispah).

[4] Wenham, (WBC 2) 280; Leupold, *Genesis:* 2:855-58 brings out the bad side of Laban's involvement here, causing one to wonder if there is anything good that might be said of Laban: (1) "Laban uses many words to cover up his untrustworthiness" (2) seeks to create the impression "that Jacob is a slippery character who has to be bound fast by a whole series of stipulations" (3) attempts to terrify Jacob "by hard and sharp terms" (4) tries to make out that the idea for the stone witness is his idea rather than Jacob's (5) implies Jacob is the bad guy who needs to be watched (6) "Whoever may be Laban's god, Laban does not require watching; but may Jacob's God (Jehovah) watch over Jacob and keep him from harming Laban" (7) Laban's comment about Jacob's treatment of his daughters is the slanderous effort born of Laban's "wicked hypocrisy" (8) His bad conscience moves him to reckon with the possibility of Jacob returning to punish him (9) Finally, note Laban's idolatry as he accuses Jacob, "but why did you steal my gods?" (v30); Laban's god is that of his grandfather, Nahor.

Unfortunately Quell, *TDNT* 2:113, allows his acceptance of the documentary theory muddy the waters of interpretation. He has Jacob calling on the God of Nahor (v53), when it is Laban speaking throughout verses 51-53a. Laban the polytheist wants Jacob's Jehovah to watch over them, suggesting Jacob alone bears surveillance. No effort is made, as Quell wrongly claims, to have the one and the same God to witness the transaction; rather, Laban desires all the gods in on the deal to guarantee its fulfillment! Note that "Jacob swore by the Fear of his father Isaac" (v53b; also v 42). *Fear* means the object of fear, or reverence. Here the word Fear designates deity; Bowling, *TWOT* 2:721: "God, as an external object of terror, is in view in the phrase 'Fear of Isaac.'" Schneider, *TDNT* 5:459: "In Israel the Law prescribed (De 6:13, 10:20) that oaths should be by Yahweh. Israel's monotheism found expression here in the fact that only the oath by Yahweh was permitted; all other gods were excluded. Hence the oath is a solemn confession of the one God."

[5] Cf. Kevan, *NBC* 98; Hartley, ibid; Sco Gen 31:49.

Patience of Job: Jas 5:11: *Ye have heard of the patience* (NKJV: *perseverance*) *of Job* (KJV).

I. Job's Afflictions

Here is the only mention made of Job in the NT. The 'myriad of misfortunes' by which Satan tested Job, combined with the charges against him by "his friends"—have led to the expression *the patience of Job.* [1] Calvin describes Job's experiences as unique troubles from which, "as far as we can learn from histories," no one else has ever experienced, "and yet he emerged from so deep a gulf." MacDonald (2241) agrees: "Job is a fine example of perseverance or fortitude. Few if any men in the history of the world have ever suffered so much loss in so short a time as Job."

Chapters 1-2 describe Job's miseries: tested by Satan, his stock (oxen, donkeys, sheep, camels) stolen or burned up; most of his servants slain by the sword or by fire; his seven sons and three daughters killed when the house they were in was struck and blown down by a great wind. Satan's second assault includes the affliction of Job's body with painful, loathsome sores (7:5); harassment by his wife; and in chapters 3-31 he is maligned by his friends who insist that his misfortunes are the result of secret sin. [2]

II. Does Job Exemplify Patience?

Those who insist that Job really was **not** patient bring his record to our attention: (1) he curses the day he was born (3:1; 10:18) (2) he describes his grief or vexation as heavier than the sand of the sea (6:2-3) (3) he complains that the LORD crushes him and multiplies his wounds without cause (9:17) (4) he indignantly refutes his friends' lack of faith in him (5) and expresses the belief that God has forsaken him, and wronged him. Job complained but did not renounce the LORD. Calvin states: Sometimes Job failed and displayed many signs of impatience, he sometimes failed through the infirmity of the flesh, or murmured within himself, yet he surrendered himself to God, and was ever willing to be restrained and ruled by Him. Still there are those who do not accept the idea of considering Job a model of patience, but rather emphasize his *impatience!*

On the surface it is not clear why Job is chosen to exemplify patience in suffering. He was anything but an example of a godly person who was patient in the midst of adversity. The characteristic Job in the canonical Scripture was not a silent party to his suffering; rather, he was one who complained bitterly to God because of his dire circumstances. (Martin, [WBC 48] 194-5) [3]

III. Correct Definition:

Two matters help us here: (1) awareness of the difference between Job's behavior in the Prologue (chs 1-2), and his experiences in the Dialogues (chs 3-31); (2) the study of the particular word translated patience in Jas 5:11. How Job copes with his problems in the Prologue is exactly what we should call patience; however in the dramatic Dialogues, Carr says Job "exhibits anything but a patient demeanor." To his visitors his words "were symptoms of an extremely sensitive, vehement and impatient character which has little of Christian gentleness in it, but excites our admiration by its passionate outbursts of exalted feeling. James does not offer the example of Job for our imitation in this sense. He is not an example of patience by the **excepted sense of the word** . . . But in his heart he knows that God whom he defies and accuses is not the real God, the God whom his inmost consciousness knew to be absolutely true and loving and just." [4]

This brings us to a major point in our use of the expression *the patience of Job*. Basically, there are two different words rendered *patience*. **First,** there is **makrothumia.** *Makros* means long, long-lasting; *thumos* means passion, anger, and outburst. Combined we have long-suffering, slow to anger, the opposite of "boiling mad, a hot-head" seeking revenge. Here is a word that describes patience when people abuse us, when we refrain from avenging ourselves, even though we have the power to do so. [5] Makrothumia speaks of our ability to be "cool-cat Christians" when folks provoke us, and not "blaze up into anger" or give folks "a piece of our mind." [6]

Second: In Jas 5:7, 8 and 10 makrothumia (or the verb makrothumeo), is translated patient, patiently or patience. However, in Jas 5:11 **hupomone** is used. *Hupo* means under (hypo); the verb *meno* means to remain; so literally, this word for patience means remaining under, to endure, thus to bravely persevere under misfortunes and trials; it is that "temper which does not easily succumb under suffering" (Thayer, 387, 644), and does not lose heart or courage. Here we have no choice but to bear certain things: sufferings, trials, religious temptation, etc.

> Hupomone-patience is endurance under imposed sufferings and religious temptation. The battle which has to be fought through is thus more inward, endurance in face of unfavorable relationships. In this respect hupomone-patience differs from makrothumia-long-suffering, which is—often at least—patience with people. The endurance of the Christian will not be complaining, weary, despondent or grumbling. It is inspired and filled by a pious and heroic will to hold firm. In persevering, the Christian is not referred to his own power. The needed power of resistance is given him by God Himself, who imparts hupomone-patience (Rom 15:5). Job is the great example of this perseverance or endurance under affliction. (Hauck, *TDNT* 4:587-8) [7]

IV. Summary: Failure to study the original language often causes trouble when two different words are given the same translation (cf. KJV: Jas 5:7-11). [8] Calvin concludes: Though his patience was somewhat deficient, "it is yet deservedly commended." Gill observes: though he afterwards let fall some expressions of impatience, yet he was humbled for them, and brought to repentance. M. Henry states: At no time did Job act amiss; he did not attribute folly to God. H. Morris, *Defender's* 1390, reminds us that James teaches that the story of Job is not fiction, or merely a "great dramatic poem" dealing with the problem of undeserved suffering. Job's patience is interpreted in the light of the purpose of the Lord. It was more than a courageous endurance of suffering and loss. The blissful conclusion at which Job arrived was that *the LORD is very pitiful, and of tender mercy*; and not only did Job discover that God has a great purpose in what happens in our lives, but that "patient endurance can sustain itself on the conviction that hardships are not meaningless." [9]

[1] Hendrickson, 396.

[2] McNab, *NBC* 1127; Clarke; Gill; Stevens, *Parallel* 2596.

[3] Martin defines endurance (the word rendered *patience* in Jas 5:11) as a rugged determination not to renounce one's faith and not to fall out of the race. Moreover, it is an activity demanding strenuous courage and firm fortitude, once we are persuaded that our lives are in God's hands even though outward circumstances seem to overwhelm. Carr, 511: Job is *not* the biblical picture of a patient man who accepts without murmuring or complaint all the evils that befall him! Cf. Fine, 28: Honesty, not patience is the real virtue of Job. There is a patient Job, and we meet him for a couple of chapters, but not after those chapters.

[4] Carr, ibid, 513.

[5] Trench, *Synonyms* 195; Christ's endurance described, Heb 12:3.

[6] Prov 15:18; 16:32; Job's wife (2:9) gives us an example of an outburst: "Curse God and die!"

[7] I greatly annotated Hauck's notes. Walker, *ISBE* 3:2263: In the NT *hupomone* carries with it the ideas of endurance, continuance.

[8] Carr, ibid, 512, 516: there is a difference between *makrothumia* long-suffering and *hupomone* endurance or fortitude. "And it is the latter and not the first which is attributed to Job." Failure to discover the different words rendered patience leads Johnson, *NIB* 12:221 to warn: "This is not the picture of Job that the dialogues in the biblical book suggests. But his reading is not completely off the mark. Job, after all, argued with God even as he looked to God for vindication, but he did not turn in spite against his fellows. . . It is this sense of purpose and pertinacity in spite of suffering that makes *hupomone* or fortitude, a higher and more inspiring quality

than *makrothumia* or long-suffering. It contains the secret of success in every endeavor." Johnson's point is indeed the main ingredient in Job's patience as defined by the Greek word used in Jas 5:11.

[9] McNab, ibid; Wessel, *Wycliffe* 1438-39.

Physician Heal Thyself - Luke 4:23: *He said to them, "You will surely say this proverb to Me, 'Physician, heal yourself!'"*

In Nazareth our Lord quotes a well-known proverb, probably in common use at that time. [1] However, His own countrymen are not happy with His discourse. They feel that He had worked miracles in other towns, but failed to dignify the town where He lived for about thirty years, the home of Joseph and Mary. And so He is held in little esteem. From their point of view He treated them with little respect, so they believe they have good reason to reject Him. His failure to perform miracles in Nazareth, while famous for the wonderful acts done elsewhere, wounded their pride. It is true that He "laid his hands on a few sick folk and healed them," apparently quite privately; but it is recorded that "He could do no mighty work there" (Mark 6:5). Unbelief prevents blessings.

Adding to their dissatisfaction with Him is their especial awareness of His ministry in Capernaum. Christ had made that city "the main center of His activity during a large part of His public ministry." [2] There in Capernaum He performed 'mighty works,' casting out demons, and healing "many who were sick with various diseases" (Matt 11:23; Mark 1:34). No wonder they were "miffed." [3] Throughout His ministry the sign-seeking Pharisees disputed with Him, seeking a sign from heaven (Mark 8:11). His own unbelieving brothers sought Him to make Himself known openly (John 7:3-5). The Pharisees again asked Him for a sign from heaven. Men who mocked, beat, blindfolded and struck Him on the face, inquired, "Prophesy! Who is the one who struck You?" Out of curiosity, Herod Antipas questioned Him, hoping to see Him perform some miracle. The sneering crowd (people, rulers, soldiers) at the cross mocked Him (Luke 11:16; 22:64; 23:8-9, 35-37).

But now in Luke 4:23 we find the Savior, having just finished reading Isa 61:1-2 is questioned, "Is this not Joseph's son?" Christ is aware of their thoughts, and responds: "You will surely say this proverb to Me, 'Physician, heal yourself! Whatever we have heard

166

done in Capernaum, do also here in Your country.'" How is the proverb "Physician, heal yourself" to be interpreted? [4] In both of the following interpretations there is a tone of sarcasm towards the Lord who is told, "Do also here." [5]

(1) Ordinarily, you would think, "Do for yourself what you have done for others." In other words, "Heal your own lameness." Since you claim to heal other folks, cure your own condition. Here we are reminded of the mockery heard under the cross: "Save Yourself, and come down from the cross! He saved others; Himself He cannot save." Even one of the robbers kept saying, "If You are the Christ, save Yourself and us!" Moffatt: Doctor, cure yourself! CEV: Doctor, first make yourself well.

(2) Another perspective suggests that "Charity begins at home" (see p 55). Thus the exhortation is, "Do here in Nazareth what we heard You did in Capernaum. If You want us to respect You, then You must help us. This is Your town, so You should take care of us! Treat us right and we will treat You well." "This would not amount exactly to a physician healing himself. We must be content with the general idea: every sensible benefactor begins in his immediate surroundings." [6]

"Christ was aware that his townsmen would object this to him, that if he was the person he was said to be, and could do the miracles and cures which were ascribed to him, he ought to do something of this kind at home, among them, who were his townsmen, neighbors, relations, and acquaintance; that is, heal their sick, lame, blind, leprous, deaf, and dumb: and that this is the sense of it, is manifest from what follows" (Gill). Luke 4:23 (LB): "Physician, heal yourself—meaning, 'Why don't you do miracles here in your hometown like those you did in Capernaum?'" Thayer also applies the proverb to Christ in this sense: "Come forth from your lowly and mean condition and create for yourself authority and influence by performing miracles among us also, that we may see that you are what you profess to be."

(3) An alternative interpretation considers the proverb is used as a personal attack or affront to the Lord, an attempt to humiliate Him. "Though in form a request, the proverb is best understood as functioning as a retort, almost an insult . . . who do you think you are to offer to us what you do not have for yourself? The request is not for an implementation in Nazareth of the ministry announced in vv 18-19. Rather it is a cynical demand for a display of dazzling miracles to dispel the impression that only Joseph's son is here." [7]

The Lord gives us the meaning of the proverb as He uses it; He understood well the response of the crowd, and knew they were anxious for Him to do miraculous works among them. I accept Barnes' conclusion:

> Suppose that a man should attempt to heal another when he was himself diseased in the same manner; it would be natural to ask him first to cure himself, and thus to render it manifest that he was worthy of confidence. The connection of this proverb, here, is this: 'You profess to be the Messiah. You have performed miracles at Capernaum. You profess to be able to deliver us from our maladies, our sins, our afflictions. Show that you have the power, that you are worthy of our confidence, by working miracles here, as you profess to have done at Capernaum.' . . . It was only a demand that he would show the proper evidence 'by miracles' why they should trust in him, and he proceeds to show them why he would not give them this evidence.

[1] Bullinger, 757; Macalister, *ISBE* 4:2394; Barnes; Stevenson, 599: Christ, as He himself indicated, was merely repeating a proverb which had been current for at least a thousand years, and which is still one of the most widely quoted of all proverbs, not only in English, but in practically all languages. Its popularity is no doubt due to the fact that it is the hardest and most unanswerable of all taunts.

[2] Ewing & Kyle, *ISBE* 1:566.

[3] Culpepper, *NIB* 9:107.

[4] Plummer, ICC, *Luke* 126, acknowledges its meaning is disputed.

[5] ATR: Do it here in thy own country and town and do it now. Jesus applies the proverb to himself as an interpretation of their real attitude towards him.

[6] A. B. Bruce, *ExpGT* 1:490.

[7] Nolland, (WBC 35A) 199-200. Culpepper, ibid, says this is the natural sense of the proverb and is consistent with how it is used elsewhere, but it does not explain the sharp shift in tone from the preceding verse.

Pride Goes Before a Fall: Prov 16:18: *Pride goes before destruction, and a haughty spirit before a fall.*

This proverb is called *synonymous* because the first half (pride goes before destruction) says practically the same thing as the second half (a haughty spirit before a fall). In an *antithetic* proverb one part says the opposite of the other part; and the word 'but' helps to identify it (Prov 16:9, 22).

I. Definition of Pride

The word translated *pride* (*gaon*) means exaltation, majesty, excellence, and is derived from a verb meaning *to rise up*. It has both a bad sense and a good sense, or "justifiable pride." [1] "The word pride (or its synonyms) can be used either positively or negatively in the OT . . . pride is not intrinsically wrong . . . Sin enters the picture when there is a shift of ultimate confidence from God as object and source to oneself as object and source." [2] The apostle Paul speaks of boasting as a healthy pride that is the opposite of that bragging that is based on outward appearance and not in the heart (2 Cor 5:12; 7:4; 8:24). [3] In Jeremiah we find an excellent example of the boasting (glorying) that pleases the Lord:

> Let not the wise man glory in his wisdom, let not the mighty man glory in his might, nor let the rich man glory in his riches; but let him who glories glory in this, that he understands and knows Me, that I am the LORD, exercising lovingkindness, judgment, and righteousness in the earth. For in these I delight,' says the LORD (Jer 9:23-24).

By far the negative trait is emphasized. This pride is bad; it is conceit, arrogance, haughtiness, presumption, "a cynical insensitivity to the needs of others"; it is puffed-up-ness, swell headedness; "a high or overweening opinion of one's own qualities, attainments, or estate, which gives rise to a feeling and attitude of superiority over and contempt for others; inordinate self-esteem." [4] One proof of our adamic nature is the fact that our vocabulary has more ways of expressing evil than of expressing that which is righteous; we are guilty even of taking a "good" word and intensifying it so that it becomes a "bad" word. As a boy I heard folks say, "I blessed him out!" meaning I gave him a piece of my mind, or cursed him. [5] Pride then, in many passages "is regarded as the basic attitude of the foolish and ungodly man. For in it we see that man desires to stand on his own feet and not to depend on God, that he builds on that which he himself can accomplish and control." [6]

II. Definition of Destruction

Destruction is the translation given to the Hebrew word (*sheber*); it means to shiver, break in pieces, fracture, breach, crush, crash or dash in pieces, overthrow, or ruin (Girdlestone, 272). It is used to describe the breaking of pottery, fracture of a limb, shattering or crushing of a wall. Murphy renders: "Before a **collapse,** pride." [7] The noun "is expressive of (physical) calamity either at the national level or at the personal level," [8] figuratively, as of an individual.

III. Definition of Haughty

The Hebrew verb (*gabah*) means to be high, exalted, lofty, or tall (as a tree or the heavens). Used in a bad sense, lofty means haughty. "Ordinarily negative, haughty can also be used positively to mean courage and daring." [9] One who has a haughty spirit exalts himself above others; he despises (looks down his nose at) others. "The contrast of pride and humility is conveyed in the imagery of high and low: haughty spirit vs. lowly spirit." [10]

IV. Definition of Fallen

The Hebrew verb (*kashal*) means to stumble, stagger or totter; the noun (*kishshalon*) used in Prov 16:18 is rendered a stumbling. Usually it is taken literally of physical falling, as from fatigue, weariness, or weakness experienced fleeing from enemies.[11] However, here it is used as a figure of speech describing ruin, failure, calamity, or misfortune.

V. Examples of the Proud Who Have Fallen

Now the Bible offers much proof of the peril of pride: (1) **Lucifer (Satan)** said in his heart, "I will ascend into heaven, I will exalt my throne above the stars of God; I will also sit on the mount of the congregation on the farthest sides of the north; I will ascend above the heights of the clouds, I will be like the Most High." For him and his angels God has prepared a Hell. [12] (2) **The Pharaoh of Egypt** told Moses: "Who is the LORD that I should obey His voice to let Israel go? I do not know the LORD, nor will I let Israel go" (Exod 5:2). The last time the Pharaoh saw Moses he said, "Get away from me! Take heed to yourself and see my face no more! For in the day you see my face you shall die!" So Moses said, "You have spoken well. I will never see your face again." (Exod 10:28-29). (3) **Goliath,** over 9 feet tall, looked down his nose at David, and said, "Come to me, and I will give your flesh to the birds of the air and the beasts of the field! . . . Am I a dog that you come to me with sticks?" (1 Sam 17:43-44; my thought: "How dare you send this flea out to me?"). With a sling and a stone David struck the arrogant giant in his forehead and killed him, then took Goliath's sword and cut off his head!

(4) **King Nebuchadnezzar** walking about his palace, boasted, "Is not this great Babylon that I have built for a royal dwelling by my mighty power and for the honor of my majesty?" While the word was still in his mouth, God spoke to him, took away his kingdom, and his mind; and Nebuchadnezzar lived like an animal for seven years. [13] (5) Then there is **Herod Agrippa I,** who on a set day, arrayed in royal apparel, sat on his throne and gave an oration to the people who kept calling, "The voice of a god and not of a man!" Then immediately an angel of the Lord struck him because he did not give glory to God. And he was eaten by worms and died (Acts 12:21-23).

(6) The **rich farmer** (Luke 12:16-20) whose land yielded such a bountiful crop that he thought within himself, "What shall I do, since I have no room to store my crops? Here's what I will do: I will pull down my barns and build greater, and there I will store all my crops and my goods. And I will say to my soul, 'Soul, you have many goods laid up for many years; take your ease; eat, drink, and be merry.'" But God said to him, "Fool! This night your soul will be required of you; then whose will those things be which you have provided?" Pride can be dangerous.

VI. Summary

We have seen examples of God's judgment upon the proud. Because "everyone proud in heart is an abomination to the LORD", it is an act of justice that those who have lifted up themselves should be laid low and humiliated (Prov 16:5; 29:23; Isa 13:11). Pride inevitably leads to destruction, brings disgrace or shame, breeds quarrels and goes before corruption and ruin (Prov 11:2; 13:10; Jer 13:9). God puts down those who are conceited. Stuck-up people usually suffer some humiliating experience, designed to deflate their ego. "It takes only a small pin to prick a large balloon." [14] "The most certain feature of pride in the Bible is that it precedes a downfall." [15] For Christians the most effective antidote for pride is to let the humility of Christ rule in our hearts and minds (Phil 2:5-8; Isa 26:3).

Thought

A man-about town was sitting in a barber's chair having a shave and a manicure. "You're cute, baby," he said to the pretty young lady giving him a manicure. Believing he was God's gift to women, he asked, "How about a date tonight?" She smiled sweetly and said, "I'm sorry, but you see, I'm married." "Big deal," said the would-be lover, "Phone the bum and tell him you'll be home late tonight." She said, "You tell him. He's shaving you." Pride can be very dangerous.

[1] Bultmann, *TDNT* 3:646; Brewer's, 856: The good is a sense of personal worth. It has further the meaning of ostentation, magnificence or anything that one can be proud of.

[2] Harris, *TWOT* 1:143.

[3] *DBI* 661-62.

[4] OED: 12: 462-3.

[5] BDB, 138-9: barak, *to bless, kneel,* with the antithetical meaning *curse* . . . a blessing overdone becomes a curse: Job 1:5, 11; 2:5, 9.

[6] Bultmann, *TDNT* 3:646.

[7] Murphy, (WBC 22) 117.

[8] Hamilton, *TWOT* 2:901; Prov 17:19; 18:12.

[9] Nelson, 1057.

[10] Van Leeuwen, *NIB* 5:161.

[11] Harris, *TWOT* 1:457; Murphy, ibid.

[12] Isa 14:13-14; 1 Tim 3:6; Matt 25:41.

[13] Dan 4:29-33; Gill: very often when a man has got to the height of his riches and honor, and is swelling with pride and vanity on account of it, he is on the precipice of ruin, and his fall is immediate; which was the case of Nebuchadnezzar, who while he was expressing himself in the haughtiness of his spirit, being in the height of his glory, his kingdom departed from him.

[14] MacDonald, 832.

[15] *DBI* 662.

Raising Cain, the Devil, and Hell

"Raising Cain," "raising the Devil," and "raising Hell" are not terms found in the Bible. You knew this, of course. But the words Cain, Devil, and Hell are found in the Scriptures and what we learn from the Bible about them helps us to some degree to understand the use of such expressions.

I. Cain: What does it mean to "raise Cain"? The Bible portrait of this firstborn son of Adam and Eve is not a pretty one (Gen 4). Cain failed to worship God the way God desired. We believe he was taught God's will in this matter by his father, Adam, but chose to worship God his own way; consequently, his sacrificial offering was not accepted.[1] Hatred for his own brother, Abel, led to the first murder. Because Cain's "works were evil and his brother's righteous," he slew Abel (Gen 4:8); and lied to Jehovah when asked of his brother's whereabouts. Cain's behavior indicated he "was of the wicked one," Satan (1 John 3:12). It is easy to see how his violent anger and fratricide is associated with the phrase that means to "cause a commotion or make a noisy disturbance." [2] To cause, rouse, stir up, or instigate trouble is termed "to raise Cain." However, I do not think this slang expression penetrates the awful depth of Cain's deeds.

II. The Devil: "Raising the Devil" may be seen as synonymous or an alternative to "Raising Cain." [3] It means 'to cause much trouble or a loud disturbance;' to cause a commotion, disturbance; to revel, celebrate wildly; make an emphatic protest or take drastic measures. To my mind "raising the Devil" is worse than "raising Cain," inasmuch as Cain was a child of the Devil. Satan is older than Cain; there is no creature in the entire world that is as wicked as Satan.

III. Hell: How many times have you heard the words, "Go to Hell!" When we were boys and someone commanded, "Go to Hell!" our response was, "What's your address?" How often have you been ordered to proceed on such a journey? [4] Where would you go? The location of Hell is important because it is a specific place. Where? I do not know. Unfortunately, there are those who do not believe Hell is a place. [5] The one word "hell" is used in the KJV to translate (1) *Sheol*; also rendered *the grave, the pit* (2)

173

Hades, the NT word corresponding to the OT word, Sheol. Both words refer to the present temporary abode of unbelievers awaiting the final judgment at the Great White Throne (Rev 20:11-15). (3) *Gehenna,* presently empty, is the future eternal home of unbelievers. *The Lake of Fire,* (Rev 20:10, 14), is another name for Gehenna. [6] (4) *Tartarus* (2 Pet 2:4), where presently certain angels are incarcerated.[7]

Summary: The expressions "raising Cain," "raising the Devil," and "raising Hell" describe rowdy or disruptive behavior. They are slang terms meaning to make a great disturbance, behave in a boisterous manner. If I would grade them for their degree of horrific and evil effect, I would make "raising Cain" the mildest. "Raising the Devil" is worse, primarily because Cain "was of that wicked one." This means Cain is identified spiritually as a child of the Devil." [8] "Raising Hell" is the strongest expression of the three, for Hell is the eternal home of Satan for whom it was prepared (Matt 25:41). Note the first inhabitants of the Lake of Fire will be two human beings, the First Beast and the Second Beast (False Prophet), Rev 20:10. Then Satan; and Cain will probably be next.

Thought
"Raising Cain": The first recorded use of the expression, in a joke printed in the *St. Louis Pennant* in 1840, shows that it was well-known at the time: "Why have we every reason to believe that Adam and Eve were both rowdies? Because they both raised Cain."

[1] Gen 4:3-5; Jude 11 calls it "the way of Cain."
[2] Brewer's 886.
[3] Hendrickson, 605.
[4] J. B. Phillips renders Acts 8:20: *But Peter said to him, "To Hell with you and your money!"* His footnote states: "These words are exactly what the Greek means. It is a pity that their real meaning is obscured by modern slang usage." "Isn't this profanity? Should it appear in a Bible translation?" Ehrenstein (*Eternity* 39) answers: "Phillips does not pretend to give a direct translation of the Greek NT. His purpose is to render the text into contemporary English, the sort of speech we might use, or hear used, today. Literally, Acts 8:20 reads, 'Your silver [money], may it [go] into destruction

with you.' The concept of 'destruction' in biblical theology would be equivalent to 'hell.' Thus, Phillips would be quite correct in saying 'to hell with you and your money.' It would not be profanity any more than any reference to hell in a biblical or theological context would be."

5 Pilgrim, Luke 16:23: The Place Called Hell. Cf. *Ebony Magazine,* "What Happened to Hell?" Jan 1961. Kenneth Bronstein, head of New York City Atheists, says that he's setting up a D.C. office called the Center for Atheism to fight for the godless. He explains: "I'm a guy who likes to raise hell, but since there isn't one, we'll lobby." Someone wrote: "Hell is a place where you don't see God, and that's what burns you up." Cf. *USN&WR,* 25 Mar 91, "Hell's Sober Comeback" 56-64.

6 "The images of darkness and fire appear contradictory, but they should be regarded as symbols pointing to a reality more horrific than either symbol can convey by itself. In fact, biblical images of Hell leave many details to the imagination, perhaps because no picture is capable of doing justice to the reality" (*DBI:* "Hell" 376-7).

7 In his book, *The Origin of Heathendom,* Ben Adam teaches those imprisoned in Tartarus shall be annihilated.

8 1 John 3:12, Nelson, 2145; H. Morris, *Defender's* 1414; F. F. Bruce, 94: he "showed his spiritual lineage."

Ram in the Bush: Gen 22:13: *Then Abraham lifted his eyes and looked, and there behind him was a ram caught in a thicket by its horns. So Abraham went and took the ram, and offered it up for a burnt offering instead of his son.*

"No other story in Genesis, indeed in the whole OT, can match the sacrifice of Isaac for its haunting beauty or its theological depth." [1] According to the story, there came a day when God tested Abraham's "sincerity, loyalty, and faith." He said, "Take now your son, your only son Isaac, whom you love, and go to the land of Moriah, and offer him there as a burnt offering on one of the mountains of which I shall tell you." Abraham obeyed, and on the third day of his journey he "lifted his eyes and saw the place afar off." In a remarkable statement to his servants, Abraham ordered, "Stay here with the donkey; the lad (young Isaac) and I will go yonder and worship, *and we will come back to you.*"

The two prepared—taking wood, a knife, and fire (probably a bundle of burning twigs or pan of embers)—and went forth. When Isaac inquired, "Where is the lamb for a burnt offering?" his father replied, "My son, God will provide for Himself the lamb for a burnt offering." Abraham built an altar, placed the wood in order, tied up Isaac his son and placed him on the altar, upon the wood.

As he stretched out his hand and took the knife to slay his son, the Angel of the LORD [2] spoke from heaven saying, "Do not lay your hand on the lad, or do anything to him; for **now I know** [3] that you fear God, since you have not withheld your son, your only son, from Me." The phrase *now I know* is accommodative language, used by the LORD to reassure Abraham of His approval of his obedience of faith. He wanted Abraham to know that He knew! God let Abraham know that he had passed his "final examination" [4] "The sacrifice was already accomplished in his heart, and he had fully satisfied the requirements of God" (K&D).

Earlier, Abraham saw the place afar off to which the LORD had told him to go (v 4). Now he lifted up his eyes and looked, and there behind him was a ram caught in a thicket by its horns (v 13). "This process testifies to a *progressively clearer seeing*" [5] and teaches us the joy of seeing what God wants us to see! Indeed, we may note here that the word ***provide*** means to see, to furnish, look at, inspect. [6] In v14, The-LORD-Will-Provide or Jehovah-Jireh, the word *jireh* comes from the same verb used in v8 rendered "provide."

Some scholars have suggested that perhaps Abraham had not seen the animal earlier because of his "intense preoccupation and mental struggle" over Isaac [7] or because the animal had struggled so long it became exhausted, and remained motionless. Then reviving, it again struggled, and Abraham heard the rustling behind him "making a noise." Where the animal came from is not known. Gill suggests it was a stray from nearby flocks. Another idea is that the ram was immediately created by the LORD for the occasion.

Finally, see the emphasis on **substitution**, for normally in the OT the idea of representation is the primary expression with respect to offering sacrifices. Representation is distinguished from "the strict idea of substitution," [8] for usually the beast represented symbolically the one(s) who offered it. However, Gen 22:13 states, "So Abraham went and took the ram, and offered it up for a burnt offering **instead** of his son." In providing the ram as Isaac's substitute, "God spared Abraham's heart a pang He would not spare His own." [9] The sacrifice of Isaac could be stopped (and was), but "the sacrifice of the Son of God on Calvary could not" [10]

Thought: In some Black-American church circles when someone is called upon at the last moment to pinch-hit for a speaker or preacher who does not show up on time or has been prevented from appearing, you may hear it said that "God has provided us with a ram in the bush." To this referral the one chosen as a substitute may respond: "Doesn't the Bible also say, 'Lay hands suddenly on no man'?" (1 Tim 5:22). I remember one night at a meeting of the Congress of Christian Education that the Reverend George Bell was scheduled to preach. When the time for preaching came and he was not there, unexpectedly I was chosen to preach. While I was preaching, Dr. Bell came in, but I continued speaking. Later, I mentioned to the congregation that prior to beginning the sermon I kept watching the door for him to enter, so that I might announce that "I had been saved by the Bell."

[1] Wenham, (WBC 2) 112.
[2] Walvoord, *BSac* (140) 102: In all probability the Lord Jesus Christ, an OT theophany (God appearing).
[3] Brueggemann (*Genesis,* 187) combines Gen 18:21 with the testing of Abraham in Gen 22:1-10 as suggestive that God wants to know something. He says, "It is not a game with God. God genuinely does not know!" His ignorance is removed in verse 12, for now He knows. Fretheim, *NIB* 1:497, supports this point of view, stating: "God does not teach; rather, God learns. For the sake of the future, God needs to know about Abraham's trust. While God knew what was likely to happen, God does not have absolute certainty as to how Abraham would respond."
   This is nonsense! Nelson 45-46: "Certainly God knew ahead of time how this event would end. But in these words, God stood beside His servant Abraham, experiencing each moment with him and applauding his complete trust (18:19)." Chafer 1:196: "If God be ignorant of the future actions of free agents, there could be no assured divine control of human destiny as pledged in every unconditional covenant God has made, and as guaranteed in every prophecy of the Scriptures . . . then He is ever coming to know things He did not know before and must be changing His plans

177

and purposes constantly . . . The divine foreknowledge does not coerce; it merely knows what the human choice will be."

[4] Pilgrim, 39.

[5] Fretheim, *NIB* 1:495.

[6] *Raah* (see) is used 1315 times; Culver, *TWOT* 2:823: "This word has extended and metaphorical meanings," one of which is the sense "'to provide,' usually of God's provision (as in English to see to something is to provide it)." Our English word, "provide," is derived from the Latin; *pro* means "ahead" or "forward" and *videre* means "to see." It is literally, to foresee, to look after.

[7] Leupold, 2:630; Nelson, 46: "With his attention solely on the awful task at hand, Abraham had not seen the ram until he looked for it."

[8] Girdlestone, 133; Pilgrim, 39: the ram is a type of Christ as the substitute.

[9] MacDonald, 59.

[10] Walvoord, *BSac* ibid; Rom 8:32.

Reap What You Sow: Gal 6:7: *Do not be deceived, God is not mocked; for whatever a man sows, that he will also reap. For he who sows to his flesh will of the flesh reap corruption, but he who sows to the Spirit will of the Spirit reap everlasting life.*

I. Other Expressions

From the OT we have: Exod 21:24: Eye for eye, tooth for tooth, etc. Job 4:8: Even as I have seen, those who plow iniquity and sow trouble reap the same. Prov 22:8: He who sows iniquity will reap sorrow. Hos 8:7: They sow the wind, and reap the whirlwind. Compare the sowing and reaping in 2 Cor 9:6. When I was 32 years of age, and visited my wife's home in Parmele, N. C., I discovered that peanuts grew under the ground. Never having lived on a farm I had learned in other ways however, the figurative meaning of such agricultural terms as—plowing, sowing, reaping and harvesting—especially the proverbial saying, "You reap what you sow."

Some examples I remember from boyhood are: (1) "What goes around comes around." (2) "God don't like ugly." (3) "Tit for tat" [1] (4) "Payback is a dog!" (5) "He got a dose of his own medicine." (6) "Chickens come home to roost." [2] This latter expression means "Curses rebound on the curses, just as chickens which stray during the day return to their roost at night." To come home to roost: "usually said of a lie, fault, misdeed or the like, which eventually rebounds on its perpetrator. [3] (7) Later in life I heard the expression "poetic justice." [4]

II. Context

Galatians 6:6 commands: *Let him who is taught the word share in all good things with him who teaches.* Perhaps my "pastoral reluctance" prevented me from instructing members of their responsibility with respect to practicing the contextual aspect of reaping and sowing. It has been said that the Holy Spirit here "is not speaking to sinners about their sins, but to saints about their meanness."

Paul exhorts believers to be generous in their help to those who teach them the Word: "Moreover, let him who is being taught (orally instructed) the Word continue to (present tense command) share with the one who is teaching him in all good things. Note it is the *teacher* of all good things who is to be the recipient of gifts from the one being taught the Word of God. The good things taught are "the spiritually and morally beneficial things" [5]

Barnes warns believers not to let "the ministers of religion" suffer starvation, "while the 'loud professor' rolls in wealth (in a Rolls Royce), and is distinguished for luxury of living, for gaiety of apparel, for splendor of equipage ('a four hundred horse-power' drawn carriage), and for extravagance in parties of pleasure." M. Henry states the apostle cautions those who because of their sin and folly endeavor by any plausible pretence to excuse themselves from doing their duty in supporting their ministers. Calvin speaks also of their 'dishonest excuses' given for withholding their help for the faithful ministers. [6]

> Unreceptive of spiritual teaching, and undervaluing it, they are unwilling to support their teachers, preferring to spend their money on themselves, they thus sow to (for the benefit of) their own fleshly natures, and the harvest will be corruption. If, on the other hand, recognizing their need of teaching and its value, they are of receptive mind towards those who are able to instruct them and willingly contribute of their goods that such teaching may continue, they are sowing to (for the benefit of), the spirit, and the harvest will be eternal life. (Burton, ICC *Galatians* 339)

III. Deception

It easy to move from the immediate context of miserly treatment of the Bible teacher to that wider sense which violates God's will by over-evaluating the temporal and material aspect of life. Sowing to the flesh is a catering to the desires of the here and now, disregarding a future life (1 John 2:16). *Do not continue to be deceived.* Our word *planet* is derived from the Greek word *planao,* a verb meaning to cause to stray, wander, and roam about. "Stop being led astray into error." [7] One who believes that he can sow to the flesh and spend money on himself, his own pleasure, and live the life of hypocrisy deceives himself.

IV. Mockery

The verb rendered to mock means to toss up the nose, contract the nose in contempt, ridicule and derision. "God is not sneered at"; [8] He is not to be "treated contemptuously" [9] "insulted with impunity" (Barnes) or "scornfully disregarded". [10] As boys we often thumbed our noses at people we disliked or dared "to mess with us." Paul wants it known that we cannot deceive or fool God. He knows our hearts. So no one can sneer at the LORD and escape punishment. We cannot outwit an omniscient God; we cannot ignore an omnipresent God.

"From its original sense of *sneer* this verb was applied in rhetorical language to the betrayal of covert ill-will and contempt by cynical gestures in spite of fair words." [11] "God is not mocked by mankind's attempts to ignore the cause-and-effect relationships of justice or to trick God into bestowing blessings instead of judgment." [12] "God will not allow His will and grace to be treated with contempt through man's obeying and trusting his carnal and sinful nature and not God.

[The Greek verb to mock] is a term used for despising God, His grace and His will, by an attitude to life which is sinful because it will not accept the Lordship of the power of the Spirit. The reference is not to verbal scoffing but to the despising of God by a man's being, by his whole manner of life." [13]

V. Sow and Reap

To sow or scatter seed is used figuratively or symbolically in the proverbial expression of Gal 6:7, and the contrast between sowing and reaping is stressed. God will judge the moral righteousness or the normal standard of what a person keeps (continues, practices) sowing. This divine assessment is inevitable, and "the obvious law of correspondence between what is sown and what is reaped provides a motive for human conduct in the present age." [14] "In Gal 6:7-8, sowing and reaping are related to man's decision" in comparison with the preaching or proclamation (heralding) of the Gospel. "Man can sow either to the flesh or to the spirit. The very different sowing will produce a fundamentally different eschatological harvest." [15]

"As a man has acted (on earth), so (hereafter by God) will he be requited (paid back), either with reward or penalty (his deeds will determine his doom": Thayer). There are those who reject all talk about judgment, and consider it "mythical and unethical." They dare call the God of the Bible "unethical"! Such belief is deception, and man stands warned by God's Word. Life is not free of the evidence of a present-tense judgment, for the carnal Christian experiences loss of rewards (but not of salvation). [16]

While we consider the future, let it be known that even in the here-and-now, "even though God forgives our sins through Christ when we repent and confess them, their physical and mental repercussions often will unavoidably continue to be experienced in this life. [17] The future NT "judgment is not capricious or emotional," but is "an inwardly necessary consequence of the sin of man. All human acts are a sowing; God's judgment is the related and self-evident reaping." [18]

The word *that* in **"that** he will also reap" indicates whatever kind of grain is sown *that* is what is reaped, not something different (ATR). You cannot sow one thing and reap the opposite or even another. There is an identity of what is sown and what is harvested. [19] You will ever get the same thing, only very much more of it. [20]

In other words, a farmer does not sow barley and then from that scattering reap wheat. "The harvest corresponds to the seed." [21] Sow to the flesh and of the flesh reap corruption; sow to the spirit and of the spirit (superintended by the Holy Spirit) reap life everlasting. Do not be deceived—this truth is irreversible. [22] Corruption produces corruption; rottenness produces rottenness. *He who is unjust, let him be unjust still; he who is filthy, let him be filthy still; he who is righteous, let him be righteous still; he who is holy, let him be holy still.* (Rev 22:11).

Thought

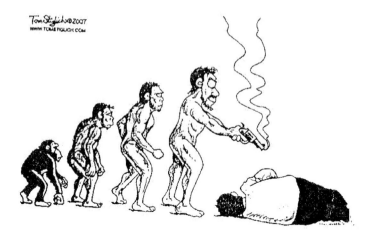

[1] "Tit for tat, kill my dog, I'll kill your cat. Now tell me, if you please how you like that?"

[2] Brewer's 278; AHD: To have repercussions or aftereffects, especially unfavorable ones.

[3] Brewer's 240. Hendrickson, 148: "Malcolm X stirred up a hornet's nest when he said this about John F. Kennedy after the president was assassinated, possibly alluding to alleged CIA attempts on Fidel Castro's life . . . The idea, of course, is that every curse or evil act returns to its originator as chickens return to their roost at night." My mother taught me early in life: "One lie leads to another!"

[4] Hendrickson 572: The first printed reference to the term, most often meaning just deserts or a fitting punishment for a crime, is found in Alexander Pope's *The Dunciad,* (1742). Brewer's 840: The ideal justice, which poets exercise in making the good happy and the bad unsuccessful . . . now used to mean little more than 'just deserts,' 'come-uppance'; ideal distribution (in an especially appropriate or ironic manner) of rewards for virtue and punishments for wickedness and vice, often shown in poetry, drama, and fiction.

[5] Lenski, *Galatians* 304.

[6] Calvin, Gal 6:7. Cf. also Gill, JFB.

[7] Hindson, *Parallel* 2400; ATR.

[8] Lenski, ibid.

[9] Bertram, *TDNT* 4:796.

[10] Hays, *NIB Galatians* 11:336.

[11] Rendall, *ExpGT* 3:189.

[12] Longenecker, (WBC 41) 280.

[13] Bertram, ibid.

[14] Hauck, *TDNT* 3:132-3.

[15] Schulz, *TDNT* 7:546.

[16] In 2 Cor 5:10 the word "bad" is *phaulos,* meaning worthless, of no account—deeds for which there are no rewards, no crowns, no commendation, no "well done." They are deeds of wood, hay and straw which will be revealed by fire and burned up (1 Cor 3:12-15), yet the believer is saved; Nelson, 1979.

[17] H. Morris, *Defender's* 1301.

[18] Buchsel, *TDNT* 3:940.

[19] Hindson, ibid.

[20]Lenski, *Galatians* 305: Sow bountifully, we also reap bountifully; sow sparingly, we also reap sparingly: 2 Cor 9:6.

[21] Preisker *TDNT* 4:719.

[22] Hughes, *Christianity Today*, 18 [318].

Run Who Reads: Hab 2:2: *Write the vision and make it plain on tablets, that he may run who reads it.*

The prophet Habakkuk [1] was disturbed over Judah's iniquity; he was in even greater distress upon learning that God intended to use wicked Babylon to chasten God's people. Our text finds the prophet, having "assumed an attitude of heart, that of anticipation and watchfulness", [2] waiting for Jehovah's response to the question, "Why would He use Babylon as the rod of His anger for correcting Judah?" The LORD's answer begins with Hab 2:2. The key verse is Hab 2:4: Behold the proud, his soul is not upright in him; but the just shall live by his faith. Basically the answer is twofold: bitter and sweet, or sad and joyous. Negatively: the bad, bitter news is that the Chaldeans (Babylonians) will invade Judah. Positively: the good, sweet news is that Judah's enemies will be defeated and Judah restored. Babylon's downfall means Judah's deliverance.

Now what is the proper explanation of the words, *that he may run who reads it?* Commentators give different interpretations. [3] (1) Read it on the run. Calvin states, "He may run who reads it, that is, that the writing may not cause the readers to stop. Write it in large characters that any one in running by may see what is written." Holt says this is grammatically possible, but obscures the true meaning. [4] (2) Moffatt: That one may read it at a glance; [5] or read it quickly, readily, quite easily. [6] (3) Run in fear of the fulfillment of the terror predicted in the vision. [7] (4) Run also means *course of life.* [8] Live in the light of God's promises. (5) The correct interpretation lies in the meaning of the verb *to run.* Whoever reads the message engraved (legibly, plainly, large, clear) is to make haste to announce, proclaim, spread the word to others. [9] To *run* means *to proclaim.* "Running is at any rate connected with the spreading of the prophetic message." [10] Running (with a message) is equivalent to prophesying. [11]

> Not the reading, but the running of the reader is the contemplated end of the revealing and the writing . . . No longer is 'running' the intended result of one's 'reading'; rather, 'running' is here the attendant circumstance of 'reading'. In the Hebrew and the more accurate translations, the revelation is given so that a reader may run; in the less accurate translations, so that a runner may read . . . If we wish to paraphrase Habakkuk so as to make his meaning accessible and not do violence to a fine and characteristic Hebrew metaphor, our choice must be something like, 'so he who reads it may live obediently' . . . Habakkuk's Hebrew demands that we understand 'running' as the end result of the act of revelation he records; it is a message that can be read and acted on by one in need of guidance . . . The main import of this figurative 'running' is doing a job, fulfilling an assigned task; in short, living one's life with its decisions and actions. (Holt, *JBL* 299, 301-2)

Thought: As a boy I heard this anecdote about a small town which had established a curfew for Negroes. They had to be off the streets and out of sight at a certain time each evening. It is said a sign was posted that warned: "Negroes, read and run. And if you can't read, run anyhow!" It is a fact that such signs existed. [12]

[1] His name means *clasp, embrace.* In the early 1950s I lived in *Hotel Tracey* while attending the University of Pennsylvania. One of the members of the cult that owned the building was named Mr. Habakkuk. Often, just to see his reaction I would call him, "Mr. Hucklebuck." He would always respond, "Now, now, Mr. Banks, my name is *Habakkuk!*" He was oblivious to the risqué, sexual

nature of this dance then popular in the world outside of Father Divine's domain and purview.

[2] Feinberg, *Habakkuk* 21.

[3] Smith, R. L., (WBC 32) 106-7; Brownlee, *JBL* (82) 320, fn. 5; T. Hiebert, *NIB* 7:641; H. Morris, *Defender's* 971.

[4] Holt, (*JBL* 83) 298.

[5] Fulghum, 106.

[6] Bauernfeind, *TDNT* 8:229; J. M. P. Smith, ICC, *Samuel* 13; K&D.

[7] White, *TWOT* 2:840: "running in terror" (Jud 7:21). Clarke: "That he who attentively peruses it may speed to save his life from the irruption of the Chaldeans." Bullinger 766 cites Hab 2:2 as a scripture among the *Misquoted Proverbial Sayings.* However, while rejecting the idea that the message on the clay tablets is to be "so plain that he who runs may read," offers the interpretation that he who reads it may flee (run) from the coming judgments. Fink, *Parallel* 1765, disagrees, and says it is better to see the dissemination of the message throughout the country, "not in fear, but in joy."

[8] Jer 23:10; White, *TWOT* 2:839, Jer 8:6: "course."

[9] Hab 2:2: Bauernfeind, *TDNT* 8:230; J. E. Evans, *BSac* (113), 58; Feinberg, 22; Fink, ibid; MacDonald; Nelson; Sco; JFB.

[10] Bauernfeind, ibid, the verb can have a transferred sense denoting *to read with ease.*

[11] P. Robertson, *NICOT* 169. T. Hiebert, ibid: Habakkuk is commissioned to record the vision in order to carry it and announce it to the people (Jer 23.21).

[12] Loewen, 65: In 1940 George and his father, an active Republican were on their way to Elwood, Indiana, to attend a rally for Wendell Willkie, the Republican presidential candidate. When they arrived at Elwood that morning before the convention, they saw two road signs posted at the city limits: "N . . . read this and run. If you can't read, run anyhow," and "N . . . don't let the sun set on you in Elwood," cf. also 69, 170, 196, photo # 4 between (pp 310 and 311); and 344.

Scapegoat

Lev 16:8: *Then Aaron shall cast lots for the two goats: one lot for the LORD and the other lot for the scapegoat* (Lev 16:10, 10, 26).

Leviticus chapter 16 reveals a ceremony not mentioned elsewhere in the OT. It is "unique, most singular, and impressive," [1] and "represents the climactic and pivotal point" of the entire book of Leviticus. [2] Later in Israel's history the event described in Leviticus 16 became known as *Yom Kippur* (Day of Atonement), "the single most important day, and most characteristic ritual, in all of the legislation of the Pentateuch." One matter to immediately dispose of is the belief that Israel (through Moses) copied this ceremony from neighboring countries. Some scholars seem unwilling to accept other nations' similarities with Israel's practices as examples of the perversion of the ritual which God gave to Israel! [3]

There are different interpretations of the significance of this ritual concerning the scapegoat; however I make much use of Feinberg's work, believing his interpretation is correct. The following order of events concentrates upon the sin offering of the two goats. [4] "One animal was insufficient to picture the entire lesson" the LORD desired to teach Israel. [5] Together the goats give us a picture of the finished work of Jesus Christ. [6] Aaron is ordered to take from the congregation of the children of Israel two kids (young goats) as a sin offering, and present them before the LORD at the door of the tabernacle of meeting. Seeking the LORD's will, he is then to cast lots, one for the goat for the LORD, and the other lot for the scapegoat. I am disappointed to read T. Simcox state, "Literally, the lots were cast so that one goat would go to the LORD and the other to the Devil." [7] It is true that one interpretation of the word *azalel* makes it refer to a demon of the wilderness. [8]

However, a demon of this kind would not possibly be placed in contrast to Jehovah in this way. Satan himself is pictured as one who fell away from God; and in no place in the Bible is he called Azazel. The Devil has no part in this ceremony! [9] The word scapegoat appears four times in the OT, all in the Book of Leviticus. We see it first in Lev 16:8. Many scholars state that the "actual use and meaning of this word is at best uncertain." [10] Wm. Tyndale (c. 1492-1536), English Biblical translator, partly completed his translation of the OT; an annotated translation of the

Pentateuch was published in 1530. He is credited with coining the word "scapegoat" as a translation of the literal words, "for azazel."

Finally, we see the goat chosen by lot for the LORD is killed for the sin offering, which is for the people (the ritual is described). The goat chosen by lot to be the scapegoat is to be presented alive before the LORD. Aaron places both of his hands on the head of the goat, confessing the sins of the people, putting their uncleanness, sins, iniquities and transgressions upon the goat's head. By so doing, Aaron symbolically transferred to the goat all of his own sins as well as those of the people. [11] Then the animal was led into the wilderness, bearing all the iniquities of the people, entering the uninhabited wilderness, never to be seen again. See in the two goats a picture of the finished work of Christ on the cross of Calvary. The procedure symbolizes all of our sins being laid upon the Lord Jesus Christ (Isaiah 53:6), our perfect High Priest and also our perfect Sacrifice. [12]

Contemporary use of the word *scapegoat* suggests there is little concept of its background, and today a scapegoat is "a person or group that is made to bear the blame of others." [13] One who is blamed or punished for the sins of others (OED 14:582); "a person or thing made to bear the blame for the mistakes or sins of others" (WBD). "Scapegoatism or scapegoating" is the act or practice of assigning blame or failure to another, as to deflect attention or responsibility away from oneself (RH). "Thus it means someone who bears the blame or burden of others." [14] Today 'scapegoat' means the one who always gets blamed or gets stuck with the task that is distasteful.

[1] Feinberg, *BSac* (115): 321.
[2] Kaiser, *NIB* 1:1109.
[3] Feinberg, ibid, 328: "The pages of the OT are strikingly free of any trace of pagan mythology."
[4] Sco: Lev 16:5; cf. Brewer's 958.
[5] H. Morris, *Defender's* 153.
[6] *DBI* 763 is in error in claiming "the scapegoat was certainly no sacrifice to God . . . by no means then as an offering but rather as a scorn." The goat sacrificed teaches us that "the wages of sin is death," and the goat carried away teaches us that our sins have been removed forever (Psa 103:12; Jer 31:34). MacDonald, 153: "The two goats symbolized two different aspects of atonement: that which meets the character and holiness of God, and that which

meets the need of the sinner as to the removal of his sins." Schultz, *TWOT* 2:658: "In Christ are consummated all the atonement concepts of the Old Testament." Lev 16:5 states the two goats constitute a "sin offering."

[7] Thomas Simcox, *Israel My Glory* 32.

[8] Barnes: "Azazel is the pre-Mosaic name of an evil personal being placed in opposition to Yahweh." Fulghum 223: "The scapegoat is sometimes called *azazel,* who is also an evil demon of the desert." *DBI* 763: *azazel* was some supernatural power, like a desert demon. Jeffrey 684-5: Azazel is the name of a demon who haunts the wilderness . . . however, the identification of the demon has remained obscure (Camille R. La Bossiere).

[9] Moeller, *ISBE* 1:343. Feinberg, ibid. 330: "There are weighty arguments against taking Azazel as a name for Satan." Cf. Barnhouse, *Romans: God's Remedy*, 2:250.

[10] Schultz, *TWOT* 2:658; Feinberg, 325: obscure etymology. *DBI* 331: lit. 'goat of removal.' Calvin: 317: It is certainly a compound word, equivalent to "the departure of the goat . . . I doubt not but that it designates the place to which the scapegoat was driven." Moeller responds, *ISBE* 1:343: But this interpretation is impossible, since the law in Lev 16 was given during the wanderings in the wilderness and accordingly presupposed a constant change in the encampment, even if this should be regarded only as the historical background.

[11] Borland, *Parallel* 225; Feinberg, ibid 324: "This is the only passage in the Bible where the significance of the imposition of hands on the head of an animal is clearly explained as the symbolical transference of the people's sins to the victim."

[12] Nelson, 202.

[13] Freeman, 151; AHD.

[14] Fulghum, 223.

Skin of My Teeth: *Job 19:20: My bone clings to my skin and to my flesh, and I have escaped by (with: KJV) the skin of my teeth.*

I. Job's Overall Physical Condition

Clines states that it is "strange that Job should suddenly be concerned about his physical distress (as nowhere else in the whole speech)." [1] It is true that Job's answer to Bildad's second speech (ch 18) has much to say about how he has been mistreated by God, brothers and relatives, close friends, acquaintances, and servants. However, the description of his deteriorating physical condition is not out of place.

A brief survey of Job's health reveals his concern is neither sudden nor trivial: He was stricken by Satan with painful boils from the sole of his foot to the crown of his head (2:7). Tossing in his sleep all night, his flesh caked with worms and dust; his skin cracked and breaking afresh (7:5). Wounds are multiplied without cause; he is not allowed to catch his breath (9:17-18).

He is shriveled up, and his leanness rises to bear witness to his face (16:8). His eyes have grown dim, and all his members [arms, legs] are like shadows (17:7). His breath is offensive, loathsome, his own children are repulsed by looking at him (19:17). His flesh trembles (21:6). Men spit in his face (30:10); His bones are pierced in him at night ("a perfect skeleton," M. Henry), and his gnawing pains take no rest (30:17). He is cast into the mire to become like dust and ashes (30:19). His skin grows black and falls from him; his bones burn with fever (30:30).

II. Job's Skin

Two uses of skin are found in Job: [2] (1) Job 2:4: "Seems to be a barter term, 'Skin for skin!' Yes, all that a man has he will give for his life." Satan's plan points to a vicious attack upon Job's body. (2) Job 20:19 may indicate a very narrow escape. The Hebrew verb rendered to cling or cleave [3] means keep close, follow closely, catch, join to, and to overtake. Clines plays down the literal physical affliction and asserts that "such language is primarily metaphorical of a psychic reality." [4]

Note the following translations, versions and paraphrases: CEV: I am skin and bones—just barely alive. KJV: I am escaped with the skin of my teeth. Fowler cautions that it is "I am escaped **with** the skin of my teeth (not **by**). [5] Moffatt: My skin is clinging to my bones, my teeth are falling out! NASB: And I have escaped *only* by the skin of my teeth. NEB: My bones stick out through my skin, and I gnaw my under-lips with my teeth! NIV: I have escaped with only the skin of my teeth (footnote: or only my gums). NLT: And have escaped death by the skin of my teeth. RSV: And I have escaped by the skin of my teeth. TLB: I am skin and bones and have escaped death by the skin of my teeth.

III. Interpretation

It is often pointed out that the exact meaning of the term "skin of my teeth" is impossible to discern, and remains obscure. [6] The phrase "skin of my teeth" has led commentators to a detailed discussion of the teeth and gums. **One** interpretation (Gill, JFB, Barnes) suggests that Satan did not afflict the mouth of Job, but spared Job's teeth, gums and lips in order that Job would reach such a low point of despair that he would still be able to cry out and curse God. Recall that one of Satan's objectives (1:11; 2:5) was to move Job to curse God. This interpretation of escaping by the skin of his teeth proposes that only the skin of the teeth, and the gums were "left unattacked by leprosy." In other words, in all this Job did not sin with his lips (2:10), but maintained his integrity, accepting good and adversity from God.

A **second** interpretation: Job's offensive breath indicates his gums are destroyed and wasted away from the teeth (K&D). Here "the skin of his teeth" is described as that which surrounds the teeth in the jaw, namely, the dense fibrous membrane covering (periosteum) the surface of bones except at the joints. The disease destroyed the gums and wasted them away from the teeth. "His body was so devastated by disease that his teeth had fallen out and only the *skin* or gums of his teeth were left intact." [7]

A **third** interpretation is that Job speaks of having escaped with absolutely **nothing!** "Job is not talking about a narrow escape here, as the adage has come to mean. Teeth, of course, have no skin, so that the expression is a paradoxical way of saying 'nothing.' Thus 'and I have escaped with (or am left with) [absolutely] nothing.'" [8] A **fourth** interpretation speaks of a close brush with death. "Job is not referring to any specific physical malady here," for the phrase "the skin of my teeth can hardly be taken literally. . . The only thing that Job has 'escaped' from is what he has not yet suffered, [namely] death." [9]

We would conclude from these scriptures that Job's body was so wasted by disease, so emaciated and exhausted that he could not help but wish that he had never been born (3:13; 10:18). "Job is already little better than a skeleton, and his hold on life precarious." [10] I believe the expression "with the skin of my teeth" signifies primarily that Job "has barely escaped death." [11] He was but a "mere hair's breadth" from death; [12] "scarcely" alive (WBD); "by an extremely narrow margin, just barely" alive (RH). He experienced "a very narrow escape" [13] with his bare life (JFB).

"The most prominent facet of meaning is of deliverance or escape from the threat of death, either at the hands of a personal enemy, or a national enemy or by sickness." [14] "Despite objections that the teeth have no skin, centuries of Bible reading have given the expression a permanent place in the language as the description of **a close escape,** though it has been altered a hairbreadth to *by the skin of the teeth.*" (Hendrickson, 122)

[1] Clines, (WBC 17) 450.

[2] Schultz, *TWOT* 2:657.

[3] Kalland, *TWOT* 1:177-8: *dabaq* is used quite often in the OT of physical things sticking to each other, especially parts of the body.

[4] Clines, ibid, 451.

[5] Fowler, 368; Stevenson 709: Almost always incorrectly quoted, "I have escaped <u>by</u> the skin of my teeth." He reckoned himself only escaped <u>with</u> the skin of his teeth that he had nothing left.

[6] Driver & Gray, ICC, *Job* 168. Newsom, *NIB* 4:477, unusually obscure.

[7] Nelson, 847.

[8] Newsom, ibid. K&D: He describes himself as one escaped with the skin of his teeth—with his flesh so completely destroyed that there is no sound skin left of him except the skin of his teeth. He has wasted away to a skeleton, and become both to sight and smell a loathsome object. *DBI* 847: "Job points to the elemental nature of teeth when he describes his current state as 'escaping by the skin of his teeth,' which means to have only what is left of your body and nothing more."

[9] Clines, (WBC 17) 451-2: "He means that he has been delivered from death but in such a state that he might as well be dead . . . Job's existence is a living death, not of course in the present context primarily because of his physical suffering, but because of his sense of abandonment." K&D in opposition to this interpretation state there is no need "for supposing that v20b is a proverbial phrase for 'I have with great care and difficulty escaped the extreme.'"

[10] Driver & Gray, ibid.

[11] MacDonald, 526.

[12] Brewer's, 166; Clarke.

[13] Schultz, ibid; Leuring, *ISBE*, 4:2814.

[14] G.L. Carr, *TWOT* 1:507.

Snake in the Grass

Early in my first pastorate, two ladies came to our home to warn me of certain church members described as "snakes in the grass," an expression I never forgot. I find no biblical evidence that is *directly* related to this characterization, but I believe the idea is inferred from the account of Satan's appearance in the Garden of Eden to tempt Eve (Gen 3:1-6). It is believed Satan possessed and controlled the serpent's body. [1] Apparently the beast had an upright bodily form; after the serpent was cursed it became a writhing, slithering creature, crawling on its belly, presumably in the grass (Gen 3:14). Satan is called *serpent* (of old) in Rev 12:9, 14-15; 20:2.

The serpent is mentioned elsewhere in the Scriptures: Old man Jacob describes his son, Dan (*judgment*), as one who shall be a serpent by the way, an adder in the path. [2] Wicked men are described as poisonous cobras (Psa 58:4); dangerous, lurking in unexpected places (Eccl 10:8; Amos 5:19); biting vipers (Jer 8:17). Christ called the religious hypocrites of His day, "Brooding [generation] of vipers." [3]

In the Millennial Age the serpents will be harmless, for in that miraculous period, the LORD decrees, "They shall not hurt nor destroy in all My holy mountain." [4] Symbolically, the *snake in the grass* is a deadly, malicious enemy; [5] a hidden or hypocritical foe; a disguised danger. He is a treacherous person, especially one who feigns friendship, clearly portrayed as a harmful poisonous creature. [6] He is described as "crafty, sneaky, and clever" (more appropriate than use of the word *subtle*).[7]

Thought
"Satan is a real person, invisible and untouchable, but real. First he is a liar, a conjurer, a trickster, and a snake in the grass . . . 'as a snake in the grass, ef you don' mind he'll get you at las.'" From the spiritual *Chilly Water* come the words: "Ol' Satan's jes' like a snake in de grass, He's watchin' for to bite you as-a-you pass." *Hard to Rise Again:* "If you don't take care, he'll get you at the end." [8]

Sally Forth: Sally describes Ralph, her former boss, at the time her co-manager:

HE'S LIKE A SNAKE IN THE GRASS BIDING ITS TIME, WITH A GRIN ON ITS FACE, READING "THE PRINCE," HOLDING A KNIFE...

[1] H. Morris, *Defender's* 11.
[2] Gen 49:16-17; cf. Varner, *Jacob's Dozen*, 56-60.
[3] Matt 3:7, 12:34, 23:33; Luke 3:7; Fulghum, 90-91.
[4] Isa 11:8; Day, *ISBE* 4:2736-38.
[5] Freeman, 429-30.
[6] Brewer's 1004.
[7] Leupold, *Genesis,* 1:142.
[8] Lovell, 299, 304-306; Johnson & Johnson, 2:114; Chenu, 207-8.

Sour Grapes: Jer 31:29, 30; Ezek 18:2, 3: *The fathers have eaten sour grapes, and the children's teeth are set on edge.*

I. The Tendency to Blame Others

Blaming others is nothing new. Indeed, we often hear the expression, "passing the buck," meaning to shift or avoid the responsibility for something, such as blame or work, to someone else. After disobeying God by eating of the tree of the knowledge of good and evil, Adam blamed the LORD for giving Eve to him; she in turn blamed the snake (Satan). [1] And what of Aaron's excuse for making the golden calf, or King Saul's reasons for his transgressions? (Gen 3:11-13; Exod 32:24; 1 Sam 13:12, 15:21). Indeed, it is "A universal mark of corrupt nature to lay the blame on others which belongs to ourselves, and to arraign [find fault with, blame] the justice of God" (JFB).

Apparently, it is easier to shift guilt upon others than to admit responsibility for our own sins. The self-righteousness of the human heart delights in faulting others and making them responsible for all misfortunes. Imagine using a proverb that teaches "Our forefathers sinned, and now we innocent children bear the results of their transgressions!" The fact is that the Israelites were not better than their fathers, but worse; [2] indeed, the ease with which they transferred to others their own guilt indicates that what suffering they experienced had no humbling effect. "Religious" people are prone to label others as "sinners," and often their misinterpretation (or ignorance) of the Scriptures is at the root. We can be sure that the judgment of God against evildoers is according to truth (Rom 2:2). It is blasphemous to charge a Holy God with injustice, and attempt thereby to deny our own culpability. [3]

II. Set Teeth on Edge

To set one's teeth on edge is to cause a tingling or grating sensation in one's teeth, as from a harsh noise. "It is literally 'made dull' but can refer to a sour sensation." [4] Calvin says (Jer 31:29): "For to eat the sour grape or wild grape has the same meaning as to set the teeth on edge; for we know this to be the effect of acidity. If any one eats a sour grape, his teeth will suffer from its unripeness." The setting on edge is also called having the teeth "blunted" [5] or the teeth will "grate." [6] Figuratively, it is to jar one's nerves or irritate one. [7] It means to induce an unpleasant sensation; to repel, irritate; to be as unpleasant or annoying as to cause physical discomfort. [8]

III. Individual Responsibility

Individual responsibility is a doctrine embodied in the words, "The soul (person) who sins shall die." [9] Both Jeremiah and Ezekiel taught that the sour grapes proverb should never be used to undermine the doctrine of individual responsibility. [10] Centuries earlier Jehovah said: "Fathers shall *not* be put to death for their children, nor shall children be put to death for their fathers; a person shall be put to death for his own sin" (Deut 24:16). [11] To His Disciples who believed the man born blind suffered his affliction because of the sin of his parents, Christ taught, "Neither this man nor his parents sinned, but that the works of God should be revealed in him" (John 9:3). [12]

Scholars inform us that "Each man will be treated exactly as he deserves; he is responsible for himself, and no one else can take his place." [13] "Sin is thus the current offence of the individual against the command of the Torah, with consequences for the man concerned both in this world and the next." [14] Add to the scholars' comments, this common saying in our churches, "Each tub stands on its own bottom." Even though we inherited the sinful nature of our parents, each of us is responsible before God how we conduct ourselves. "Experiencing hardship as a consequence of the sins of ancestors was not the same as judgment for one's own sins. Suffering caused by another's sins does not excuse willfully sinful behavior." [15] It is true that innocent children may suffer because of a parent's wickedness. A drunken father smashes his automobile, and the son riding with him loses both legs in the accident. But the child is not held guilty for the drunken driving of his father.

Exod 20:5, "For I, the LORD your God, am a jealous God, visiting the iniquity of the fathers upon the children to the third and fourth generations of those who hate Me" (cf. Exod 34:7; Num 14:18) This verse does not contradict the principle of individual responsibility, and should not be used to undermine that truth. Often the words, *of those who hate Me* are overlooked. It is a fact that children tend to repeat the sins of their fathers (Matt 23:32-36). But if we are guilty of the same sins our parents committed, we cannot call God unjust for punishing us. "The proverb contained a most dangerous and fatal error, for which the teaching of the law concerning the visitation of the sins of the fathers, etc., was not accountable . . . God will visit the sins of the fathers upon the children who hate Him, and who also walk in the footsteps of their fathers' sins; but to those who love Him, and keep His commandments, He will show mercy to the thousandth generation" (K&D, Ezek 18:2).

An interesting point concerns the response of the Jews who cried, "His blood be on us and upon our children!" (Matt 27.25). God heard those words. "They imprecated his blood upon them, and upon their children . . . who are under the power of the same sin of unbelief, and will remain so, until the veil is taken away, and they turn to the LORD" (Gill, Jer 31:30). Jews, and Gentiles— **all mankind**—took part in the crucifixion of Christ (Acts 2:23). But never forget that He was smitten of the Father (Isa 53:4, 6, 10)! No man took His life (John 10:17-18). Those who have written about the anti-Semitism of the NT apparently do not believe the NT is the Word of God; or they forget that the Lord

Jesus Christ is a Jew after the flesh, a Son of David—and that the writers of the NT, excluding Luke, were Jews.

IV. Differences between Jeremiah and Ezekiel

Jeremiah's ministry extended approximately from 626 to 586 B.C., making him a contemporary of the prophet Ezekiel. In chapter 31 he speaks of the New Covenant with Israel (fulfilled by the Lord Jesus through His work on Calvary) and deals with changed hearts and minds. His emphasis is upon the future; in coming days no longer will be heard such words as, "The fathers have eaten sour grapes, and the children's teeth are set on edge." Such skepticism of the exiles is repudiated by Jeremiah's amplification of "individual moral responsibility," and by predicting that people will be punished for their own sins. [16]

"In the future when the Lord repopulates and rebuilds the land, the complaint quoted here will be silenced." [17] For Ezekiel, who prophesied approximately 593 BC to 571 BC, the historical back-ground is different. Whereas Jeremiah emphasizes judgment, warning Jerusalem of its coming destruction, Ezekiel encourages the exiles—those Jews who had been deported by the Babylonians. At that very moment the country was on the verge of ruin; and so Ezekiel preached that the antidote for their present bad situation was to repent both individually and as a nation. [18] What Jeremiah declared would cease in the future, Ezekiel preached was to cease right then! [19]

V. Contemporary Use

Prior to Aesop, the 6th century fabulist who wrote of the fox that in an effort to save face dismissed as sour grapes those he could not reach, the people of Judah blamed their sins on the failure of their ancestors. Today the expression is a pretended dislike or disdain for something because one does not have it or cannot have it. It is said proverbially, "when a person is heard to disparage something which it is suspected he would be glad to possess if he could"; sourgrapism is the action or practice of disparaging something because it is out of one's reach. [20] The expression *Sour Grapes* has come to mean any belittling, envious remark. [21] It is an effort to save face (RH). It is the denial of the desirability of something after one has found out that it cannot be reached or acquired (AHD); or a thing that a person pretends to dislike because he cannot have it (WBD).

Thought

A hungry Fox one day chanced to come into a vineyard where he saw some fine ripe grapes hanging at a good height from the ground. He jumped at them, and made many other vain attempts to reach them. Finally he walked off grumbling to himself, "If those grapes had been good I would be disappointed. But they are green and sour." *It is easy to despise what you cannot get.* [22]

[1] My late pastor (Dr. WHR Powell) told this anecdote: The Devil was sitting on the curb outside of a church, crying. A man walked up to him and asked, "What's the matter?" Satan replied, "Them old people in that church blame everything on me!"

[2] Cooke, ICC, *Ezekiel* 195.

[3] Gaebelein, *Ezekiel* 123: Charging God with injustice and cruelty was an impious, impudent and insolent act; Rom 3:23.

[4] Nelson, 1359.

[5] Feinberg, *Ezekiel* 99; and Cooke, ibid 194.

[6] Brownlee, (WBC 28) 282.

[7] Brewer's, 974.

[8] Jeffrey, 732.

[9] Ezek 18:4, 13, 18, 20, and 24. Death here is physical. Feinberg, ibid, 100: "Life is used to mean continuance in this world, and death means removal from it." MacDonald: 1051-2: "The punishment is *temporal,* not eternal. It is *physical* death because of sin now." It is not eternal life, for salvation is not by works (Eph 2:8-9).

[10] Fulghum, 78: "Jeremiah and Ezekiel taught individual responsibility as against inherited or group guilt." Lindars, 452-3, cites the "important distinction between *criminal responsibility,* which is a matter of social legislation, and the responsibility of *the individual before God,* which carries with it ideas of the divine retribution of rewards and punishments."

[11] K&D: Deut 24:16 "shows how remote such a perversion of the truth was from the Law of Moses."

[12] Schrage, *TDNT* 8:290-1: The disciples' thought was "in accordance with the common OT and Jewish view."

[13] Cooke, ibid; FG Kroll, *Parallel* 1481: "not God's anger, but the sins of the people, that had brought judgment upon them." Jantz, *Parallel* 1566: "While there are cumulative effects of sin, the LORD here declares that each individual is accountable for his own sin."

[14] G. Stahlin/W. Grundmann, *TDNT* 1:290.

[15] Nelson, ibid.

[16] Harrison, R. K., 137; Cooke, ibid 195: "Such talk will cease to be uttered in the ideal future".

[17] Keown, Scalise, & Smothers, (WBC 27) 129. Cf. P. D. Miller, *NIB* 6:811: "In this future time when sin occurs it will be dealt with, but it will be a community that is not shaped by a long history of disobedience." Brownlee, (WBC 28) 282: Such a visitation of the sins of parents upon their offspring can have no place in the ideal tomorrow; indeed, this proverb is already invalid. Only the wicked will be judged; the righteous will be spared, and will constitute the Israel of the future. McClain, *BSac* (112) 120: "The kingdom will be ethical in its effects . . . Moral retribution at last will become an individual matter." Men shall no longer say this proverb, "thus removing one of the greatest present stumbling blocks to rational belief in a moral universe."

[18] However, Feinberg states, *Ezekiel*, 99: "Ezekiel was not at this time dealing with the problem of the suffering of the innocent, vicarious suffering or corporate suffering. He had foretold national punishment, but he had to bring home to them an individual sense of sin. He deals with individual responsibility elsewhere" (Ezek, chs 9 and 14). Joyce, 187-191: Instead of smugly suggesting they are not to blame, there is the urgent need to accept responsibility— in other words, repent!

[19] Cooke, ibid 197: "Ezekiel, on divine authority declares that the proverb must be dropped at once." Bullinger 277: Hebrew is lit.: "Ye proverb this proverb" means "Ye have this proverb in constant use." Keown et al, (WBC 27) 130: Neither one's past sin nor that of one's ancestors "can prevent that person from choosing to turn away from wickedness to righteousness and life."

[20] OED 6:761, 16:60; Brewer's, 1011.

[21] Hendrickson, 677.

[22] The Fables of Aesop, "*The Fox and the Grapes,*" 116.

Sow the Wind, and Reap the Whirlwind
Hos 8:7: *They sow the wind, and reap the whirlwind.*

I. Definitions
Figuratively the word *wind* speaks of the nothingness of human exertions, signifying utter failure. [1] At the very heart of chasing after the wind (Eccl 1:14) is idolatry, for idols are pure vanity. [2] In

198

Israel's case, the wind represents senseless, heartless, vain, empty worship, [3] its unprofitable conduct demonstrated by its alliance with false gods, and dependence upon foreign nations rather than upon the true and living God. Calvin says of Israel's impiety and idolatry that sowing the wind is an appropriate figure that shows "how unprofitably the Israelites exercised themselves in their perverted worship." Without faith their service was but wind, "an empty show," vain confidence, frivolous counsels "though the outward aspect of their service differed nothing from the true and legitimate worship of God."

A whirlwind is defined as any rotating air mass, where two currents from opposite directions meet, and a circular motion results. This includes tornadoes and cyclones, but it is "more strictly applied to the smaller swirling atmospheric phenomenon commonly known as dust devil or dust whirl, which occurs mostly over deserts and semiarid plains during hot, calm days" (Encarta). Desert sand is drawn up, small particles of water from the ocean condense and some of the moisture in the clouds forms a great funnel-shaped column. [4]

II. Result

Sowing to the wind can result in a destructive, scattering whirlwind. Reaping always follows sowing. Paul reminds us of this in Gal 6:7-8: *Do not be deceived, God is not mocked; for whatever a man sows, that he will also reap. For he who sows to his flesh will of the flesh reap corruption, but he who sows to the Spirit will of the Spirit reap everlasting life.* God's principle is: If we sow something, we must reap something. This law ever remains true. Morally speaking, the nation had planted wind to result in whirlwind or coming judgment. Israel's impiety and idolatry would reap judgment just as other nations that forget God have reaped (Psa 9:17). Sow to false gods, and reap the wrath of the true and living God! Sow the seeds of unrighteousness, and reap a harvest of judgment. Only in Christ can we find today protection from the whirlwind. He paid our penalty with His blood and we need not fear the time of reaping. Instead, we rejoice, knowing that our Savior is able to make all things work together for our good (Rom 8:28).

III. Psa 58:9: *He shall take them away as with a whirlwind, as in His living and burning wrath.* The word *whirlwind(s)* occurs some

29 times in 13 Books of the Bible (OT). [5] In this imprecatory
psalm (invoking evil, calling down curses or calamity), David
cries for divine vengeance. It is his desire that the demise of his
(Israel's) enemies will be as sudden as a whirlwind snatching them
away, ruining all their plans. The language used reflects the
experience of those who travel in the desert. While preparing their
meal, before the pots can feel the heat from the burning thorns,
before the meat is cooked, God scatters the pots, sweeps away the
fire and the fuel (dry thorns or brambles), and destroys the food, as
with a churning whirl-wind. [6]

Other verses using the same Hebrew words refer to:
Jehovah's violent, grievous, furious judgment upon the wicked
(Jer 23:19), continuing, angry tribulation judgment upon Babylon
and the nations (Jer 25:32, 30:23), and the power of the Beast is
described as he attacks (Dan 11:40). There is the scattering of
Israel's enemies (Hab 3:14), both scattering and deliverance, Zech
7:14; translation of Elijah 2 Kgs 2:1, 11, and the LORD's Presence,
answering Job face to face, Job 38:1, 40:6. The same words refer
to God's stormy wind that carries away evildoers like dry stubble
or chaff (Isa 40:24), Jehovah's irresistible scattering (Isa 41:16;
Zech 9:14), and the vision of Theophany, and God's glory (Ezek
1:4).

IV. Hos 8:7: *They sow the wind, and reap the whirlwind.* [7] The
Hebrew word translated whirlwind or 'storm-wind' is *suphah*. [8]
Israel will not reap just what they have sown but will harvest much
worse. In a gentle breeze farmers would throw their seed upon the
tilled ground, spreading it evenly. But if a storm came up it would
scatter the grain, making useless all of their efforts, bringing to
naught their planning. [9] Such disastrous consequences are
examples of reaping the whirlwind; for if you "sow moral
bankruptcy" you will "reap coming judgment." [10] This is the
principle that was applied with great fury to ancient Israel. [11] Sow
a wind and reap a hurricane. A breeze becomes a tempest. A drop
of water becomes a flood. A tossed away cigarette becomes a
forest fire! Out of their futile actions of the nothingness of folly is
produced "the nothingness of devastation." [12] Reaping the
whirlwind speaks of an inevitable awful, deadly increase.

Other verses using this word, *suphah*: God's wonder and
greatness in nature (Job 37:9); the sudden destruction of the fool
(Prov 1:27); annihilation of the wicked man's foundation (Prov

10:25); the rolling tumbleweed, blown-around-by-the-wind flight of Jehovah's enemies (Isa 17:13); conquest that is like the violent, tempestuous winds from the great Arabian Desert (Isa 21:1); crushing defeat under the wheels of God's war-chariots (Isa 66:15); swiftness of the judgment invasion of Jerusalem (Jer 4:13); fiery, tempestuous judgment of Ammon (Amos 1:14); the LORD's holiness avenging sin (Nah 1:3); the chariot wheels of Israel's enemies are like a whirlwind (Isa 5:28). [13]

Thought: In Bradenton, Fla., L. R. Jenkins fell asleep and lost control of his car. He struck a power pole, and the accident caused the following chain reactions: Power was knocked out for 6,000 Florida Power and Light Company customers; lines were down for 43 blocks; and 600 insulators were smashed. In addition, 54 streetlights were ripped down; a tourist center roof was dented; two traffic lights were smashed; power was cut off temporarily at the courthouse and jail. Jenkins was jailed in lieu of $85 bond for failure to have his vehicle under control and driving with an improper license. He told police he had dozed off.

[1] K&D; Harper, ICC, *Amos & Hosea* 317; Stuart, (WBC 31) 134; Eidevall, 130: "engage in an inane project."
[2] Gill describes their sowing to the wind as idolatry, a vain, glorious and ostentatious show of religion and devotion.
[3] Feinberg, *Hosea* 65; Jacob, *TDNT* 9:628.
[4] Joy, *ISBE* 4:3083.
[5] Also: tempest, storm, and windstorm: Patterson, *TWOT* 2:629.
[6] Leupold, *Psalms*, 438, 440: His wrath is described as "something like hot anger." Kirkpatrick, 329: "It is another figure for the swift destruction of the wicked and their schemes."
[7] Sow to the wind, reap the whirlwind is a fine, bold, and energetic metaphor (Clarke).
[8] Possibly from a verb that means to come to an end, or to cease; or that makes an end; Patterson, ibid 2:620. However, Stuart, ibid: 128 states: "There is no evidence that *suphah* means 'whirlwind'."
[9] Stuart, ibid. 133; Yee, *NIB* 7:261: "sowing seeds when it is windy is an exercise in futility."
[10] OED: 20:250.
[11] Morris, H., *Defender's* 935.
[12] Eidevall, 145; 130: "For they sow a wind, and a gale they shall reap." Cheyne, 88: Unprofitable conduct's requital [avenge, repay-

ment] shall be actual destruction. Jeffrey, 732: "Sinful seeding will yield a monstrous crop." Brewer's 1012: Heedless actions provoke serious consequences; Hendrickson, 678. Stuart, ibid. 127: "Though they sow with a wind, they will reap in a storm." Clarke: As the farmer reaps the same kind of grain which he has sown, but in far greater abundance, thirty, sixty, or one hundred fold; so he who sows the wind shall have a whirlwind to reap. The rental seed shall be multiplied into a tempest; so they who sow the seed of unrighteousness shall reap a harvest of an irresistible divine judgment. Cf. *DBI* 943. Stevenson, 2177: "He that sows thistles reaps thorns."

[13] Horses with hoofs like flint were harnessed to the two-wheel chariots used by the Assyrians in ancient warfare. They moved with such rapidity that it appeared they were whirlwinds themselves. The violent velocity of the turning wheels destroyed everything in their paths. This is a terrifying description of the enemies of Israel coming in judgment against that nation. Such wheels are swift as the wind, and raise a cloud of dust like a whirlwind.

Strain out a Gnat and Swallow a Camel: Matt 23:24*: Blind guides, who strain out a gnat and swallow a camel!* KJV: *Ye blind guides, which strain at a gnat, and swallow a camel.*

I. Definitions
Strain: This verb, used only once in the NT, means to filter through, strain thoroughly, pour through a filter. Note that the verse speaks of those who strain *out* the gnat, rather than strain *at* the gnat. [1] To strain at something is to make a "violent effort," to scruple at; in other words, to make a difficulty of swallowing or accepting something. [2]

> It is probable that the translators of 1611 did not make a mistranslation, but simply adopted a rendering which had already gained currency in the popular speech of the time, meaning, 'which strain the liquor if they find a gnat in it.' However, the phrase was soon misapprehended, and was taken to mean to make a difficulty or swallowing or accepting something. (Stevenson, 966) [3]

Swallow: *Katapino* means to drink down, to gulp. The literal and figurative meanings merge into one another. In line with its root it denotes swallowing whole (e.g. Jonah 1:17) rather than grinding and consuming (Gal 5.15; Rev 11.5)." [4] **Gnat:** This word (*konops*) also is found only once in the NT: The wine-gnat or midge (see the word midget) that is bred in evaporating wine.

II. Background

From Lev 11:20-23 we learn that certain flying insects, including gnats, were considered unclean, and were not to be eaten by the Jews; it was permissible however to eat locusts, crickets and grasshoppers. It became necessary to meticulously filter or strain water, but especially wine, through a cloth or fine wicker basket before drinking it, for tiny creatures actually bred in the wine. [5] A sharp contrast is made between the gnat and the camel to stress an impossibility, one that is variously described by the commentators as humorous; [6] a figure of speech unsurpassed for its expressiveness [7] oriental hyperbole; [8] or exaggeration [9] and monstrous supposition, but relevant. [10] The camel was the largest "Levitically unclean" animal in Palestine. Imagine gulping down a camel!

Our Lord called the Pharisees, **Blind Guides**. It is one thing to be a guide or leader of those who are blind, to be "a teacher of the ignorant and inexperienced" (Rom 2:19), but it is something else to be a blind leader or blind guide of the blind. Christ condemns those who "while themselves are destitute of a knowledge of the truth, offer themselves to others as teachers," for as our Lord points out, "if the blind leads the blind, both will fall into a ditch" (Matt 15:14; 23:16, 24). From the Pharisees' perspective one is blind who is ignorant of the Law of Moses and tradition. What *they* do not realize is that they are blind to God's will and ignorant of the true purpose of the Law. [11]

> The Pharisees make out that they are the guides of others, but they themselves are blind. They will necessarily miss the right way and lead astray those who trust in them. It does not need to be assumed that the Pharisees regard those whom they seek to lead as blind and in need of leaders, for even those who see can seek guides when they do not know the way. Nevertheless, the judgment on the Pharisees in Matt 15:14a . . . shows

that Jesus is probably thinking of blind leaders of the blind in 23:16, 24. (Michaelis, *TDNT* 5:99)

III. The Mistake Made by the Pharisees

They made a fuss about trifling matters (Calvin) or minor misdeeds, but committed offences of real magnitude, while leaving weightier matters unattended to. [12] Concerned with "the excessive amplification of the ritual precepts of the law," [13] they lost their sense of proportion as to what was little in the law and what was great. Spiritual blindness led them to commit sins of deceit, hypocrisy, dishonesty, cruelty, oppression, lust and greed; their anxious scrupulosity led them to an utter lack of scruple.

Their table became their trap! By neglecting justice, mercy, faith, righteousness, [14] it was easy to swallow the camel of sin. [15] And what a camel it was—a beast full of extortion [16] self-indulgence, corrupt teaching and living; devouring widows' houses; quarreling with the disciples for eating with unwashed hands; praying long self-righteous prayers; for fear of being defiled, refusing to enter the Judgment Hall; and haggling over what to do with the betrayal money that Judas returned to them.

IV. Contemporary Interpretation and Usage

To strain out a gnat (or as commonly heard, 'strain *at*' a gnat and swallow a camel) means to fuss about trifles while ignoring more serious matters (RH); it is to object to some small or very trifling thing (WBD). Figuratively, in allusion to Matt 23:24, the camel is "anything large and difficult to 'swallow' or 'do away with.' [17] It signifies much solicitude about little things, and none about greater (Gill); it is "concern for the small and relatively insignificant . . . accompanied by the ignoring of something enormous in size or importance." [18]

---

[1] Brewer's, 1032-3; Fulghum, 243; Hindson, *Parallel* 1945; ATR.
[2] OED 16:829.
[3] Cf. Bullinger, 759.
[4] Goppelt, *TDNT* 6:158.
[5] Byatt, 45-6; Manson, 236.
[6] Hagner (WBC 33B) 670: "a humorous analogy that was perhaps a proverbial saying." Cf. Tasker, 221; Boring, *NIB* 8:436: Matthew's critique is that in being concerned to filter out minor violations—major ones plop in unnoticed.

[7] MacDonald, 1290.
[8] ATR; Manson, ibid: "frankly hyperbolical" [exaggerated].
[9] Nelson, 1619.
[10] A. B. Bruce, *ExpGT* 1:283.
[11] John 9:39-41; Schrage, *TDNT* 8:292: "The blind leaders of the blind are blind to God's will and to the word of Jesus at which they take offence." Lenski, *Matthew* 909 describes their condition as "double-edged: blind men who yet pretend to show others the way; and others who consent to be guided by blind men."
[12] Brewer's, ibid; Day, *ISBE* 2:1240.
[13] Tasker, 217; Hagner, ibid, 671: "By dwelling on the minutiae and neglecting the more important matters of the law."
[14] Michel, *TDNT* 3:594; Rice, 359.
[15] Manson, ibid: The saying then pillories (exposes to ridicule and abuse) the elaborate precautions taken in minor matters and the carelessness about big things.
[16] Hindson, ibid: In Matt 23:25, instead of full 'of' extortion, read full 'from' extortion." The Pharisees' living was obtained by extorting wrongfully from others.
[17] OED: 2:804.
[18] Hagner, ibid.

Thief in the Night

Thief in the night is a phrase that **does not apply to the return of Christ for believers.** It refers rather to that stage of His Second Coming suddenly and unexpectedly in judgment for **unbelievers.** "The first phase of the Lord's coming is as a bridegroom and the second phase is as a thief. He does not come upon His bride as a thief and He does not come upon the apostates and unregenerate world as a bride-groom." [1] There are three OT verses connecting the words *thief* or *thieves* with the word *night.* [2] However, our exposition deals primarily with NT Scriptures.

"Nowhere in Scripture are believers warned against the coming of the Savior as a thief . . . Mark you, the Lord does not come to believers as a thief, but to professors only." [3] We repeat this thesis because we observe a very common mistake in referring to Jesus Christ coming for His Church as a *thief in the night.* The phrase is actually intended to show that the coming of the Day of the LORD in judgment will be sudden and unexpected. A thief's coming is ordinarily not anticipated. As the early saints (and true of believers today) expected Christ's coming in the air for them at any time, so the coming as a thief in the night does not involve us. It is rather the unbelievers who will be caught napping and unprepared.

1 Thess 5:2: *For you yourselves know perfectly that the day of the Lord so comes as a thief in the night.* First Thess 4:13-18 refers only to Christians, while 1 Thess 5:1-4 refers to the judgment of unbelievers (those in darkness and of the night). Naturally, the knowledge of this coming judgment has an effect upon the Christian. The fact that the saints will escape the wrath of the Day of the Lord is calculated to bring comfort to the believers (1 Thess 5.11). In other words, it would make little sense for Paul to say in one breath, "Christ may come at any moment" for Christians, and then say in the next breath, "His coming for Christians is unexpected!" The clue to the proper interpretation: the expectedness and the lack of expectedness have to do with two different kinds of people and two different times.

There are critics who claim the idea of a two-fold stage of His coming is not scriptural and altogether untenable.[4] However, we firmly believe that Christ's coming in the air (the Day of Christ) **for** believers is looked for **by** believers; it is imminent. There are no predicted events which still must be fulfilled before this occurs. On the other hand, His coming to the earth to judge unbelievers (the Day of the Lord) is not expected and will not be looked for by the ungodly.[5]

Paul develops in 1 Thess 5:1-11 the idea affirming "that the true Christian will be watching for the return of the Lord. If he is not, he is putting himself into the same class with the unbelieving world." [6] Unbelievers will be entirely unprepared for the event occurring after the true Church is removed (raptured) from this earth. It is this period of judgment called *Tribulation* that is described as a part of *The Day of the Lord.*

> [This Day comes as a thief in the night]. The only way it will **overtake** anyone is **as a thief**, and the only persons it will **overtake** will be those who are in the night, that is, the unconverted. It will not **overtake** believers at all, because they **are not in darkness**. At first reading, this verse might seem to say that the Day of the Lord will overtake believers but *not as a thief.* But this is not so. It *will not overtake them at all* because when the thief

comes to this world's night, the saints will be dwelling in eternal light. (McDonald, 2040-1)

Use of the phrase thief in the night heightens the element of surprise. The very moment men cry, "Peace, peace!" they shall experience sudden destruction! [7] *Kleptes* (thief) is sneaky; he gives no notice of his approach, for stealth is a major aspect of his *modus operandi* and one key to his success. Understand then that the apostle "contrasts absolutely the state of the Church with that darkened state of carnal security, in which the Lord's coming catches the world as a snare." [8] His coming in judgment is unexpected, sudden, and without warning.[9]

2 Pet 3.10: *But the day of the Lord will come as a thief in the night.* Reference here does not emphasize His personal coming, but is used impersonally of events and of time, especially the purging of the heavens and the earth at the end of the Millennium.

Rev 3.3: *Therefore if you will not watch, I will come upon you as a thief, and you will not know what hour I will come upon you.* The members of the "dead" church at Sardis are warned that the consequence of spiritual deadness is sudden and unexpected judgment. This visitation of condemnation is not the coming of the Lord **for** His church. Members of the church at Sardis whose names were on the church roll but not in the Lamb's book of life are described as dead. Mere professors are described as church members whose works before God were anything but perfect; had their hearts been right, they would have paid attention to God's Word, would have received and heard with believing hearts and ears, and would have repented.[10]

Rev 16:15: *Behold, I am coming as a thief. Blessed is he who watches . . .* Scholars disagree whether this passage, Rev 16:13-16, is parenthetical. [11] If you are watching, though His coming is sudden, it is not to you as the coming of a thief. He comes here to the world, and rather than being changed and snatched up, their carelessness leaves them naked and numbered among "the earth-dwellers." [12]

Summary: The phrase *thief in the night* does not refer to Christ's coming for the Church. His imminent coming for us is our blessed hope! We are warned to be vigilant, looking for and yearning for His return. Along the way we see signs we believe confirm "the patient hope of the watchful." [13] Furthermore, we are moved to evangelize, knowing what awful tribulation lies ahead for this sin-cursed world.

Thought: A wife constantly begged her husband to secure all doors and windows so that no burglar could intrude their home. One night the husband was awakened by a noise. He investigated and was confronted by a burglar. He said to the thief, "Sir, please come upstairs and meet my wife. She's been expecting you!"

[1] Barnhouse, *Revelation*, 70.

[2] **Job 24:14**: The murderer rises with the light; he kills the poor and needy; and in the night he is like a thief. **Jer 49:9**: If grape-gatherers came to you, would they not leave some gleaning grapes? If thieves by night, would they not destroy until they have enough? **Obad 5**: If thieves had come to you, if a robber by night . . . The prophecies of Jeremiah and Obadiah are similar in their announcement against Edom (the nation that descended from Esau) for its enmity against Jacob (Israel).

[3] Feinberg, *Parallel* 2698 (Rev 16:15); 2665 (Rev 3:3).

[4] Berkhof, 695-6.

[5] Dr. Mason states the Day of Christ is one phase of the Day of the Lord, thus suggesting the Day of the Lord begins with the translation of the church and ends with the cleansing (purgation) of heaven and earth mentioned in 2 Pet 3:10-12. "While generally 'day of Christ' and its variants are used concerning the church's translation to heaven, and 'the day of the Lord' comes into the New Testament with heavy overtones from the Old Testament concerning God's dealings with Israel and the nation[s] (Zec 14:1-4, 9), the difference is not primarily one of time or of words but rather of emphasis" (*Prophetic Problems* 147-8). Cf. Bigg, ICC *Peter & Jude* 296.

[6] Tenney, *Interpreting Revelation,* 64.

[7] Leon Morris, *Thessalonians* 91: "clearly it is unbelievers in general who will be thinking that all is at peace . . . they will be saying these things at the moment that doom comes upon them."

[8] Newell, *Revelation* 258. Incidentally, the two men crucified with our Lord are robbers (ληστης), men who "appropriate what is not theirs . . . by violence and openly," whereas the thief (κλέπτης)

208

does so by fraud and in secret (Trench, 157). "A thief will steal the shortening out of cornbread and never break the crust." "Thieves" (KJV) in Matt 27:38, 44; Mark 15:27 is better rendered "robbers" (NKJV, NIV, NASB, RSV, Moffatt, Montgomery, and Weymouth) In JBP and NEB, it is "bandits." "Malefactors" (KJV, RSV) in Luke 23:32, 33, 39 is better rendered "criminals" (NKJV, NIV, NASB, NEB, JBP, Moffatt, Montgomery and Weymouth).

[9]Frame, ICC, *Thessalonians* 180; Barnes, 1 Thess 5:2, adds that "all attempts to determine the day, the year, or the century when He will come, must be fallacious."

[10] Ironside, *Revelation,* 64.

[11] Levy, 185, says it is not; Gaebelein, *Revelation* 96, says it is a very brief parenthetical vision. Cf. Sco, Rev 16:13-16.

[12] Newell, ibid.

[13] JFB, 1 Thess 5:2.

The Truth Shall Set You Free

John 8:32: *And you shall know the truth, and the truth shall make you free.* John 18:38: *Pilate said to Him, "What is truth?" And when he had said this, he went out again to the Jews.*

I. Used and Misused

The proverbial phrase "you shall know the truth and the truth shall make you free" is often misused; usually the problem has to do with the definition of the word, truth. "The words express a great principle, which is applicable in many directions, and which has been enunciated by Jewish and heathen teachers as well as by Christian." [1] Elijah Muhammad, late leader of the Black Muslims, said:

> The New Testament and Holy Quran's teaching of a resurrection of the dead can't mean the people who have died physically and returned to the earth, but rather a mental resurrection of us, the black nation, who are mentally dead to the knowledge of truth; the truth of self, God and the arch-enemy of God and his people. That is that Truth that will make us free, whereof John (8:32) doesn't say what truth shall make you free; therefore leaving it questionable and to the advantage of the enemy. (*Message to the Blackman in America,* 97)

II. Pilate's Question

Pilate asked, "What is truth?" and walked away. "This question had long agitated the world. It was the great subject of inquiry in all the schools of the Greeks. Different sects of philosophers had held different opinions, and Pilate now, in derision, asked him, whom he esteemed an ignorant fanatic, whether he could solve this long-agitated question" (Barnes). It is uncertain with what design Pilate asked this question (M. Henry), but consider some (overlapping) reasons offered **why he did not wait for an answer:** (1) "The question was not seriously put (human irony)." [2]

(2) It is what is labeled *Interrogating*: This figure is used when a speaker or writer asks animated questions, but not to obtain information. Instead of making a plain and direct statement, he suddenly changes his style, and puts what he was about to say or could otherwise have said, into the form of a question, without waiting for an answer. Instead of declaring a conviction, or expressing indignation, or vindicating authority, he puts it in the form of a question without expecting any reply. (Bullinger, 943; in reproach, 955)

(3) Contempt [3] (4) curt dismissal [4] (5) a contemptuous *jest* at what he considered impractical abstract truth. (6) A way of dismissing the subject since he learned what he wanted to know, namely, Christ is no revolutionary [5] (7) "an indifferent worldling", he did not seek to learn about *the* truth, or about any religious truth whatever [6] (8) simply the question of the practical pagan skeptic (9) a sneer (ATR) with a shrug of his shoulders upon leaving (10) A cynical denial of the possibility of knowing truth; useless speculation, for he believed that no one could answer his question. (11) "Difficult to say what Pilate meant. Was he puzzled, or sarcastic, or interested?" [7] (12) confused about Christ's spiritual purpose (13) "perhaps wistful rather than cynical or careless" [8] (14) he may have asked in a mocking way; not staying for an answer indicates that he either despaired of getting a satisfactory one, or that he was indifferent about it (Clarke) (15) such a question would lead to endless and unreasonable inquiries, and Pilate had business that demanded rather prompt action (JFB) (16) the clamor and outrage of the priests' mob at his gate obliged him abruptly to let fall the discourse (M. Henry) (17) it seems "Pilate

saw that Jesus had no concern for politics or affairs of state and was far removed from a warlike spirit, and so he terminated the interview." [9]

III. Truth Defined [10]

"Truth is not in fragments. Truth holds together. There is no phase of Truth that is not related to every other phase of Truth." [11] (1) All of the "I AM's" of Christ are related, and constitute truth. [12] (2) God's Word is Truth (John 17:17) (3) God *is* Truth; the revealed will of God is Truth [13] (4) Truth is that pearl of great price which the human understanding has a desire for and is in quest of (M. Henry) (4) Jesus Christ, the Son of God, is Truth (John 14:6). (5) Truth is 'reality'; "the Greek article here indicates the specific reality and actuality that exists in God and in Jesus." [14] Philosophy treats both the meaning of the word *true* and the criteria by which we judge the truth or falsity in spoken and written statements. For thousands of years philosophers have attempted to answer the question, "What is truth?"

Theories abound, e. g.: (a) True statements correspond to the facts; they agree with reality, while false statements do not. But then, "Is falsehood a truth"? (b) Others assert that truth is that which experts will agree upon when their investigations are final. But then there is the question, "Which set of beliefs finally will be agreed upon?" (c) A third theory states that a set of beliefs is true if the beliefs are comprehensive, that is, that they cover everything, and do not contradict each other (d) A fourth theory dismisses the question, "What is truth?" Paul cautions: "Beware lest anyone cheat you through philosophy and empty deceit, according to the tradition of men, according to the basic principles of the world, and not according to Christ." [15] "Philosophers have searched for truth all through the ages but, like Pilate, have never found it . . . men will be 'ever learning, and never able to come to the knowledge of truth' (2 Tim 3.1, 7). But for those who sincerely desire the truth, 'the Spirit of truth,' through the 'scripture of truth,' will lead them to the Lord Jesus who is 'the truth'. [16]

IV. True Freedom

Consider the very heart of the matter of Truth setting us free. Sin, the **great enslaver**, shackles all humans. Paradoxically, freedom to sin is slavery, and false concepts of true freedom add to our bondage. So strong is the concept of works in our old nature that we do not even realize we are in bondage. Sin blinds us; when we do as we please we think we are really free. True freedom involves taking us outside of bondage to another person, such as a slave to his master. [17] Our Lord does not speak to the Jews of their political freedom from the Roman government; but to their "inner position, their inner freedom" [18].

To describe true freedom we have to explain how it is obtained. We cannot free ourselves from sin's death-grip by good works, self-discipline, education, or the study of philosophy. By asserting our self-sufficiency, and religious pride we prove our enslavement. I have heard men use John 8:32 in their determination to achieve freedom from racism, government authority, financial stress or poverty, the ghetto, the white man, European colonialism, Eurocentrism, etc!

However, true freedom involves breaking the shackles that bind the soul. A dope-taker may know the truth of what dope is doing to him, the havoc it plays with his mind, and the wreckage of his body. But if he does not know the truth about his own sin nature, and his need for spiritual cleansing, he will never be liberated. "Truth by its very nature cannot be imposed by external compulsion, nor can it be validated by anything other than itself. One either sees the truth for what it is, or one does not." [19]

Now this saving truth is bound up with the Person and work of the Lord Jesus Christ. [20] Only by faith in His shed blood is it possible to end the enslavement to sin; this freedom is won by Christ alone (ATR). Only He can break the dominance of sin, and enable us to sing: *"He breaks the power of canceled sin, He sets the prisoner free; His blood can make the foulest clean; His blood availed for me"* (Charles Wesley). "True freedom is not simply the random, directionless life, but the genuine humanness that reflects the image of God. This is found under the Lordship of Christ. And this Lordship makes demands that are as testing and difficult as they are actually liberating . . . true freedom" is slavery to God." [21] Freedom is affected only "by the intervention of a higher power outside" of ourselves; the slave "has no control over his own fate. He has no claim to be liberated." [22] The word free refers to freedom from the grievous bondage of sin that expresses itself in ignorance, error, legalism, superstition, prejudice, evil passions, corrupt propensities, inordinate desires, false notions, darkness—the list is interminable. Unless this power is destroyed by Jesus Christ there is no emancipation from sin's slavery. "To know Truth is to know the True God in Jesus." [23]

When He justifies us, we are freed from sin's guilt; when He sanctifies us we are liberated from corruption's bondage (M. Henry). Calvin states: It is evident that we are by nature the slaves of sin . . . so long as we are governed by our sense and by our natural disposition we are in bondage to sin. When the Lord regenerates us by His Spirit, he makes us free. Loosed from the snares of Satan, we willingly obey righteousness. We recognize then the importance of the Bible, the Word of God, in this matter of true freedom. "Belonging to Him, abiding in Him, is dependent on the abiding of His words in them. To abiding, knowledge of the truth is promised (John 8:32) . . . If knowledge relates to truth, faith relates no less to him who is the truth (14:1, 6)." [24] "Abiding in His Word gives greater knowledge of the Truth and sets one free from sin." [25] "True freedom is submission to God's Word . . . Critics who submit to Scripture only in part are not wholly free for truth. Their fancied freedom of non-subjection to God's Word is really intellectual anarchy . . . an academic lawlessness." [26]

[1] Bernard, ICC, *John* 2:305.

[2] Bullinger, 813; 807: "The speaker intends to convey a sense contrary to the strict signification of the words employed; not with the intention of concealing his real meaning, but for the purpose of adding greater force to it."

[3] Barnes; Carver, *ISBE* 4:3025: "Probably only the contemptuous thrust of a skeptical attitude."

[4] F. F. Bruce, 354, for discussing the nature of truth formed no part of Pilate's business.

[5] Leon Morris, *John* 771.

[6] Lenski, *John* 1235-36.

[7] MacDonald, 1562.

[8] Bernard, ibid, 2:612.

[9] Harrison, E. F., *Wycliffe* 1116.

[10] Cf. Bernard, ibid. 1:25-26 for exposition of the word Truth. Carver, *ISBE* 4:3025: "No term is more familiar and none more difficult of definition."

[11] Barnhouse, *Illustrating*, 259; Lenski, *John*, 631: Truth is a unit, consisting of many united and unified parts.

[12] Lategan, *Neot* 2, 72: "The different attributes that are linked with *eimi* [*I am*, from the verb *to be*], must be understood as being

on the same level and mutually interchangeable. The different Christological descriptions must be seen as complementary to and explanatory of one another. 74: *ego eimi* [*I am that I am*] is used three times in absolute form: John 8:24, 28, and 58.

[13] Carver, ibid: "In the Bible the known will of God is final for man as a standard of truth, not as arbitrary," but expressing God's nature.

[14] Lenski, ibid: *the* truth.

[15] Col 2:8; Acts 17:18.

[16] H. Morris, *Defender's* 1167 (John 18:38).

[17] OED: 6:157.

[18] Lategan, ibid: 76. Bultmann, *TDNT* 1:246: "Freedom does not mean the freedom of the human mind but freedom from sin." Lockerbie, *BSac* (143) 104: "Free from narrow-mindedness and parochial bias; free from denominational supposition; free from received opinions and traditional ignorance; free from shackles restraining redeemed intellectual curiosity and redeemed imagination; free from cant and shibboleth and prescribed terms of speech. Free to begin thinking like a Christian! Free to enter wholly into all those good things that the loving heavenly Father welcomes believers to enjoy. Free to become conscious, thankful recipients of God's bounteous grace, wherever one finds it and however it may be mediated to him." Schlier,*TDNT* 2:496: the NT defines freedom from sin (Rom 6:18-23; John 8:31-36), from the law, and from death. Freedom is liberation from an existence which in sin leads through the law to death.

[19] F. F. Bruce, 196.

[20] Leon Morris, *John*, 457.

[21] Wright, *NIB, Romans*, 10:548.

[22] Lategan, ibid.77-8.

[23] Schweizer, *TDNT* 6:439. Harrison, E. F. *BSac* (113) 40-41: "The acme of the concept lies in its application to Jesus Christ. To be set free by the truth and to be set free by the Son are two ways of saying the same thing." Divine truth is in the person of Christ (cf. Eph 4:21).

[24] Bultmann, *TDNT* 6:226-27.

[25] Dobson, *Parallel* 2097; H. Morris, *Defender's* 1149: True freedom results from continued study of the Bible and obedience to it.

[26] Unger, *BSac* (121) 65.

Twinkling of an Eye: 1 Corinthians 15:51-2: *Behold, I tell you a mystery: We shall not all sleep, but we shall all be changed –in a moment, in the twinkling of an eye, at the last trumpet.*

I. Blinking

To blink is to look with the eyes opening and shutting, to rapidly close and open one or both of the eyes, or to wink. Figuratively, to blink means to ignore, look at with indifference. As we shall see, *twinkling* is not as the TEV puts it, "as quickly as the blinking of an eye," although often so defined. [1] "The average blink of the human eye lasts about one twentieth of a second. . . . Studies show that humans blink every two to ten seconds on average . . . occasionally we blink voluntarily as part of our body language. For example, we wink or 'bat an eyelash' in order to send flirtatious messages to another person. We also blink to express astonishment." [2]

II. Winking [3]

Psa 35:19: *Let them not rejoice over me who are wrongfully my enemies; nor let them wink with the eye who hate me without a cause.* The word rendered *wink* is from the Hebrew verb *qarats* and means to nip or pinch. [4] Psalm 35 is an imprecatory Psalm, one in which severe curses are found, and the writer prays for the defeat of the wicked. [5] David pleads, "Since they have no reason for hating me, give them no reason for a victory celebration." Winking of the eye describes the enemy's "derision"; [6] "malicious signals of satisfaction at David's misfortune". [7] It is an arrogant expression of joy at the harm inflicted upon David, their congratulatory sign to one another that they have triumphed completely over their victim. Winking is called "the low-bred sign of congratulation at the ruin of their victim . . . The Hebrew word here has no sufficiently expressive substitute in English." [8] David prays that he will escape experiencing their scornful gesture. [9]

Prov 6:13: *He winks with his eyes*, and **Prov 10:10:** *He who winks with his eye causes trouble* are two verses which have in them the elements of craftiness, malice, and mischief making. The winking describes haughtiness, frowardness (lying, crookedness), self-confidence, deceit, cunning, subterfuge, and maliciousness. Here is a lively description of "the silent, underhand procedures of mischief-makers, the hints, suggestions, provocations, and signals that are effective in hatching quarrels or giving insults." [10] The winking eyes of these "malicious tattlers and scandalmongers" [11] indicate their speeches are full of lies, never to be taken at face value. Trouble and heart-sorrow are the inevitable results of the insincere conduct of these eye-winkers! Winking suggests conspiracy; one or more accomplices are involved. It is the sneering and contemptuous gesture of a deceitful man, the attempt to entice others to join with him; and his winking signals the appropriate time to do harm to the one hated.

Job 15:12: *Why does your heart carry you away, and what do your eyes wink at* (literally, *"And why do your eyes flash?"*), *that you turn your spirit against God, and let such words go out of your mouth?"* Here we find the Hebrew verb (*razam*) means to wink, flash or roll the eyes, or the eyes to move to and fro. [12] Eliphaz rebukes Job, and what he says about Job's winking may indicate "the expression of pride, haughtiness, and arrogance," insolence (Barnes) and rebellion—all expressions which in some way may be conveyed by the winking of the eyes. [13]

III. Twinkling
1 Cor 15:52: *We shall all be changed—in a moment, in the twinkling of an eye, at the last trumpet.* Twinkling is an archaic word—old fashioned, antiquated, once common but no longer current. Aside from the words, "Twinkle, twinkle, little star, How I wonder what you are! Up above the world so high, Like a diamond in the sky," [14] we seldom hear the works twinkling or twinkle. When commonly used, *twinkling* means a winking, blinking, or an instant. In a twinkling is defined as immediately, or in a very short time. [15] Clarke says it is "as soon as a man can wink." It is the "fluttering of an eyelid" [16] "The phrase has been thoroughly secularized, and appears in modern literature almost exclusively without allusion to its biblical source." [17]

The change that will occur in the believer's body when the Lord Jesus comes in clouds for His church (the Rapture) will **not be a process of evolution!** As Adam was created in an instant, so Christians who are resurrected instantly receive new bodies! The casting of a glance takes an extremely short time. "The marvelous change from death to life and from mortal to immortal will not be a long process, but instantaneous; and it will be final." [18] "It is true that the words 'secret rapture' do not occur, but if, as is stated, the whole event will be over in 'the twinkling of an eye,' clearly only those taken away will know of it at the time, though their absence will doubtless be noticed later. They will be delivered thus from the Great Tribulation." [19]

Three vivid phrases define this aspect of the Rapture, that moment when Christ returns to snatch (pluck, force, or catch) off of this earth all who truly belong to Him. (1) **In a moment**: *en atomo. Atomos* means without cutting; the prefix 'a' means not or without (amoral, agnostic, amillennial). 'Tomós' means cutting, sharp, sharper. [20] NIV and NEB render "in a flash." From *atomos* is derived the word atom, which was considered indivisible because of smallness. This was before the day of electrons, protons and neutrons. In the Temptation Story (Luke 4:5) Satan shows the Lord "all the kingdoms of the world **in a moment of time.**" Here the phrase is *en stigma chronou*—in a dot, prick, puncture, point of time (chronology), and so is not the same term used for the Rapture.

(2) **In the twinkling of an eye** is *en rhipe ophthalmou.* An ophthalmologist is an MD who specializes in treating eye problems. *Rhipe* is used only here in the NT, and is defined as a throwing, a beat or stroke, a rapid movement or jerk (Barnes; Thayer, 563). The verb *rhiptō* means "throwing" things. [21] Here we have a time that is faster and more accurate than a blink or a wink; it is literally a "casting of a glance." "Scientists now have an instrument which measures 'the twinkling of an eye.' It is many times faster than a 'blink'. . . . **It is "three hundred thousandth of one second** . . . this doesn't leave any time for unfinished business." [22] Finally, on this twinkling idea, see it as the throwing, rapid movement of the eyes—the **casting of a glance,** an excellent way of describing this extremely short time or sudden motion. [23] It expands "in a moment" to include instantaneousness; thus 1 Cor 15:51-52 helps us to better understand our Lord's promise, "I come quickly" (Rev 22:7, 12, 20). He does not say, "I am coming back right away," but, "Whenever I do come, the coming will take place rapidly, quickly, instantly."

(3) **At the last trump.** This sounding of the trumpet has nothing to do with the timing of the blowing of the trumpets in the Book of Revelation. Do not make the mistake of confusing them. From chapter 4 on, the book of Revelation deals with what happens *after* the Church is snatched up. The last trumpet describes the solemn finality of the change or transformation that takes place at the Rapture. It is the war-trumpet used for signals

and commands. Since there will be no advance notice, let us rejoice as we wait *on* Him while *in* Him who cleansed us with His own blood (1 John 3:2, 3; Heb 9:28; 2 Tim 4:8).

Thought: Winking and Blinking are not the same as Twinkling!

[1] 1 Cor 15:52, Byatt, 222: "But then [Paul] added an illustration to make his meaning clearer; not exactly synonymous, but close enough for his purpose, to convey a very rapid and speedy event, far shorter than a second. So he described it as a 'blink of an eye.'"

[2] Juan, 67, 72.

[3] Acts 17:30: Truly, these times of ignorance God overlooked (winked at: KJV), but now commands all men everywhere to repent." A. W. Evans, *ISBE* 3089: "The use of 'winked' in this connection would in our day, of course, be considered in bad taste, if not actually irreverent, but it is an excellent example of the colloquialism of the '1611 Authorized Version of the Bible'." Used only once in the NT, the Greek word (*hupereidōn*) means to overlook, take no notice of, not attend to; disregard. God is calling all men everywhere—not just believers or Jews—to repent, to "do an about-face" (MacDonald, 1639), to "turn to the true God from their idols and their ignorance with an inward change of heart" (Lenski, *Acts* 736).

[4] Pinch the eye, i.e. wink maliciously. Coppes, *TWOT* 2:817: "'Winking' is not a felicitous translation since it connotes merriment rather than hostility. Perhaps [the phrase] 'narrow the eyes' would better represent a deceitful and malicious look."

[5] Sampey, *ISBE* 4:2494.

[6] Luering, *ISBE* 2:1069.

[7] Kirkpatrick, 181.

[8] Spurgeon, *Treasury* (Psa 35:19): 1:144, 155.

[9] W. M. Kroll, *Parallel* 1024; Calvin: they *wink with the eyes askance in mockery.*

[10] Toy, ICC, *Proverbs* 126.

[11] Hawkins, *Parallel* 1208.

[12] *TWOT* 840; Young's Concordance.

[13] A. W. Evans, *ISBE* 4:3088.

[14] Ann Taylor & Jane Taylor Nursery Rhyme.

[15] Brewer's, 1103.

[16] S. L. Johnson, *Wycliffe* 1258.

[17] Jeffrey, 790.

[18] Robertson & Plummer, ICC, *1 Corinthians* 377.

[19] Hoste & Rodgers, 64; Calvin: 1 Cor 15.52: For in all the change will be sudden and instantaneous, because Christ's advent will be sudden, and to convey the idea of *a moment,* he afterwards makes use of the phrase *twinkling (or jerk)* of the eye . . . Paul has selected a movement of the body, that surpasses all others in quickness; for nothing is more rapid than a movement of the eye.

[20] *MCED,* 1293. Note in English: appendec**tomy**; tonsillec**tomy**; 'ec' [ek] means 'out,' and 'tomy' means cut.

[21] Bieder, *TDNT* 6:991-3.

[22] Sword of the LORD, 22 Dec 00.

[23] Often in teaching 1 Cor 15:52, I stand before my class and tell the students to watch my eyes, as I change directions or switch glances, without moving my head. It is not, however, a demonstration of what it means to be "shifty-eyed," thus "displaying or suggestive of a tricky, deceitful character, evasive or untrustworthy" (AHD; WBD).

Wicked Cease from Troubling, and the Weary Are at Rest—Is This Heaven?
Job 3:17: *There the wicked cease from troubling, and there the weary are at rest.*

Description of Job
Job was a good man, God-fearing, and avoiding evil. Out of nowhere devastation comes; his animals are stolen, most of his servants slain, his seven sons and three daughters killed, and he is physically afflicted with boils. In addition, he is plagued with a foolish-speaking wife, and some troublesome friends. He is full of misery and despair. Agonizing over his situation, he raises questions no human being can answer adequately.

Suffering may be used for the chastisement of believers in order to draw them to Christ and make them more like Him. God may use troubles to humble us and teach true submission; He may use us as examples (of faith, perseverance, humility, etc.) to encourage others, or to warn unbelievers (1 Pet 4:17). Suffering helps us to establish proper values; it could well be used to prepare us to die. The problem of human suffering is complex; there are too many factors, too many variables for us to pinpoint and determine in any given case why the righteous suffer. Man can see only so far; he cannot fathom the ways of God. Through all the adversities of life we take God at His word that "all things work together for good to those who love" Him (Rom 8:28).

Despair

Losing his taste for life, Job wished he had never been born. Recall that Jeremiah also cursed his day of birth, so discouraged was he over the sins of his people and the way they persecuted him for preaching against their evil ways (Jer 20:14-18). Job expresses his despair by stating it would have been better if he had not been born at all. He sees his birth as a disaster, and wishes he had died at birth. From his perspective the grave is the place to be.

Death

Job was of the opinion, such was his misery, that death would have been a sweet relief, an escape from life's agony. He considered "Death is the great leveler;" [1] "Death equalizes everything." [2] All the inhabitants of death's dormitory—kings, princes, statesmen, the distinguished, famous, world renowned, stillborn children, the wicked, slaves, small and great, as well as prisoners—are at ease, freed from their toil—for there the wicked cease from raging (NASB, Moffatt), stop their evil (TEV), cease from turmoil (NIV), bustle no more (NJB: *New Jerusalem Bible*). All who are there find relief from troublesome human beings; and so with the thought that only death is desirable, Job seems to enhance the attraction of *Sheol*:

> Job sees death not as the enemy, but as the bearer of rest. He is a sick man, and his views are warped by his condition. His extreme suffering has blinded him, at least for the moment. Satan must have rejoiced to hear God's faithful servant speak so; and since the result of Job's testing was unknown to the adversary (Satan is not all-knowing), he may have even cherished the idea of snatching victory from the jaws of defeat. (Matheny, *Parallel*, 940)

Definitions

Wicked: The word *rasha* "is supposed originally to refer to the *activity*, the *tossing*, and the *confusion* in which the wicked live, and the perpetual agitation which they cause to others" (Isa 57:20-21). [3] Wickedness is more than being in a state of sin or of living in condition of emotional turmoil. There is an active, restless desire to harm others. In short, acting antisocially, wickedness always produces victims.[4] **Troubling:** Means excitement, quivering, quaking, trembling, and perturbing; raging or "strong agitation." [5] The thought behind the word for 'trouble' is paroxysm. [6] This turmoil or wrath "Can refer either to external disturbances or troubles or to inner emotional agitation as in anger. Job uses this term for external disturbances (3:26; 14:1)." [7]

He contends that at death and in the grave all such activity will cease. [8] Troublers will no longer be able to cause trouble. Dead persecutors can no longer persecute (M. Henry). Liars cease to have an audience; dope-pushers no longer have any customers; and mischief-makers are idle. The Sabeans and Chaldeans will have ceased raiding, plundering and killing. And contrary to what we often hear nowadays, Satan will not be in charge, but a victim, no longer able to tempt or destroy.

Weary: means to toil, grow or be weary; the adjective, the toil-worn, "exhausted of strength"; [9] "wearied in strength" (Barnes). **Rest:** *Nuach*; "relates to rest in death as is seen in Job 3:13, 17, where Job bemoans his existence and lauds stillbirth (cf. Prov 21:16)." [10] Sheol or underworld is variously translated in Job: grave (5x), hell (2x), and pit once. Zophar uses the word once (11:8); Job, seven times. The verses depicting Sheol as "dark, gloomy, without return," are described as "all being alike 3:17-19." [11]

Decision

Our study leads us to conclude that it is not proper to use Job 3:17 as a description of Heaven. Of course, it is true that there will be no trouble-makers in heaven. However, Sheol is not heaven; indeed, heaven never has been and never will be populated with mischief-doers. Christians need not pray as Job prayed, for our lives (including suffering) are in God's hands. Through faith in the shed blood of the Lord Jesus Christ, the death of the saint (all believers are saints) is precious in His sight (Psa 116:15). What Job sought in his misery, the Lord Jesus gives to us now (Matt 11:28). Furthermore, the fact that dead evildoers are incapable of harming others, by no means suggests that they individually enjoy peace and rest. There is no peace anywhere to or for the wicked. The grave is but the entrance way to Hell and more suffering for all who reject the love of God shown in Christ. All my church life

I have heard this passage pulled out of context and made to describe heavenly peace, bliss and rest. Accurately exposited it has no such reference. It relates only to the grave; its inhabitants are no longer capable of causing trouble.

[1] MacBeath, 24.

[2] Bultmann, *TDNT* 2:851. See *A Living Dog Is Better Than a Dead Lion,* p 165.

[3] Girdlestone, 81: In the Book of Job the wicked are represented as triumphing for a time, but as finally put out into darkness; fn 1: The word *wicked* is supposed by some etymologists to be connected with *quick,* and to mean *lively*; if this be its true significance, it answers admirably to *rasha.*

[4] Newsom, *NIB* 4:369: "Wicked is a term with not only moral tones but also specific antisocial overtones."

[5] K&D: "contained etymologically [a word's true sense] in the word for *wickedness*"; Clines, (WBC 17) 96; Driver & Gray, ICC, *Job* 37.

[6] Sudden, intense, sharp, severe; MacBeath, 23.

[7] Bowling, *TWOT* 2:831.

[8] Cf. Yamauchi, *TWOT* 1:264: cease, stop, forbear, desist, and forego: "most often means to cease doing something." Pratt, *ISBE* 1:586: to leave off. "Few words illustrate better the fertility of the Hebrew in expressing limitless shades of meaning, impoverished by the use of one English word." 'Cease' well expresses this extensive variety.

[9] Clines, ibid: 73; R. H. Alexander, *TWOT* 1:362: the primary meaning of the verb is "to work until one is tired and exhausted."

[10] Coppes, *TWOT* 2:562.

[11] MacBeath, ibid; Matheny, ibid.